Somebody Feed Phil The Book

Somebody Feed Phil The Book

Untold Stories, Behind-the-Scenes Photos and Favorite Recipes

Phil Rosenthal

and Jenn Garbee
Location Photography by Richard Rosenthal
Food Photography by Ed Anderson

Simon Element
New York · London · Toronto · Sydney · New Delhi

SIMON
ELEMENT

An Imprint of Simon & Schuster, Inc.
1230 Avenue of the Americas
New York, NY 10020

First Simon Element hardcover edition October 2022

SIMON ELEMENT is a trademark of Simon & Schuster, Inc.

For information about special discounts for bulk purchases, please
contact Simon & Schuster Special Sales at 1–866–506–1949 or
business@simonandschuster.com.

The Simon & Schuster Speakers Bureau can bring authors to your live event.
For more information or to book an event, contact the Simon & Schuster
Speakers Bureau at 1–866–248–3049 or visit our website at
www.simonspeakers.com.

Interior design by Debbie Berne Design

Manufactured in China

10 9 8 7 6 5 4 3 2 1

Library of Congress Cataloging-in-Publication Data has been applied for.

ISBN 978–1–9821–7099–8
ISBN 978–1–9821–7100–1 (ebook)

I hope I've been a good traveling companion.

—BRUCE SPRINGSTEEN

Foreword

IN FEBRUARY 2019, Phil and I organized by text message a meeting in Los Angeles. I had no doubt he would choose a cool spot, but when I read his last message, saying he was going to take me to an "avant-garde place," I cringed. I was on a forty-eight-hour trip from Italy to cook over Oscars weekend, and between the jet lag, interviews, and other engagements, I didn't have much room left for avant-garde.

Phil and I had met years earlier at the Albinelli Market in Modena. As we walked from stall to stall, I understood immediately that this guy was interested in one thing only— Good Food. You can put all kinds of labels on gastronomic movements and styles of cooking, but in my book, food always falls into one of two categories: Good Food or Bad Food. It didn't matter to Phil if he was eating a sandwich in a bar, a mushroom directly from the vendor's basket, or a meal at a three-star Michelin restaurant. He wanted to taste it all and to know everything he could about why that bite was better than the last.

When we pulled up to Sumo Dog on Western Avenue, which was attached to a dive bar, a big smile came over my face. The Korean hot dog stand famous for its Asian-flavored hot dogs and collaborations with LA chefs was my kind of avant-garde. Phil ordered everything. We passed hot dogs around, comparing one to another. The conversation was rich with gourmet exclamations like "Oooooh!" "Oh my God!" "No way!" and "Try this one!" Then Nancy Silverton's dog came along, with its American-Italian notes: American Wagyu beef, Calabrian sausage, and Caciocavallo cheese. Everyone ate in silence. Too good for words.

A year later I was back in LA for the Oscars again. It would be the last trip I took before the COVID-19 pandemic hit. Unable to travel outside Italy, I became quite nostalgic about that kind of "avant-garde" curbside adventure. The shared hot dogs, the unmasked laughs, and the ease of gathering, which we took for granted at the time. Thank you, Phil, for this lasting memory.

The recipe I've shared, Five Ages of Parmigiano Reggiano in Different Temperatures and Textures (page 109), has nothing to do with hot dogs. It has everything to do with the quality of the ingredients and, even more important, the quality of the ideas.

And that's exactly why *Somebody Feed Phil* is such an addictive television show. Phil never just scratches the surface or simply reports on what he sees and eats. I can testify from various experiences on set that every moment is unscripted, real, and raw. Phil dives in and begins getting to know the guests, the places, and the food through his curiosity

and questions. When Phil shows up, the pressure is on to show him your favorite food angles, big and small, and the secret flavors, ingredients, and customs that make your life delicious. And in return, Phil shows you his favorite hideouts and hot dog stands. The relationships we form around food are some of the most meaningful (just think about our attachment to our mothers), so when you have Good Food and Good Conversation at the table, there is always magic.

Somebody Feed Phil the Book brings to life the dynamic intersection of cultures, people, landscapes, ingredients, and ideas. Phil shares not only his travels and culinary adventures but also the recipes he loves most so that everyone can experience extraordinary places and fabulous people—and delicious food. And that, really, is what the best cookbooks do. They animate places we've visited or read about or dream about traveling to someday; they remind us of people we've met, cooked with, and broken bread with; and they connect us to one another, no matter how great the distance between us.

—MASSIMO BOTTURA

Introduction

WELCOME EVERYBODY, to *Somebody Feed Phil the Book*. I'm trying to do two things here: make a great companion book to the series, and give you some of the best recipes from our favorite chefs and places on the show.

Let me make this clear—these are not my recipes. I'm not a chef. I don't have the temperament or talent to make anything from this book. All I care about is whether the recipes here taste as close as possible to what I ate around the world, and they do. But—and this is the message of the book and the show—you should still go to these places and try the originals. One thing I've learned after eating things all over the world: a dish never tastes the same at home as it does when you're traveling. Because it's all connected: the sights, the sounds, the smells, the people you're with, the experience—are all connected to your tongue. So the best thing that could come from this book is that at some point you drop it and call your travel agent.

My favorite part about doing the show has been the people I've met, not just during filming but also those of you who watch it and reach out to me. It's been my calling card to the world and one of the greatest pleasures of my life. It feels like a fantasy, but what I'm telling you is that everything you see me doing is 100 percent real, and you can do it, too. In fact, the name of the show could be *If That Guy Can Do It, Anyone Can.*

How it all started . . .

My parents weren't exactly adventurous people. When my brother, Richard, and I were young, they moved from a small New York City apartment to Rockland County, New York. Moving to the suburbs was

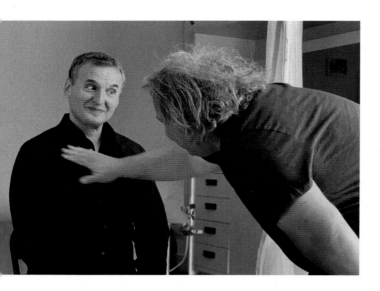

understandably all the adventure they needed after the Holocaust. Rockland was a nice, safe place to raise their family. In our neighborhood, every house was built by the same company and looked exactly the same, other than the color of the paint. (One advantage: when you went to a friend's house, you didn't have to ask where the bathroom was.)

Delicious meals and travel were not the priorities in our house. Safety and affordability were. But my parents did buy Time Life Books' *The Great Cities* series, twenty-five volumes highlighting incredible places: Athens, Venice, Paris, Istanbul, San Francisco . . . They intended for Richard and me to use them as a geographic encyclopedia, but to me, the pages were filled with magical places that seemed better than where I was living. And we never went to any of them.

But when I was nine, my parents announced we were going to my cousin's bar mitzvah. The great thing was this cousin did not live in New York, but in a far-away place with a mysterious name that sounded like a lost city: Atlanta. I could not have been more excited. I don't remember a single thing about the bar mitzvah. What I do remember is not long after we got there, my cousins took Richard and me to a store that was open from seven in the morning until eleven o'clock at night. It looked like a store for astronauts, filled with candy and food in wrappers, and a magical machine like some sort of carnival soft-serve ice cream dispenser. You pulled the handle and out came a Coke, only thanks to cutting-edge science it was transformed into the most amazing thing: a sweet, cold slushy food/drink. I thought, "This place is great! I love Atlanta!" I had two Slurpees a day for the three days we were there, and the idea of trying new foods, and celebrating other cultures, was born.

A few years later, another milestone: My parents said we were going to spend a week at an uncle's apartment in Miami Beach. (My dad couldn't say no: the apartment was free.) Miami Beach was okay, but it was hot. We went to the Everglades, where I saw an alligator that just laid there. I could see that at the Bronx Zoo. Fortunately, this was 1972, and as every child knew, a whole new world was upon us: Walt Disney World. It wasn't even finished yet, but Richard and I begged our parents to stop in Orlando on the way home. They kept saying no, improvising rationales that millions of future parents would later use: it's too expensive, it's too far away, the last thing we want to do is wait on line with a whole "world" of screaming kids. But we had a week to wear them down, and we got to go for one whole day. I spent that day running around the Magic Kingdom. It was entirely different from the New York tristate area, different from Atlanta, different from any place I'd ever been. It was thrilling. I was hooked on travel. This is what Disney is for.

The first real city I fell in love with abroad was Florence. I ended up there because of my good friend Rob Weiner. After college, we shared an apartment in Washington Heights in upper Manhattan. Rob is far more cultured than I will ever be and expanded my life by introducing me to a world of art, culture, and travel that people our age could appreciate. I could only contribute one thing: a love of good food. Our birthdays were one week apart, so I thought it would be great if we saved up our money all year to go to a four-star restaurant. The rest of the year we'd live off of tuna sandwiches, hot dogs, pizza—anything cheap but also delicious (at the time, we were both struggling to get into theater, working at the Metropolitan Museum of Art, Rob at the front desk and me as a guard, to pay the rent). My parents thought I was out of my mind spending $100 on a single meal at Le Bernardin or Lutece, or wherever else Mimi Sheraton, the *New York Times* restaurant critic, had deemed worthy of a coveted four stars. They acted like I had a drug habit. Why would you spend money on such a transitory thing? But it was totally worth it to me. It was an entire vacation in one night. Rob and I couldn't each afford dates, so we would split one girl. But I dreamed of going to the source, to the places in Europe these restaurants were inspired by.

Rob heard about a deal DHL was offering in the early eighties. DHL had a courier program: their cargo would fly as a normal passenger's excess baggage, in exchange for which they would get a free round-trip ticket to one of their worldwide destinations. Not only was this totally legal, it was phenomenal. Rob and I ended up on Lufthansa flights a day apart to Frankfurt with two whole weeks until we had to get on the return flights. We immediately took a train to Paris, where Rob had a friend with an apartment we could stay in. I got to see the Eiffel Tower. I ate croissants, baguettes, and snails, and even the roast chicken tasted different from any I'd ever had. I thought Paris was fantastic, but then, we went to Florence because my mom had said it was the most beautiful place she'd ever been. She was right. Florence was somewhere past heaven. It felt like being inside a painting. As much as I was enthralled by the scenery, I fell in love with the people. On the train from Paris, Rob and I met two Italians, Dania and Dario, who were the same age as us. We instantly bonded and stayed up all night doing what young people do best:

drinking and talking. It didn't matter that Dania only spoke a little English and Dario only spoke Italian. When we got to Italy, we visited the bakery that Dania's father ran. He insisted we taste all his specialties, then all their friends from around the neighborhood came by with their specialties. A woman came with a bowl of freshly made pasta, another woman came with chocolates. A few years later, I brought my new girlfriend Monica there (via DHL) to meet them. And then Dania and Dario came to New York to visit us. They all—Dania and Dario, their baby Ginevra, and their parents—stayed in our one-bedroom apartment. Monica and I are still friends with Dania and Dario. That story is the story of not just our series, but my life: how travel and the people you meet change you.

One person's life I wanted to change through travel was my good friend Ray Romano. I asked him where he was going when we were on hiatus after the first season of *Everybody Loves Raymond*. He said, "We always go to the Jersey Shore." I told him that was great, but had he ever been to Europe? "Nah." I asked him why not, and he said, "I'm not really interested in other cultures." I couldn't understand how someone could

This did not become the poster for the show.

to the character that I wrote actually happening to Ray the Person. And watching my friend experience the joys of travel for the first time was as good as doing it myself. I actually remember thinking, "If only I could do this for other people."

So after *Raymond* ended, and several futile attempts to do another sitcom, I decided to pursue my dream. And you know what? Nobody wanted it. "Why are you doing this? Stick to sitcoms" is something I would hear from everyone, including my agents and my parents. But I kept trying for years. I wanted to use everything I learned about how to tell a story in the service of everything I loved in life: Family, Friends, Food, Travel, and Laughs.

Finally, the nice people at PBS saw some clips I had made of some travel videos and liked them, and I got a meeting. Here's how I pitched the show: I said, "I'm exactly like Anthony Bourdain, if he was afraid of everything."

After the meeting, I called Richard. I told him that PBS was giving me six episodes on the air where I would try to get you to travel by showing you the best places in the world to eat. He said, "Really? What are they going to call the show? *The Lucky Bastard*?" I told him to quit his job (he was already a TV producer) and come produce this show with me, and we'll call our production company Lucky Bastards. We got Zero Point Zero (the production company that did Anthony Bourdain's shows) to join us, and that show became *I'll Have What Phil's Having*.

feel that way. Not even Italy? Ray's family was Italian. I knew instantly it was a story I wanted to tell on *Raymond*, do an episode set in Italy and send his character, Ray Barone, over there, this guy who doesn't want to travel. He'd come back as Italian as Roberto Benigni, or me, someone who's been transformed by the magic of travel—the food, the people, the beauty, especially of Italy.

So after lots of convincing, we got Raymond on a plane and filmed the episode in Rome and outside the city in a little town called Anguillara Sabazia on the Lago di Bracciano, the lake there. After shooting one night, Ray and I, along with thirty members of the cast and crew, ate at a huge table in the middle of the piazza in Trastevere, the old Jewish ghetto in Rome. Ray saw a gelato store in the corner of the plaza and said, "We'll probably get dessert here, but we should get gelato after, right?" As he and I were enjoying our second dessert of the night, he saw a pizza place and said we then had to try that. Then he saw another gelato place and said, "The best combo is coconut and chocolate. Shouldn't we try that here, too?" I saw what happened

We brought my parents into each episode, and they have always been not just supportive and fantastic but a great source of comic material. You can see their debut in my 2011 documentary about my trip to Russia to try to help them turn our sitcom into *Everybody Loves Kostya*. It's called *Exporting Raymond*. And what you see on those video calls to my folks is really how they are. I realized those calls home are the modern-day equivalent of a postcard from wherever you're traveling. And we realized they're comic geniuses on camera. My mom was a complete natural and absolutely hysterical. (Unlike Dad, she never wanted to be on TV, but later, she did enjoy people recognizing her. I loved that.) Then we had Dad with his jokes. He had done some stand-up here and there when he was younger. He always amazed me, because he did get very nervous going up there, but then he owned the stage. He had accumulated a lot of jokes over the years, but as the series went on, Monica would tell me that Dad would go to the Internet and look up old Jewish jokes before I called. He wanted to make sure he had the joke right so that it appeared to the audience as if he just happened to remember it. The dynamic of the two of them together, my mom and dad, first on *IHWPH* and on our first four seasons of Netflix's *Somebody Feed Phil*, was incredible. They're just as funny in this series, being themselves, as the actors who portrayed versions of them in *Raymond* were on the sitcom. They weren't just the best part of the show, they were one of the best parts of my life. This book, like everything else I'm lucky to do because of them, is dedicated to them, Max and Helen Rosenthal.

It's also dedicated to the rest of my family: Monica, Ben, and Lily, Richard and his family, Monica's family, and my extended family: our crew and production staff, all the chefs and friends we've made, and all of you, who should really be dropping this book just about now.

1

Bangkok

So what's Thailand? Sweet, savory, salty, sour, and spicy, sometimes all brilliantly in one bite. There's very little bitterness.

WHEN YOU'RE WRITING A TELEVISION SHOW, you have to know how you're going to start the whole thing. But this whole show is improvised. When I screw something up, it's in the show. Whoever or whatever made a moment great is part of it. Bangkok was the first place we went for *Somebody Feed Phil*.

Bangkok can be a little daunting at first, starting with the traffic. There are spectacular things everywhere you look. Even the van we had to take everybody around was packed with trinkets and decorations. It

was like a souvenir shop exploded inside. Then you've got these areas that are so peaceful and serene, it's absolutely stunning. "The Venice of the East."

The food is like that, too, all these flavors together, and you're having them at the same time. That's not how I usually eat. And still my favorite dish from the entire show came from here, something I'd never had in my life. More important, some of the most special people I met anywhere were from here. Such kind, wonderful people.

Every great city has a market, a microcosm of daily life.

When we started *Somebody Feed Phil*, it had been two years since *I'll Have What Phil's Having*. The very first scene we shot was the very first scene you see in Bangkok, the boat ride through the floating market. Five minutes in, my brother said, "We're back."

Richard will tell you that was one of the hardest scenes for the crew. They had one camera on shore and two in a follow boat behind us. You've got the traffic on the river.

The camera boat had to be as steady as the boat I was in. And we were in this really hot, humid tropical place. Richard will also complain to you that one of the hardest jobs on the show is "keeping Philip comfortable." I tell him that's his most important job.

But here, none of that mattered. How do you not fall in love with this place? You're on a boat, in a floating market, going from one side to the other, eating these fantastic creations. Disney's got nothing on this ride. The whole experience becomes a multisensory adventure. But it's all part of their majestic daily life. We have zero like this. *This* is why you travel.

Phil: Dad, you know what you would like here? Soup. I've had at least four or five different kinds of soup, some of the best I've ever had in my life. And Ma, you know what you'd like? The fruit.

Helen: Oh yes.

Phil: Maybe the best fruit in the world. Let me show you something you've never seen. Do you know this?

Helen: Yes.

Phil: Tell me what it is then, Ma.

Helen: It's a fruit, and you open it up.

Phil: You're like a genius.

Helen: Is that a cherimoya?

Phil: No this is called a longan. (*opening it*) Oh, it squirted me. Look at that. It looks like a crystal or something. (*next*) That's a pomelo, like a grapefruit only like a basketball.

Max: I'm getting hungry.

Phil: Okay, look at this—you know what that is?

Helen: I have no idea.

Phil: This is one of the best things I ever ate in my life. Look at this. This is called a mangosteen.

Helen: A mango what?

Phil: A mangosteen. It's like a Jewish mango.

Helen: Mango . . . steen.

Phil: The best in the world.

Helen: Oh, that looks delicious.

Phil: It is. I wish I could feed you through the screen. Richard loved them. You haven't mentioned Richard today. Why? Don't you care about Richard?

Helen: Who says we don't care about Richard?

Phil: Not once have you asked me about Richard.

Max: We're very fortunate and lucky to have two nice boys.

Helen: What?

Phil: I don't know if you remember, but whenever I would ask what Dad would like for his birthday, he would say, "All I want is two nice boys."

Helen: And he's still saying that.

Phil: Okay, I say goodbye with a kiss of mango.

Pink Pad Thai

Serves 4

Phil and I enjoyed a version of these noodles fresh from the wok while on a rickety wooden boat floating on the river. It was the best possible setting! The original recipe was supposedly the result of a 1940s cooking contest in an attempt to make noodles (considered solely Chinese at the time) more "Thai" by using Thai seasonings. Of course, a minister's wife won the contest.

The noodles are pink in color because of the tamarind paste, which is an integral ingredient in Thai food along with fish sauce, fresh limes, and bird's eye chiles. In this version developed with my cookbook coauthor, Lauren Lulu Taylor, the eggs are cooked with the shrimp, but you can also fry them up whole in a separate pan and put them on top of the noodles just before serving like we had on the boat. Thai-style sriracha, which has pickled garlic, is mellower and a little sweeter than the California-style sriracha common outside of Thailand. If you can't find it, a brand like Huy Fong works. Use one or up to three bird's eye chiles, depending on your heat tolerance. —**Chawadee Nualkhair ("Chow")**

8 ounces (225g) pad thai or similar dried, thin rice noodles

2 tablespoons vegetable oil

16 to 18 (12 ounces/340g) large tail-on shrimp, deveined and shells removed

4 large eggs, lightly beaten

Pad Thai Sauce, recipe follows

2 green onions, thinly sliced

Thai chile powder (optional)

½ cup (75g) roasted unsalted peanuts, finely chopped

2 cups (9 ounces/255g) mung bean sprouts

1 lime, cut into wedges, for serving

Put the noodles in a large bowl, cover with lukewarm water, and soak until softened, about 30 minutes, then strain.

Heat the oil in a wok or large sauté pan over medium-high heat until very hot, about 30 seconds. Add the shrimp and stir or toss in the wok for a few seconds. Add the eggs, strained rice noodles, and about a quarter of the Pad Thai Sauce and cook, stirring constantly, until the noodles soak up the sauce, about 15 seconds. (If using a sauté pan, use tongs to help lift up the noodles and redistribute them in the sauce.) Continue adding the sauce in three more batches, letting the noodles soak up the sauce after each addition. If the noodles are still firm, add 2 to 3 tablespoons of water and stir until the noodles have softened.

Add the green onions, mix well, then divide the noodles and shrimp among four serving bowls. Sprinkle the chile powder, if using, to taste over the pad thai, scatter the peanuts and arrange the mung bean sprouts on top, and serve with the lime wedges.

This pad thai on the boat with Chow, it wasn't just the best pad thai I'd ever had on a boat, it was the best pad thai I'd ever had.

Pad Thai Sauce

Makes about 2 cups (480ml)

2 tablespoons tamarind pulp

½ cup (120ml) Thai sriracha, preferably Sriraja Panich or Shark

3 to 4 tablespoons palm sugar or loosely packed light or dark brown sugar

2 tablespoons good-quality fish sauce, such as Red Boat

2 teaspoons distilled white vinegar

2 garlic cloves, roughly chopped

2 whole Thai-style pickled garlic cloves, roughly chopped, plus ½ cup (120ml) pickled garlic brine

2 Thai bird's eye or other small hot chiles, seeds removed

Rehydrate the tamarind pulp in ¼ cup (60ml) of hot water, set aside for 5 minutes, then smash the pulp with a spoon or between your fingers until softened. (Discard any hard seeds.) Put the tamarind pulp and any excess water, sriracha, palm or brown sugar, fish sauce, vinegar, fresh and pickled garlic cloves, pickled garlic brine, and chiles in a blender and blend until smooth.

Transfer the sauce to a medium saucepan, add 2 cups (480ml) of water, bring to a low boil, and cook, stirring occasionally, until thickened and reduced by about a third, about 15 minutes. Use the sauce immediately or cover and refrigerate for up to 3 days.

Tips

- Tamarind pulp is pure dried tamarind, often sold in blocks and available at most Asian and Indian markets (avoid tamarind paste, which typically contains sweeteners).
- Unlike more widely available European-style cured garlic (cured in oil) or Korean pickled garlic (cured in soy sauce), Thai-style pickled garlic, available at most Asian markets, is pickled in a sweet vinegar brine.

Maybe my favorite things to discover are the different street foods of the world.

There's a simple reason why every culture has it: It's cheap and quick and delicious. The original fast food.

I'd never experienced anything like the street food markets in Bangkok. The stalls have every kind of food group imaginable, even those with antennae. Just getting soup in a bag was an experience. Anyone can put soup in a cup.

Bangkok is not easy to get to know. It's very big, it's very confused, it's very hot. Then at night, you go out and bang! It's a pleasure garden. The city turns into an extraordinarily enjoyable spectacle.
—Lawrence Osborne

I have to confess something: I don't watch cooking shows.

It's because I love magic, and once you know how the trick is done, it's a little less magical. It's like explaining a joke.

But I've never been as excited about the process of cooking anything as I was when we were filming at Jay Fai's place. It was dynamic. And watching her, it was like the sleight of hand was happening right in front of me. I felt like she and I had a real connection.

And just look at this woman. She looks like Snoopy with those goggles, going to fight the Red Baron. She's manhandling these two giant woks that are over tremendous fires. She's the coolest person I've ever seen. How does she keep the shape of the eggs while she's turning them? How do they stay together? And then you eat the crab omelet, and it's one of the best things you've ever eaten. It's practically a football filled with crab, and not just any crab. The freshest, most delicious crab anywhere. If you want to try making it like Jay Fai, watch the show. Let me know how it goes.

A meal like this is only good if you can share it.

Gaggan Anand is a true artist. His restaurant was voted best in Asia four years in a row.

Richard had sent a photo of our fixer in Thailand, Aunchalee Burkhart, who goes by "Nok," back to our family while we were at the Golden Mount Temple at Wat Saket. He captioned it "best fixer yet, Nok." A fixer is somebody local who helps us with all the logistics, connects us to everyone local, and Nok was amazing. When I found out it was her birthday, and that she'd never been to a place like Gaggan, I wanted her to experience it. And I wanted you to experience it through her eyes.

Watching that scene, you can see Gaggan's vision of the five senses—sweet, spicy, salty, sour, and the surprise—all right there in her beautiful facial expressions. And when it was over, she uttered the kindest words I've ever heard. "I'm so glad I get to sit here and enjoy this special meal with you . . . instead of Richard."

Ha ha, Richard.

Everyone goes to Chiang Mai, Northern Thailand's largest city, because it's so beautiful and serene.

That temple, Wat Suan Dok, is out of a movie. But what I really wanted to do was to spend time with the monks.

We don't think of monks as being real people, and then you get to know one. They spend all day, every day, stuck in the same place, with the same people. They probably can't wait for meditation time. I love that Boonchai gets annoyed sometimes with his fellow monks.

. . . .

If I had to pick a single dish from the series that was a true discovery, this would be it. That khao soi that chef Ian Kittichai took me to try at his favorite place was one of the best things I have ever eaten. It was so good, I said a bad word on the show. And this, one of the most delicious things in the world, costs $1. You can't find these places if you don't ask somebody local, and if the local is a chef, even better.

I think I ate more in that scene than I ever ate anywhere else in the entire series. The number one question I get is how do I eat so much and not weigh four hundred pounds? Well, you know how they film a dog food commercial? They don't let the dog eat until the commercial. That's me. I'm the dog. I want to be excited when the food comes, and they say being hungry is the best appetizer. Also, I usually just take a few bites of what we feature and then pass it on to either my brother or the rest of the crew. This way, I can taste a lot more things, and my pants thank me.

But when the owner at this nice little shack, Prakit, wanted me to taste the chicken *and* the beef version of his khao soi, I threw all my rules out the window. I was gonna finish both bowls. Everyone had to get their own.

If I implore you to make or try one dish from this book, it's this one.

Khao Soi

Serves 6

Khao soi is a very popular dish in Northern Thailand. I took Phil to one of my favorite shops, Khao Soi Loong Prakit Gard Gorm ("Uncle Prakit's Khao Soi at Gard Gorm Market") in Chiang Mai. I was happy he enjoyed the khao soi there as much as the locals do. When I asked Prakit, the owner and cook, to come to say hello, Phil offered a hug to him. In general, we Thais do not hug very much, so everyone was a little surprised when Prakit gave Phil a hug back. It was a sweet moment.

This version is inspired by Prakit's. The amounts of noodles, chicken, and coconut milk are starting points; adjust them depending on how you like yours. Please do use boxed UHT (ultra-high temperature treated) coconut milk, which is pure coconut milk heated to a high temperature to naturally preserve the milk; it makes for a much better texture and flavor than canned coconut milk. This is true for all Thai dishes when fresh coconut milk is not available. Pickled mustard greens and Thai chili oil are typically available at Thai and Chinese markets. You can double the amount of curry paste and store the extra in the freezer for another meal. —**Ian Kittichai**

20 ounces (560g) dried lo mein or other thin egg noodles

2 tablespoons vegetable oil, divided, plus more for frying the noodles

Curry Paste, recipe follows

1½ to 2 pounds (680 to 900g) bone-in chicken thighs

8 cups (64 ounces/about 2L) UHT coconut milk, such as Aroy-D

2 tablespoons coconut sugar or lightly packed light or dark brown sugar

4 to 5 tablespoons good-quality fish sauce, such as Red Boat

2 teaspoons liquid seasoning sauce, such as Maggi, or soy sauce

½ teaspoon fine sea salt

2 medium shallots, finely chopped

1 small bunch fresh cilantro, leaves only, roughly chopped

2 limes, sliced into wedges

Pickled mustard greens, for serving (optional)

Thai chili oil (optional)

Cook the noodles according to the package instructions, strain, and rinse under cold water to cool. Transfer the noodles to a large bowl. Add 1 tablespoon of the oil and toss the noodles until well coated in oil. Cover the bowl with a kitchen towel to keep them from drying out.

Heat the remaining 1 tablespoon of oil in a large Dutch oven or stockpot over medium-low heat. Add the Curry Paste and cook, stirring often, until fragrant, about 5 minutes. Add the chicken thighs and stir until well coated in the Curry Paste, then stir in the coconut milk, coconut or brown sugar, and ½ cup (120ml) of water. Bring the coconut milk mixture to a boil, reduce to a simmer, and cook, stirring occasionally, until the chicken meat beings to separate from the bone and the coconut milk has taken on the rich colors of the Curry Paste, 35 to 45 minutes. Use a spoon to skim off some of the fat that has risen to the top of the stew, if desired (or leave the fat for a more richly flavored stew), and add the fish sauce, liquid seasoning or soy sauce, and salt. Transfer the chicken thighs to a bowl and keep the stew warm over low heat.

Meanwhile, to make the fried noodle topping, line a sheet pan with paper towels and transfer about a third of the cooked noodles to plate. In a large frying pan, heat about 2 inches (5cm) of vegetable oil over medium-high heat until very hot. Add a handful of the noodles to the pot in a single layer, fry until golden brown on the bottom, about 2 minutes, and use tongs flip the noodles (they may stick together like a pancake). Fry the opposite side until golden brown, 1 to 2 minutes, and transfer the noodles to the sheet pan. Use a spider or small strainer with a handle to scoop out any remaining noodles from the oil, and fry the remaining noodles on the plate the same way.

Shred the chicken meat (discard the bones) and return the meat to the stew with the reserved boiled noodles to rewarm for a few minutes and adjust the flavor and consistency of the soup with a little coconut milk or water, if needed.

Alternatively, keep the soup warm on the stovetop for up to 1 hour and stir in the noodles a few minutes before serving.

Divide the broth, chicken, and boiled noodles among six serving bowls. Scatter the shallots and cilantro over the khao soi, lay a handful of fried noodles on each, and serve with the lime wedges, pickled mustard greens and Thai chili oil, if using, on the side.

Curry Paste

Makes about 2 cups (480g)

8 medium (2 ounces/55g) dried Anaheim (California) chile peppers

½ cup (80g) peeled and roughly chopped ginger (about three 4-inch/10cm pieces)

½ cup (80g) peeled and roughly chopped turmeric (about three 4-inch/10cm pieces)

1 cup (220g) roughly chopped shallots (3 to 4 medium)

2 garlic cloves

Zest of ½ lime

½ small bunch fresh cilantro, preferably with roots attached (or 1 bunch cilantro, both leaves and stems), roughly chopped

1½ tablespoons Thai shrimp paste

3 tablespoons whole coriander seeds

1½ teaspoons curry powder

1 teaspoon coarse sea salt

Soak the chiles in cold water for 30 minutes, strain, and remove the stems and seeds.

Put the chiles, ginger, turmeric, shallots, garlic, lime zest, cilantro, shrimp paste, coriander seeds, curry powder, and salt in a blender. Add ⅓ cup (80ml) of water and blend until smooth. (Do this in batches if needed.) Use the curry paste immediately, cover, and refrigerate for up to 5 days, or freeze for up to 1 month.

Tips

- You can make the curry paste ahead and refrigerate or even freeze it for a quick weeknight dish; the fried noodles can also be made ahead.
- UHT coconut milk (a shelf-stable milk) is available at most Asian markets and online in various size boxes (do not substitute refrigerated coconut milk, a beverage diluted with water and flavorings).
- Prepared pickled mustard greens are also available at most Asian markets.

- Thai prik chee fah (spur) chiles, a moderately spicy chile, can be difficult to find; here, more readily available dried Anaheim (California) chiles are used.
- Cilantro with roots attached are often available at Asian markets; the roots have a more peppery flavor than the top stems and leaves (the stems can be substituted).

Everyone loves a happy ending.

The Elephant Nature Park is a retirement home for elephants that weren't treated well in the logging or tourism business. I was only on an elephant once, and that was when I was six years old. When you went to the Bronx Zoo in the 1960s, the animals were in this very primitive display, cage after cage. Lions, tigers, elephants, other animals. It wasn't a nice place for those animals to be. Kids would ride a camel and an elephant, then go home.

Here, you immediately get the sense these giant animals are happy. I love that scene right after they

take a bath and then go roll around in mud. It feels like they're having fun being a little naughty, rolling around in the mud right after their bath. (I later learned the mud is like sunscreen for the elephants.)

Sometimes when you're filming, you get lucky. I would say the luckiest moment of Richard's life as a producer was when I was almost crushed to death by two elephants, and upon backing out from between them, the elephant on the left whacked me on the head with his tail. It just happened to be perfectly framed for the camera.

There are moments in your life when you can't believe where you are.

I saw some of the happiest, sweetest, gentlest faces I've ever seen in Thailand. If you visit this place, you will get to witness that, too. Why is everyone smiling? Go, and you'll find out. The people here can make you believe that all things in life are possible.

2

Saigon

Vietnam is a country with a rich cultural history and beauty, incredible food, and a great future. It's a country defined by the spirit of its people.

I HAVE TO ADMIT, BEFORE GOING TO VIETNAM, I had some preconceptions. And I rattled them off at the beginning of the episode: *Apocalypse Now, The Deer Hunter, Coming Home, Full Metal Jacket, Casualties of War, Platoon.* That had been my education.

But every person I know who had been to Vietnam said it was their favorite place they'd ever been. How do I reconcile that? The only way to change your preconceptions is to learn new conceptions. And the best way I could do that with Vietnam was to go there.

Then you get to the beautiful city of Saigon, and the first thing you notice walking down the street is not only are people making eye contact with you.

They're all smiling at you.

When people share something that's important to them, you make a connection.

We do a lot of research before we head out somewhere. Where we might go and, of course, what I'll be eating. I knew Saigon had some of the best street food in the world. Bánh mì and phở (pronounced "fuh") are probably Vietnam's two most famous exports. I'd had both many times before; LA has some of the best Asian food in the world. But eating something in the place it's from is a whole different experience. You're standing at a food cart that somebody literally hooked onto their motorbike a couple hours before. They made this food for you and brought it here.

One thing I didn't know about was bò lá lốt. That one we got at Quán Ăn Cô Liêng was great. The restaurant had been there twenty years. In Vietnam, that's a really long time. People have had to adapt. They've had to be resilient. It's an understatement to say that war changes a place.

To locals, it is important to call Saigon by its proper name, not Hồ Chí Minh City. Hồ Chí Minh City is just a formal name we must use to fill out forms. The name is only spoken by foreigners and Vietnamese who are not from Saigon. Many people here felt as if they lost their country the day South Vietnam was lost to the communist North in the Vietnam War. Their home had been called Sài Gòn for hundreds of years. Saigonese are extremely proud of their city and its history; calling Saigon by another name is like losing that city's identity, its culture, its way of life. —**Nikky Tran**

As I always say, the bread is half the sandwich. Gotta have good bread.

People here appreciate that. My kind of people. A bánh mì isn't on a basic roll like the ones you get here. The roll has a really good crust. You know when you eat it that it is their excellent version of a French baguette. You see that French colonial influence everywhere.

The food writer Calvin Godfrey took me to his favorite bánh mì stand across the street from a phở place, Phở Bò Phú Gia. (You should go there.) When Calvin moved back to the States, his wife, Nhàn, re-created it here. Calvin has tasted so many bánh mì, he knows who makes the best.

A bánh mì in Saigon is a simple snack, omnipresent and cheap as cheap can be. Street vendors may adorn each crispy baguette humbly. A bánh mì may contain a triangle of Laughing Cow cheese or a fried egg, a slab of pork liver pâté, a tin of sardines in tomato sauce, or the very lowest of lunch meat chả lụa (think: New Jersey pork roll). A squirt of Maggi, a sprig of cilantro, a few cucumber batons, and well-placed pickles render these sandwiches impossibly greater than the sum of their parts. They are life affirming and sustaining, and invite all fillings. Lately, since we moved back, I've added cold meatloaf, smoked char siu, and a semi-dry, semi-fermented sweet bologna from Central Pennsylvania. And yet, I insist on observing my wife, Nhàn's, four pillars of bánh mì excellence. —**Calvin Godfrey**

You get it all here. Good bread, good fillings: pickled vegetables, lunch meats, chicken liver pâté, and Vietnamese aioli, which is basically homemade mayonnaise with a stick of butter. Even the French aren't bold enough to do that. You can't get any more diverse than this sandwich.

Bánh Mì
with Chicken Liver Pâté
Serves 4 to 6

You can put almost anything in a bánh mì and eat it pretty much anywhere. But in my mind, there are four essential pillars that make it Vietnamese: light, crisp, pillowy loaves of bread; chicken liver pâté inspired by my mother-in-law (its richness eschews Western herbs like thyme, rosemary, or sage); rich sốt dầu trứng ("egg oil sauce," or aioli sans garlic); and tangy đồ chua (quick-pickled carrot and daikon).

If you've gone to the trouble to make the bread, pâté, aioli, and pickles (make more loaves for the leftovers, or they're all good in other dishes), I'm hesitant to tell you what meat to put in your sandwich. Use whatever you have on hand, but be sure to slice or chop it. In America, I've taken to using supermarket ham, Italian cold cuts, and (best of all) the sweet bologna ("Lebanon bologna") found in Central Pennsylvania. **—Nhàn Văn Godfrey**

Chicken Liver Pâté, as needed (page 28)

4 bánh mì loaves (page 29), hero, or hoagie rolls

Vietnamese-Style Aioli, recipe follows

8 ounces (225g) sliced lunch meats: ham, mortadella, coppa, or good-quality bologna

Carrot-Daikon Pickles, recipe follows, strained

2 green onions, finely chopped

½ medium cucumber, peeled and thinly sliced

½ small bunch fresh cilantro, tough stems trimmed

3 to 4 teaspoons liquid seasoning sauce, such as Maggi, or soy sauce

Vietnamese chile sauce or 3 to 4 thinly sliced Thai bird's eye or similar small hot chile peppers, for serving (optional)

Remove the Chicken Liver Pâté from the refrigerator 30 minutes to 1 hour before making the sandwiches.

Slice the bánh mì, hero, or hoagie loaves along one side, lengthwise, about two thirds of the way through the loaf to make a pocket for the fillings.

Use a small rubber spatula to spread about 1½ tablespoons of Vietnamese-Style Aioli inside each loaf. Spread 3 to 4 tablespoons of Chicken Liver Pâté inside each loaf and lay the lunch meats on top of the pâté. Stuff a small handful of the Carrot-Daikon Pickles inside each loaf followed by the green onions, cucumber, and a few cilantro sprigs. Drizzle the liquid seasoning or soy sauce over the fillings, cut each bánh mì in half, and serve with the chile sauce or peppers, if using, and the remaining Chicken Liver Pâté and Carrot-Daikon Pickles on the side.

Vietnamese-Style Aioli

Makes about ¾ cup (180ml)

2 large egg yolks, room temperature

½ teaspoon kosher salt

½ cup (120ml) vegetable oil

2 ounces (½ stick/55g) unsalted butter, room temperature

Put the egg yolks, salt, and 3 to 4 drops of water in a blender and blend on low speed until the yolks are pale yellow, about 5 seconds. With the blender running, drizzle in the oil a few drops at a time until the mixture emulsifies, then slowly pour in the remaining oil in a steady stream. Transfer the aioli to a medium bowl and whisk in the softened butter, about a third at a time, until fully incorporated. Use the aioli immediately, or cover and refrigerate for up to 3 days.

Carrot-Daikon Pickles

Makes about 3 cups (720ml)

2 medium carrots, peeled

1 4- to 5-inch (10 to 12cm) piece daikon radish (about 4 ounces/110g), peeled

½ cup (120ml) unseasoned rice vinegar

3 tablespoons granulated sugar

½ teaspoon kosher salt

Slice the carrot and daikon radish lengthwise into thin strips about 3 inches (7.5cm) long. Stack several slices of both on top of one other, then thinly slice the stack lengthwise to make matchstick-like pieces. Slice the remaining vegetables the same way. You should have roughly equal amounts of carrot and daikon radish slices.

In a medium bowl, combine the rice vinegar, sugar, and salt and stir until well incorporated. Add the carrot and daikon and toss the vegetables with your hands until well coated. Let the vegetables rest at room temperature for 15 minutes, or pack the vegetables into a large jar with enough brine so they are fully submerged; cover and refrigerate for up to 1 week. (Strain the pickles before using.)

Tips
- You can make all the sandwich components—the Chicken Liver Pâté, aioli, and Carrot-Daikon Pickles—a day or two ahead.
- Daikon radishes, available at most Asian markets, can be the size of small carrots (often sold in bunches) or larger than the average zucchini (typically cut into smaller pieces); either works for this recipe.

Chicken Liver Pâté

I prefer the texture of fully cooked liver, but you may prefer yours cooked medium rare (still slightly pink in the center) as it creates a creamier pâté texture. I leave that for you to decide. This recipe makes more pâté than you'll need for the sandwiches. Serve the leftovers with salad and (good) bread later in the week. —Nhàn Văn Godfrey

8 ounces (2 sticks/225g) unsalted butter, divided	2 medium shallots, roughly chopped
1 pound (450g) chicken livers, trimmed of fat and gristle	1 tablespoon brandy
1 teaspoon kosher salt	⅓ cup (80ml) heavy cream
½ teaspoon freshly ground black pepper	1 medium tart apple, such as Granny Smith, peeled and roughly chopped

Cut 4 ounces (1 stick/110g) of butter into roughly ½-inch (12mm) pieces and set aside until softened, about 30 minutes.

Rinse the livers under cold running water, lay the livers on paper towels to dry, and sprinkle evenly with salt and pepper over both sides.

Melt 2 ounces (½ stick/55g) of the butter in a large saucepan over medium-high heat. Add the shallots and cook, stirring occasionally, until softened and beginning to brown, 3 to 4 minutes. Add the livers and cook, stirring

constantly, until the liver is evenly browned, about 2 minutes, then add the apples. Continue to cook the mixture, stirring occasionally, until the liver is medium, or still slightly pink in the center (to test, cut one of the larger pieces in half), about 3 minutes. (If you prefer them well done, cook the livers until no longer pink in the center, 2 to 3 minutes longer.) Use tongs to transfer the livers to a food processor.

Increase the heat to high, let the pan juices heat for a few seconds, then pour in the brandy and simmer until reduced by about half, about 2 minutes. (Be careful, the brandy may ignite.) Turn off the heat and stir in the cream.

Add the apples and warm pan juices to the food processor with the livers, pulse two or three times, then add the softened butter. Process the mixture, scraping down the sides of the bowl once or twice, until almost smooth, about 45 seconds.

Season the pâté with salt and pepper. Spoon the pâté into an 8x4-inch (20x10cm) loaf pan or small casserole dish and use an offset spatula to smooth the surface.

Melt the remaining 2 ounces (½ stick/55g) of butter in a small saucepan over medium-low heat and cook, without stirring, until the white solids rise to the top of the yellow butterfat, about 10 minutes. Remove the saucepan from the heat, allow the butter to cool for 5 minutes, then skim off and discard the foam on the surface. Pour the clarified butter through a fine mesh strainer on top of the pâté. Refrigerate the pâté, uncovered, until the butter is firm, about 1 hour, then cover and refrigerate overnight or for up to 3 days.

Tip To create a mousse-like pâté consistency, make sure the butter is at room temperature before adding it to the food processor with the liver.

Wanna make the bread?

Bánh Mì Loaves

**Makes 4 extra-large loaves
(enough for 4 to 6 bánh mì servings)**

Bánh mì actually means "bread" in Vietnamese, but most recipes outside Vietnam leave that part out. The bread is our version of a baguette, crispy on the outside but fluffy in the center (it usually has eggs and a little oil or butter). I've found it possible to re-create the crusty shell that holds a Saigon sidewalk sandwich together using an instant "sourdough" starter similar to the hidden bánh mì bakeries that perfume my hometown. Here, I've simplified the process with a preferment using instant yeast.

Parchment paper generously dusted with flour stands in for a baker's couche, but you can use the latter if that's what you prefer. (The parchment paper doubles as an easy way to not have to transfer the delicate risen rolls to a separate baking sheet.) You could also proof the loaves in a baguette pan and pop the pan in the oven to bake. —**Nhàn Văn Godfrey**

3¼ cups (390g) bread flour, divided, plus more for dusting

2¼ teaspoons (1 packet/7g) instant yeast

1 teaspoon coarse sea salt

1 large egg, lightly beaten

1 tablespoon vegetable oil, plus more for greasing

Use your fingers or a fork to mix together ¾ cup plus 1 tablespoon (90g) of the bread flour, the yeast, and ⅓ cup plus 1 tablespoon (100ml) of water in a small bowl. The preferment should just hold together; if it is very dry, add 1 tablespoon of water. Cover the preferment with plastic wrap and set aside in a warm spot until very bubbly, at least 1 hour or up to 4 hours.

Put the remaining 2½ cups (300g) of bread flour and salt in a large bowl. Add the egg, the preferment, and ⅔ cup (150ml) of water, and mix with a fork until shaggy. Then use your hands to mix until a very loose dough forms.

Wash any sticky bits of dough off your hands and turn out the dough onto a very lightly floured work surface. Knead the dough with the palms of your hands, lightly sprinkling the dough with a very small amount of flour only as needed, for 3 minutes. The dough will be very sticky, but try not to add more than 2 tablespoons of flour to the work surface or your hands (the dough will be easier to work with after resting). Let the dough rest, uncovered, for 10 minutes.

Use a bench scraper or spatula to lift the dough off the work surface. Clean off and very lightly dust the work surface with flour and knead the dough for 5 minutes. It's best not to add any more flour at this point, if possible, even if the dough slightly sticks to the work surface or your hands. The dough should be smooth enough to shape into a ball; if not, knead it for another minute or two. Use the bench scraper to cut the dough round in half, then cut each half in half to make four equal pieces, and shape each into a ball.

Spray one side of a large sheet of plastic wrap with cooking oil or rub your hands with vegetable oil and run your hands across one side of the plastic wrap to coat it. Cover the dough rounds loosely with the plastic wrap, oiled side down, and let rest for 5 minutes.

Meanwhile, tear off a sheet of parchment paper that is about 1½ times the length of a sheet pan (if your parchment paper is precut, use several pieces). Turn the sheet pan horizontally, then pinch and raise the parchment paper vertically in three places to create four evenly spaced "furrows" or troughs for the loaves. (The furrows will hold their shape better once dough is placed inside each.)

To shape the loaves, use your fingers to press each ball of dough into a small oval, then use your palms to roll the dough into a larger oval about about 4 inches (10cm) long. Fold the dough in half lengthwise, then use the heel of your hand to seal the seam to form a baguette 7 to 8 inches (17.5 to 20cm) long. Leave the ends of the loaves softly rounded (not pointed like a baguette). Place each loaf, seam side down, in a parchment paper trough, evenly spacing the loaves throughout the sheet pan so each has room to rise. Re-apply oil to the plastic wrap, loosely cover the loaves so the plastic is not too close to the surface of the loaves, and set the loaves in a warm place to rise until nearly doubled in size, about 45 minutes.

Meanwhile, preheat the oven to 475ºF (245ºC). Put a baking rack in the top and bottom thirds of the oven and place a sheet pan on the bottom rack. Fill a clean spray bottle with water.

When the loaves are ready to bake, lightly spray the loaves with water and use a sharp razor blade or bread lame to make three slashes about 2 inches (5cm) wide at even intervals on each loaf. (Or, use kitchen scissors to notch the bread.)

Carefully pour 2 cups (480ml) of water into the hot sheet pan on the bottom rack of the oven, lightly spray the loaves with water again and bake the loaves for 8 minutes. Reduce the oven temperature to 450ºF (230ºC), quickly spray the loaves with water again (be careful, the oven will be very hot), rotate the pan from front to back, and bake the loaves for 5 minutes. Spray the loaves with water one more time and bake until golden brown, 2 to 3 minutes longer (for a total baking time of 15 to 16 minutes). Transfer the loaves to a baking rack to cool completely and use immediately, or cover tightly with plastic wrap and store at room temperature for up to 12 hours.

Tips

- While these generously sized loaves require time to make, the most difficult part of making a baguette (shaping the dough) is more forgiving as they will be sliced and stuffed with sandwich fillings.
- Especially with such a moist dough, the amount of flour needed will vary depending on your climate (temperature, humidity), but it's key not to add much flour during the kneading process to create a light, pillowy interior.
- It helps to both rise and bake the loaves on the same surface, like the parchment paper used here, as the loaves can easily become misshapen when moved after proofing. You'll also need a clean spray bottle filled with water to mist the loaves as they bake.

. . . .

On opening night at Nikky Tran's restaurant, Cậu Ba Quán, the chef didn't show up. That's like lining up at the dock to get on a cruise ship and there's no captain. You're supposed to turn around and go home . . . and

cry. But Nikky took over and cooked what she knew, and it turned out she's a great chef.

This looks like a simple salad: different vegetables and fruits and some beef. The magic happens as you work your way around the plate. Each bite is like tasting a mix of flavors as you travel across the world with your fork.

Happy Salad
Serves 4

I grew up Saigonese and I'm proud of my heritage. I like to use traditional ingredients in nontraditional ways, like the passion fruit in this salad dressing. I make the salad with ingredients that aren't commonly paired together—a combination of raw white eggplant, skin-on calamansi, pineapple, lemongrass, and mint. The stir-fried beef is in the center of the plate. You can eat the salad by mixing everything up together or by choosing your own combinations and experimenting with flavor pairings. Each bite will taste different depending on the combination of ingredients you've chosen.

After the show, fans came to my restaurant in Saigon seeking out the Happy Salad. (I did change the name—it makes everyone happy!) It was the first thing placed on the menu of my Houston restaurant, Kau Ba.
—**Nikky Tran**

1 pound (450g) boneless beef rib eye or tenderloin

½ large pineapple, peeled

6 small calamansi or kumquats, or 2 mandarin oranges

2 small Asian eggplants, preferably Vietnamese white or green

2 lemongrass stalks

2 tablespoons vegetable oil

2 tablespoons good-quality fish sauce, such as Red Boat

½ cup (120ml) Passion Fruit Dressing, recipe follows

½ small bunch fresh mint

2 tablespoons toasted sesame seeds

Slice the beef into 2- to 3-inch pieces (5 to 7.5cm) about ¼ inch (6mm) thick and lay the beef on paper towels to dry.

Slice the peeled pineapple in half lengthwise through the core, then cut half in half lengthwise so you have four quarters. Remove the core from each quarter and cut each into 1-inch (2.5cm) thick triangle-shaped slices.

Slice off the ends of the calamansi, kumquats, or mandarin oranges, then slice each into wheels about ⅛ inch (3mm) thick.

Slice off the stem and base of the eggplants and thinly slice each about ¼ inch (6mm) thick.

Peel off the tough outer layers of the lemongrass, trim the ends, and thinly slice the tender shoots (discard the tough upper stalks).

Arrange the fruits and vegetables on a large serving platter or on four individual plates, leaving room in the middle for the beef.

Heat the oil in a wok or large sauté pan over high heat until very hot, about 30 seconds, then add the beef. Stir or toss the beef in the wok to separate the pieces and cook until medium rare (the meat should still be very pink in the center), about 1 minute. (If using a sauté pan, use tongs or a spoon to help toss the beef.)

Transfer the beef to a medium bowl, drizzle the fish sauce on top, and toss until well combined.

Arrange the beef in the center of the fruits and vegetables. Drizzle about half of the Passion Fruit Dressing evenly over the fruits and vegetables and tuck the mint leaves alongside. Scatter the sesame seeds on top of the beef and serve the salad with the remaining Passion Fruit Dressing on the side.

Passion Fruit Dressing

Makes about ¾ cup (180ml)

6 passion fruits	Generous pinch fine sea salt
2 tablespoons honey	

Cut the passion fruits in half and scoop out the flesh (discard the skins); you should have about ⅔ cup (150ml). Put the passion fruit pulp and seeds, honey, and salt in a blender and blend until smooth. Use the dressing immediately or cover and refrigerate for up to 5 days.

Tips

- The seeds in the passion fruit add tartness and texture when ground. If you can't find fresh passion fruit, use ⅔ cup (150ml) frozen pulp, such as Goya, plus 2 tablespoons of poppy seeds if the pulp is seedless. Avoid shelf-stable passion fruit purees that often have added sugar.
- Calamansi, also known as a Philippine lime, are small sour orange-like fruits available at many Asian markets and farmers markets; kumquats are the best substitute, but sweeter mandarin oranges can also be used.
- Vietnamese white and green eggplants, available at most Asian markets and many farmers markets, are very small varieties with a mild flavor. Any Asian eggplant variety can be used (large, purple globe eggplants are typically too bitter).

The lotus flower is the national flower of Vietnam, a beautiful symbol of optimism and resilience.

Thanh Da Island is a suburb of Saigon that's really a man-made peninsula that connects the Saigon River directly to the city. It's a place you'll also find a lot of lotus flowers. Every morning, the flowers rise up from the water to bloom, then at night, they close and disappear beneath the muddy water. The next day they come up again and re-bloom into perfectly clean, beautiful pink blossoms.

Today the area is known for its fish farms, which are at people's homes. A lot have restaurants built right outside their homes overlooking the water. It's a really special place. If you saw this scene, you know you should go there and eat lunch with these people.

Here's what they don't tell you. These ponds are so thick with mud it's like there's a monster at the bottom pulling your legs, refusing to let you go. And you're doing this at four a.m. when you should still be asleep. Stupid Richard.

Phil: Hello!

Max: Hello, Vietnam!

Phil: Yes, exactly. You took the movie *Good Morning, Vietnam* and changed it now to *Hello, Vietnam*. So it's even better now. Hey, you want to see my fruit of the day? Ready?

Helen: Oohh, what's that.

Phil: A rambutan.

Max: Can you eat that stuff with the pricks on it there?

Phil: No, I try to avoid them whenever possible. (*cuts fruit with a knife*)

Max: Oh, okay.

Helen: You're going to cut yourself.

Phil: It's a butter knife, Ma. You peel that, look inside . . . (*opens up fruit*). It's like a lychee, right?

Helen: Oh, I see, like a lychee nut.

(*Phil shoves entire fruit into his mouth.*)

Max: Oh, I see . . . And it's soft?

Helen: He can't talk now.

Phil: Sweet and juicy and fantastic. Oh, and you know what's great? They'll take a coconut and put it in the refrigerator for a while, and the water in the coconut is like this delicious ice-cold drink. It's so refreshing.

Max: When I buy a coconut, I always drink the inside before I crack it open.

Phil: Are you buying a lot of coconuts in New York?

Max: No.

Helen: He hasn't bought any.

Max: When I was in the Philippines, I used to eat a lot of coconuts. You had to watch it, they could fall on your head.

Helen: I have a feeling they did.

Phil: So, we go out to an island in Saigon, and on this island are these ponds. The moment you step into this pond, you sink up to your knees in mud. So, I'm hanging on to your other son, Mr. Producer, to help me, and Richard loses his balance. Now, I can barely stand, he's fallen over, and I can't pull him up. And I'm pulling on Richard, pulling, pulling, and Richard says . . . "Go on without me!"

Max: It's like a sitcom.

Phil: So, I left him there, so you won't see him anymore.

I was against doing this scene. First of all, I don't do anything at four a.m., let alone go hip deep into the middle of a pond, in the middle of an island, in the middle of a river, in the middle of Vietnam. But if I hadn't gotten up at four a.m. that day, I wouldn't have met this beautiful family. That they even let someone like me, someone whom they'd never met, into their home opened up my world.

So don't tell Richard, but he was right.

When you go somewhere like a public park, you can interact with locals in a way that you can't anywhere else.

I love parks. The parks in Vietnam are a whole different experience, like a social club, not just a place you go to be in nature. We went to Tao Dan Park in the morning, when the men bring their pet birds. They hang up a cage, sometimes two or three, with their featured bird of the day, and while the men talk the birds learn each other's songs. And when they go back home, the birds sing the beautiful new song they learned from the other birds at school that day. My kids never did that.

Here the ladies sit separately from the men and have their own social hour. It's like a private men's club on one side, a women's club on the other, so I visited both sides. When one of the ladies kindly said I looked like Rowan Atkinson's *Mr. Bean*, I knew I was in.

And now, a treat:

Vietnamese Coffee

Here the coffee is brewed right into your cup. The grounds go into this metal filter called a phin, you pour in the hot water, and the coffee drips into your cup. They add sweetened condensed milk so it's basically a coffee milkshake. I like my coffee black, but wherever I am I always try something the way locals prefer it at least once.

Get a phin or other pour-over coffee maker. Put some coffee grounds into the drip filter, add some hot water, then add a little sweetened condensed milk and some ice if you like it cold.

We're back!

As I said in that scene riding in the Doppel Mayer Cable car in Vũng Tàu, the last time I was in as romantic a situation was at the top of a Ferris wheel in the Tuileries Gardens in Paris…with a cameraman named Marshall.

The people you don't see on-screen are the ones who really make this show—any show—work. We've got our local fixers, drivers, and guides; they've all been fantastic. But the people who are there every day with me make the show. It's a real collaboration. And it's as fun as it looks.

John Bedolis, our director, had been at Zero Point Zero, but he had also worked for Stephen Colbert, so he had a comedy background as well. The moment I met John, I knew we would have been friends in elementary school. Henry Tenney has been our supervising post producer for all four seasons, then you've got the guys behind the cameras, our DPs (directors of photography). These brilliant craftsmen capture everything you see: James Adolphus, Matt Garland, John Kelleran, Todd Liebler, Ian McGlocklin, Paul Niccolls, and Marshall Rose. They've all worked on food shows, but many have also done many documentaries, nature shows with wild animals, all of that. Yet nothing had ever prepared them for having to watch me eat.

Traveling somewhere, doing anything, bound by preconceived notions is like jumping off a high diving board for the first time.

It's a little scary, but it has the potential to make the biggest splash in your life.

The whole Saigon episode really became about that. Nikky taking over her restaurant kitchen when the chef didn't show up. Sam Maruta and Vincent Mourou meeting on that jungle survival adventure in the Mekong Delta, moving to Vietnam, and opening up a chocolate place when they had no idea how to make chocolate. (By the way, that hot chocolate at Maison Marou is still the best I've had outside Paris.)

I can tell you probably one of the hardest things I ever did was go in front of those school kids in southern Vietnam. I've given commencement speeches and talks onstage and been on TV, but I had never talked to an elementary school class before, especially in another country. I was petrified.

I spoke to someone who had taught English to kids and he gave me that food game to play. That broke the ice. Then I thought of the song to sing, which was much longer than what you see in the cut. And just to make sure they would like me, should all else fail, I had a secret weapon: ice cream.

And here's what I learned: kids are kids are kids are kids are kids.

Cảm ơn, Vietnam.

Oh, how I love this country, these people. Connecting with people I'd never thought I'd meet, falling in love. Look at their smiles. That's Vietnam.

When something is so good that I can't describe it, sometimes I say, "C'mon!" In Vietnamese, the phrase "*cảm ơn*" means thank you.

Thank you, Vietnam.

3

Tel Aviv

The world so often today focuses on the fault lines, highlighting differences and amplifying only the most extreme voices. If you want to know what a place is really like, what Israel is really like, walk the streets, eat the food, and most important, meet the people.

Best prison food I've ever had.

I haven't been fed like this since I was three years old.

THE TEL AVIV EPISODE WAS ONE OF THE MORE personal ones for me, being Jewish. We all probably have some conflict about how we feel about our "own" people. I made some jokes about how annoying "we" can be at the beginning of the episode.

I start by telling you that my first trip to Israel reminded me of Hebrew school. I was being led around by someone with an agenda. It permeated everything. The food choices, the scenic choices. I couldn't interact with the local people. Those are very good reasons to not be on a tour all the time. Mini tours are a good idea, a half-day tour here and there. You want the inside scoop on a castle or an architectural wonder or the food at the market. But to be on a tour the entire time, I would say that's a mistake. You're at the whims of someone's agenda, so the agenda is never going to be exactly what you want. I'm so glad I went back. When you love something for your reasons and not somebody else's, you get it. That's what happened in Israel.

I love the people, the history, the diversity. The news only focuses on conflict, and what I found in reality, on the ground in Israel, are people who for the most part are not only co-existing, but celebrating each other's differences. The food draws it all together. There is spectacular artistry, even certain ingredients in the food are beautiful. The food is a mash-up of all the cultures in the Middle East and beyond and, therefore, representative of how people all over the world get along.

Sabra

1. The Hebrew name for prickly pear cactus fruit that's covered in tiny, painful little thorns that lodge in your skin and are impossible to get out.

2. Slang for a Jewish person born in Israel.

Max: Did I tell you the story about the Wailing Wall?

Helen: The Western wall.

Max: The story about the wall. So this guard was seeing this man, he comes every day to pray. He walks over and says, "Mister, I see you here every day, what are you praying for?" "Uh, I pray for health, I pray to make a lot of money. And I pray for peace." He says, "That's great, does it help?" He says, "You're talking to a wall."

Phil: I think maybe you meant, "It's *like* talking to a wall." I don't want to rewrite your jokes, but do the joke again for us. Ma, I want you to try to pretend you like this joke.

Helen: For the fiftieth time?

Phil: Sorry, you married him. This is what you get.

Max: He said, "I pray for health, making money, and I pray for peace." He said, "Does it help?" "I think you're talking to a wall."

Phil: Again, you said it wrong. It's *like* talking to a wall!

Max: It's like talking to a wall.

Phil: By the way, this is a very apt joke to work on with you, because telling you to do it the right way is like . . .

(*long pause from Max*)

Phil: (*laughing*) Do you want one more shot at it? It was good until the end.

Max: I think if you're talking to a wall, honestly, it's just as good.

Helen: No, it's not just as good. You messed up.

I'm not someone who actively seeks out strictly vegetarian food. I'm certainly not against vegetarian or vegan food, it's just not something I get all excited about. "Hey look, a beet!" Zakaim might be the one place that changed my mind. It may have even blown my mind. Tell me these mushrooms don't taste exactly like meat.

Grilled Oyster Mushrooms

Serves 4

As a vegan chef, I find myself dealing more and more with the simplicity in the kitchen. I try to understand how to get the most of every vegetable by finding the right method to use in as few steps as I can on the journey to the final dish. My goal is to give each and every vegetable the stage and the honor it deserves. It makes me feel very proud thinking about all the farmers that put all their effort and energy in their craft. My ideology gives me the obligation to put the vegetables in the center, and from that a new understanding comes to life: vegetables are no longer side dishes. This recipe is the perfect example of how it can be done, one main ingredient followed by deep understanding and using the ideal cooking technique. The texture, the smell, the flavor—you've got it all.
—Harel Zakaim

1 pound (450g) oyster mushrooms	1 teaspoon freshly ground black pepper
2 teaspoons ground turmeric	½ cup (120ml) extra-virgin olive oil, plus more for grilling
1 teaspoon ground fenugreek	
1½ teaspoons kosher salt	½ large white, yellow, or red onion, halved

Starting at the thick stem end, use your hands to gently tear any large mushrooms in half or thirds, lengthwise, so all are fairly uniform in size. Put the mushrooms in a large bowl.

In a small bowl, mix together the turmeric, fenugreek, salt, and pepper. Sprinkle about a third of the spice mixture over the mushrooms and gently toss the mushrooms with your hands until the spices are well incorporated. (Don't use a spoon; the mushrooms tear easily.) Continue adding the spices in two more batches, then add the olive oil the same way, a third at a time, tossing the mushrooms with your hands after each addition until the oil is fully absorbed.

Thread the mushrooms onto several metal skewers by first piercing through the thickest stem end of each, then through the caps, so they are securely fastened and lay almost flat. (Try not to pack the mushrooms too close together or they won't cook evenly on all sides.) If not grilling the mushrooms immediately, put the skewers on a sheet pan, cover the pan tightly with plastic wrap, and set aside for up to 2 hours.

To prevent the mushrooms from sticking, clean the grill grate of a charcoal or gas grill of any charred debris and prepare the grill for direct cooking over medium-high heat. Put the onion half, cut side down, in a small bowl and add about ½ inch (12mm) of olive oil.

When the grill is hot, pierce the top of the onion with a barbeque fork or prong that is long enough to hold the onion away from the grill surface and any flames. Rub the oil-soaked onion over the grill grate two or three times, then return the onion to the bowl with the oil.

Place the mushroom skewers on the grill and cook until lightly charred, about 2 minutes. Use gloves or tongs to flip each skewer and dab the surface of the mushrooms gently with the olive oil–soaked onion. Continue to grill the mushrooms, flipping the skewers about every 2 minutes and dabbing the mushrooms with the onion, until tender and charred, 10 to 12 minutes. Use tongs or a paper towel to carefully slide the mushrooms off the skewers (the metal will be very hot) and serve immediately.

Tip If you don't have a grill, the mushrooms can be blackened directly on a gas stovetop the same way the vegetables for the Lutenitsa (page 74) are charred, or simply grilled until golden brown in a stovetop grill pan.

The world is interconnected, for better and worse. We need each other.

There's this magical place in Israel where ladies meet. It's called the mall.

Richard and the crew arranged for a table of ladies. "Would you mind if Phil sat with you and gave you some pastries?" They said, "Sure."

I didn't want to talk to them before. I wanted it to be genuine. So, I picked up some pastries, walked up to the table of ladies, and said, "Hello! May I join you?"

The ladies looked at me, sized me up, and said, "No."

I looked over at Richard and he tells me I'm at the right table, but they don't want me anymore. I didn't know what else to do, so I went to the next table, and these other ladies said I could join them. This wasn't the table Richard had arranged, but this is what's in the show.

Then, I find out the ladies at these two tables have been coming to the same spot for years, and they had never spoken to each other. Not once. So, I invited whoever wanted to come over from the first table to the second table. Only one lady came over, but they started talking as if they had been friends for life. And this is how I solved the Mideast crisis.

. . . .

The single best thing I ate in the Israel episode was that herring sandwich at Sherry Ansky's restaurant in the Tel Aviv port market, Shuk HaNamal, that her daughter, Michal, and several other locals passionate about food founded. It's not a fancy sandwich, which is true about most things I like. It was just so good. We went back there with the crew a couple more times. When we go back to a place off camera, that must mean it's our favorite thing; we go back to what we loved when nobody is watching.

Sherry has spent a lifetime tasting herring to find the very best. She's written this beautiful explanation for you about herring and why you need the very best—and how in the United States, we usually get it very wrong. (My people.) Get a whole salted herring or make your own (good luck) or go to a Jewish deli and ask for their schmaltz herring fillets, the kind you can get at Russ & Daughters (from the New York episode), then make this sandwich. I'm sorry, but this one is never going to be as good as Sherry's. You should still make it, but you'll also have to go to Tel Aviv and eat it there. And then tell me it's not one of the best sandwiches you've had in your whole lousy life.

Pickled Herring Sandwich

Serves 2

My sandwiches hold flavors I inherited from my eastern European ancestors and heritage, along with the memories of our grandmother's herring here in Israel. They are based on the Dutch idea to sell herring at a food stand, though the concept goes through me as well. It includes all that I have learned about cooking techniques, my passion for food and the culinary arts, and even what I know about the life expectancy of the herring shoals in front of Holland's shore (where I import my herring).

It took us a few months until we got the high quality and fine ripeness of the fish we sell at our food stand today. The main difficulty is that herring is a non-civilized fish. (Herring is one of the few truly wild, rare things we consume. In other words, it is purely organic.) That means there are natural differences in the quality of the fish, depending on where they are caught, the sorting process, and the size of the fish. There is also a difference in the final flavor depending on the pickling process (a wet or dry curing method), the concentration of salt, and the duration of the salting process. In Western and Northern Europe, the herring is preserved in a mixture of salt water at a concentration of between 2 percent and about 20 percent; this is almost "unsalted" compared to those in the United States, which are salted by a method known as the "Jewish recipe." All this means is that there is no uniformity in taste and quality among products; you must taste to find the best. Take care that your other ingredients are also the best: the baguette, fine butter, tomatoes that are firm and a bit sour (sweet tomatoes are not suitable), the sour cream, and the spicy peppers—the connection between the Eastern European–style and the Mediterranean Israel–style herring sandwich.

We do not rinse the fish or soak it to remove any salt, but you may need to rinse yours depending on how salty the herring is and if you cannot find whole herring fillets (ours is almost as salty as anchovies). And be patient when removing the bones; there are more than two hundred bones in a herring's body. You want to place the best pieces of herring (the slices from the belly) so they are the first and the last bites in the sandwich. These are the most important moments of enjoyment: the first impression when meeting the sandwich, and the last, when finishing it. Done right, the taster will get a mouthful of different flavors and textures in each and every bite, each holding a surprise: a hint of sour cream or fresh tomato juice, followed by a bit of the edgy, spicy peppers along with the crisp white onion and the fresh flavor of the green onions. —**Sherry Ansky**

2 whole salted young herring fillets, preferably Dutch, or six 1-inch (2.5cm) slices of schmaltz herring (16 ounces/450g)	¼ small white onion, thinly sliced
	4 to 5 tablespoons sour cream
1 good-quality baguette	3 green onions, thinly sliced
1½ ounces (3 tablespoons/42g) good-quality unsalted butter, room temperature	½ small jalapeño or similar moderately hot chile pepper, seeded and thinly sliced
	6 grape tomatoes or other firm, tangy small tomatoes, halved

Taste the herring to determine the saltiness. It should be about as salty as anchovies (rinse the fish gently in water if needed). If using whole herring, use tweezers to remove all the bones. Slice the herring fillets width wise into about eight 1-inch (2.5cm) pieces. Or, if using schmaltz herring, put the fillet pieces in a strainer, rinse under cold running water, and transfer the fillets to paper towels to drain.

Slice off both ends of the baguette (discard the ends) and slice the baguette in half to make 2 sandwich loaves. Slice each loaf along one side lengthwise, leaving one edge intact so the sandwiches can be opened like a book. Spread the butter all over the insides of the baguette halves.

If using whole herring, place the two middle slices of each fillet (the belly) at opposite ends of each loaf ("the first and last bites") and space the remaining slices evenly throughout the sandwiches. If using schmaltz herring, evenly space the pieces on the baguettes.

Arrange the white onion on top of the herring and spoon several dollops of sour cream down the length of each sandwich. Scatter the green onions, jalapeños, and tomatoes evenly inside the sandwiches, gently close the sandwiches, and serve.

Tip   If you can't find good-quality salted herring, look for fresh (not jarred) schmaltz herring at Jewish delis. The term "schmaltz herring" refers to extra-fatty fish caught just before spawning, but also more generally to salt-pickled herring; rinse the fish well before using.

. . . .

People ask me why we didn't include Jerusalem in the episode. We did go to Jerusalem, about forty minutes north, on our day off. We couldn't fit it into the show. It would have to have been a whole separate episode. And I didn't want to focus on the political center.

We did go to Galilee or, as I like to call it, the Israeli Catskills. We were back in the country where my friend Michael Solomonov, the great Philadelphia chef, was born, and he's making an incredible lunch in this idyllic setting. Every single bite of that meal was fantastic, and none of it he had ever made before. *That's* what makes a chef great.

(By the way, I did have the best chicken pita I have ever had in my life in Jerusalem. It was at a place called Steakiyat Hatzot. Look it up. Our production assistant, Yoav, who happens to be Netanyahu's nephew, took us there. We didn't talk about politics. Only the chicken.)

Phil's Duck Stew

Serves 2 to 4

So here's the thing. You could essentially take anything from Mitzpe Hayamim, light it on fire, toss it in salt and some olive oil, and it would taste good. This duck dish is that sentiment and much more because it represents what Phil and I saw, touched, and, more than anything, smelled on that beautiful morning hike in the Galilee. Thank G-d the weather was nice because otherwise, I might have just opened a bag of Bamba and a can of Coke and called it a day.

My biggest tip for this weeknight-friendly version using more accessible ingredients is to simply make sure you take your time with searing the duck. The fond (the brown bits on the bottom of the pan) from searing the skin builds the essential flavor for the stew. The dish serves two or up to four people, depending on how ravenously hungry you are—and whether Phil is there. Make sure to save the excess duck fat for future latkes!
—**Michael Solomonov**

2 8- to 10-ounce (225 to 280g) skin-on, boneless duck breasts	1 cup (6 ounces/170g) canned whole tomatoes, drained
1 teaspoon kosher salt	1 quart (950ml) chicken stock, homemade or low-sodium store-bought
1 medium white or yellow onion, thinly sliced	
1 medium carrot, peeled and thinly sliced	8 dried apricots, halved
4 garlic cloves, thinly sliced	½ small bunch fresh parsley, leaves only, roughly chopped
2 tablespoons smoked paprika	Juice of 1 medium lemon
½ teaspoon urfa pepper	Juice of 1 medium orange
½ teaspoon ground cinnamon	¾ cup (120g) unsalted pistachios, toasted and finely chopped
1 15- to 16-ounce (about 450g) can chickpeas, drained	

Use a sharp knife to make three to four shallow scores on the skin of each duck breast; be careful not to pierce the meat. Sprinkle the salt on both sides of each breast and set aside at room temperature for 45 minutes to 1 hour.

Pat the duck breasts dry with paper towels. Heat a Dutch oven or large sauté pan with a lid over medium-low heat and add the breasts, skin side down. Slowly cook the breasts until the skin is golden brown and crispy and the fat has rendered (the meat should still be very rare), 12 to 15 minutes. Transfer the breasts to a plate and pour off all but 1 to 2 tablespoons of the duck fat (reserve the fat for another use).

Increase the heat to medium. Add the onion, carrot, garlic, paprika, urfa pepper, and cinnamon and cook, stirring occasionally, until the onions are soft, about 5 minutes. Add the chickpeas, then add the tomatoes, crushing them between your fingers, and cook until the liquid evaporates, about 5 minutes. Add the chicken stock and apricots. Use a wooden spoon to scrape any caramelized bits off the bottom of the pot, then bring the stock to a boil, reduce to a simmer, and cook until the liquid is reduced by half, 12 to 15 minutes. Stir in the parsley and lemon and orange juices. Season the stew with salt, if needed, and reduce the heat to low.

Meanwhile, slice each duck breast crosswise into roughly ½-inch (12mm) pieces and lay the slices, skin side up, on top of the stew. Cover the pot and cook the stew until the duck is medium rare and a digital thermometer inserted into the flesh reads 135°F (57°C), 2 to 3 minutes. Then transfer the duck slices to a plate.

Divide the stew among serving bowls, lay the duck slices on top, sprinkle the pistachios over each, and serve.

Tip Urfa pepper, or Urfa biber, is a smoky, slightly sour, and mildly spicy seasoning made from sun-dried peppers traditionally grown in the Turkish town of Urfa.

There was a street vendor in the old market district in the ancient port city of Acre, or Akkō (how locals spell and pronounce it), where I had a falafel sandwich that you eat with preserved lemon.

It changed my life. I have no idea the name of the vendor. Richard couldn't remember, either. Another reason to go to Israel. Please find out his name for me. I love him.

Golden Ball Falafel

Order a falafel sandwich from someplace really good. You need really good falafel on a really good pita (find somebody who makes their own) and that yogurt sauce they put on it. Open a jar of preserved lemons, slice some up, and stuff those into the pita with the falafel. Enjoy your new life.

Things will always return, you just gotta be patient.

"We'll be back." I said that a lot during the pandemic. A lot of my friends are in the restaurant business. It was a terrible time for so many. But I knew we'd be back. Just like it's been throughout human history, there will be this weird period of adjustment, but slowly and surely, life will return.

A great example of that is Uri Jeremias. You don't meet people like him often. I said in the episode he's the historian, the restauranteur, the hotelier, and the guy handing out ice cream to the kids. He's all that, and more. Akkō is also one of the most integrated cities in Israel, populated by both Jews and Arabs. There are no police there because it's not needed.

But just when the pandemic was getting better here, the violence was growing in Israel. Uri's restaurant was set on fire by rioters targeting Jewish places. It was terrible. He started rebuilding the restaurant in a few days with the help of all the people in the city who love him, love this place. Jews and Arabs. If we'd never gone there, seeing what was happening on the news wouldn't have meant the same. Travel changes you, your perspective. It can make world news personal.

There is one main ingredient that makes it possible to live together. And this is respect. —**Uri Jeremias**

. . . .

Going to Uri Buri is about the experience. You're in this building that's been there for longer than anything we have here in the States, in the entire country. You're a part of that history, sitting in this place.

Uri's Mediterranean Fish

Serves 4 to 6

Shalom everybody, this is Uri speaking from the Old City of Akkō. You are welcome to come anytime to Uri Buri and taste our original and unique fish and seafood. In the meantime, I wanted to share with you one of my favorite recipes for Mediterranean-style fish. The ingredients and preparation are quite simple and manifest an incredibly tasty dish that has been a customer favorite since opening our doors in 1989. This recipe is a true encapsulation of my style of cuisine: fresh, simple, and food I like to eat. As you make it, you can witness the transition from raw material to crispy and delectable in real time. It is ideal for a family meal that needn't take much time to prepare.

You can make this with any good Mediterranean fish like grouper, snapper, or Spanish mackerel (or whatever is local). Get the fish cut into fillets, but with the skin still intact on one side. And if you are a garlic lover like Phil, use the larger amount. —**Uri Jeremias**

2 pounds (900g) skin-on fish fillets, such as grouper, snapper, Spanish mackerel, or similar	½ Thai bird's eye or similar small hot chile pepper
	1 to 1½ tablespoons finely chopped garlic
1 teaspoon coarse sea salt	
⅓ cup (80ml) extra-virgin olive oil, plus more for frying	2 teaspoons good-quality fish sauce, such as Red Boat
	1 medium lemon, halved
1 medium red or yellow sweet bell pepper, deveined and sliced into rings	Freshly ground black pepper
	¼ small bunch fresh cilantro, leaves only, finely chopped

Use tweezers to remove any fish bones from the fillets, if needed, and sprinkle the salt over both sides of the fillets.

Heat a large cast iron skillet or sauté pan over medium-high heat until hot and add a thin layer of olive oil. When the oil is very hot, add 2 or 3 fish fillets, skin side down (or however many fit in the pan in a single layer without overlapping), and sear until the skin is golden brown, about 2 minutes. (Resist the temptation to lift up the fillets with a spatula while the skin is searing as the skin tears easily.) Use a spatula to gently lift and flip each fillet, and cook the other side just until the flesh around the edges flakes but the flesh in the center is still translucent, 30 to 90 seconds longer, depending on the thickness of the fillets. Transfer the fillets to a plate.

Wipe out the skillet with paper towels, add another thin layer of olive oil, and cook the remaining fillets the same way, wiping out the pan again after frying the fillets.

Add the remaining ⅓ cup (80ml) of olive oil, reduce the heat to low, then add the bell pepper, Thai bird's eye or other chile pepper, and garlic and cook, stirring often, until the garlic is fragrant, about 1 minute. Add the fish sauce and the juice of half the lemon, and season the sauce with salt, pepper, and more lemon juice, if needed.

Return the fish fillets to the pan (do this in batches if needed), and sear the fish until the meat flakes in the center, about 30 to 90 seconds, depending on the thickness of the fillets. Use a spatula to carefully transfer the fillets to a large serving platter, pour the hot pan juices evenly on top, sprinkle the cilantro over the fish, and serve.

Tips

- Depending on the variety of fish you use, you may have multiple smaller fillets or larger whole sides of a fish; choose a pan large enough to accommodate the fish so the flesh lies flat in the pan and the skin can become crispy.
- The cooking time will vary depending on the variety of fish and thickness of the fillets.

Everywhere I go, I find that most people are so much better than their governments.

It can become all too easy to develop preconceived notions about a people or a place. That couldn't be more true of Israel. The people I meet are so much kinder, are such loving and caring people, than what we read. Why don't our governments reflect most people's hearts?

I was welcomed here with warmth and openness from everybody. I witnessed how shared experiences are helping forge a bond based on mutual respect. I discovered a sense of joy and communion at the Israeli table. It's a table that celebrates the tastes and values of everyone. If anyplace can show you how delicious food has the power to bring us together, it's here.

L'Chaim!

May your home always be full of guests.
—Persian saying

4

Lisbon

Lisbon is all about the joys of discovery. And that, of course, is the best thing about traveling.

LISBON WAS NEVER REALLY ON MY TRAVEL LIST. I always thought of Portugal as the New Jersey of Spain. It doesn't get the attention that Spain does. Then you go, and it's the best of all worlds. I was walking around at night and suddenly said to myself, "I could live here." And it's true. If everything went to hell at home, I could be happy here.

It was one of the places where I had that feeling you get when something is so new and exciting but also familiar. First, it's a nation of explorers; you can see the influences from all around the world. It's on this beautiful river that opens out onto the Atlantic. So many explorers traveled here: Bosco de Gama, Magellan; and my favorite, as you know, Helen Rosenthal, sailed from here after WWII.

In many ways, it's more livable than many major European cities, and it has some of their best qualities. It's got cafés like Paris and piazzas like Rome. It's closer to Africa than the rest of continental Europe. To me, it feels most like San Francisco with the hills, and the bay, and the bridge, and the trolley cars. It's also got a massive stone statue of Jesus like Rio. It's a wonderful place to walk around.

Here's something from Lisbon I'm glad I did but don't need to do again: the ride in the sidecar. My bones were really rattled. I will say it was slightly better than riding that camel in Morocco, which felt like someone was punching my undercarriage with every step.

· · · ·

Lisbon is known for its pastries, so one of the first things I wanted to do was try their most famous, pastéis de nata, the little custard tarts that have been around for hundreds of years. You go to these places and have it as a snack with the local espresso. You take a minute out of the day to just enjoy a little thing. We don't do that enough here.

We started at Manteigaria, a newer bakery in the city. The next day we went to Pastéis de Belém, probably the most famous and one of the oldest pastéis bakeries and loaded with tourists for a good reason. I bonded with some wonderful folks from Madrid there.

Places that specialize in one thing like to keep recipes a secret. My friend Célia, who showed me around, has a family recipe she gave you to try at home. You need to eat them right out of the oven. You may start with one pastél, but I promise you, it's gonna be pastéis.

Pastéis de Nata

Makes 24 mini custards

This recipe is based on one that Lucy Pepper and I adapted from a family recipe for our book, Eat Portugal. *The biggest challenge is oven temperature, as our domestic ovens don't go as high as bakery ovens. Frozen puff pastry is a good solution for this problem, though puff pastry is made with more "turns," or folds, in the dough than the usual custard tart dough, so the texture will be lighter. Eat these slightly warm, sprinkled with icing sugar and cinnamon on top, as is traditional at Pastéis de Belém, the famous café where they use an egg custard recipe from the Jerónimos monastery.* —**Célia Pedroso**

1 9x9-inch (22.5cm) sheet frozen puff pastry (about 9 ounces/260g)

Cooking spray or vegetable oil, for the muffin tins

2/3 cup (135g) granulated sugar

1 tablespoon all-purpose flour

1 cup (240ml) whole milk, divided

1 2-inch (5cm) piece lemon peel (avoid the white pith)

3 large eggs, at room temperature, divided

1 tablespoon powdered (icing) sugar

1/8 teaspoon ground cinnamon

Thaw the puff pastry according to the package instructions. Lightly oil a 24-cup mini muffin tin, preferably nonstick, and fill a small dish with water.

Starting at the bottom, roll up the puff pastry into a tight log. Slice the log in half, then slice each half in half, and cut each quarter into six pieces about 1/3 inch (8mm) thick and save any scraps.

Put a pastry round in each muffin cup and use your fingers to press the rounds into the bottom and up the sides

Here's Richard testing out the ride first, and loosening some bolts.

of each cavity, dipping your fingers in water as needed to prevent the dough from sticking to your fingers. The dough should be slightly thinner on the bottom and come almost all the way up the sides, but not on top, of each pastry cup. Cover any holes in the pastry bases, if needed, with small pieces of the reserved scraps. (If the dough becomes too soft as you shape the final few crusts, put the muffin tin in the freezer for a few minutes to firm up.) Refrigerate the pastry shells while you make the filling, or up to 2 hours. Or, cover the muffin tin tightly with plastic wrap and freeze the pastry shells for up to 3 days (let thaw at least 1 hour in the refrigerator before using).

Preheat the oven to 425°F (220°C) and set a rack in the top third of the oven.

In a small saucepan, combine the granulated sugar and ⅓ cup (80ml) of water. Bring to a low boil over medium-high heat (do not stir) and cook until the sugar has dissolved and the mixture has slightly thickened, about 3 minutes; it will thicken more as it cools. (Do not let the syrup brown on the edges; it will solidify if caramelized.) Set aside the syrup to cool for a few minutes.

Meanwhile, in a small bowl, whisk together the flour and 3 tablespoons of the milk until smooth. Pour the remaining milk into a medium saucepan and whisk in the flour mixture. Bring to a simmer and cook, whisking constantly, until slightly thickened, 3 to 4 minutes. Remove the pan from the heat, add the lemon peel, and let steep for 5 minutes. Remove the lemon peel and pour the custard through a fine mesh strainer into the sugar syrup and stir until well combined.

In a stand mixer fitted with the whisk attachment or with a hand mixer, whip 2 egg whites (reserve the yolks) on medium speed until light and foamy, about 1 minute. Transfer the egg whites to a small bowl.

In the stand mixer fitted with the whisk attachment, add the 3 egg yolks (discard or save the remaining egg white for another use), turn on the mixer, and very slowly add the hot custard mixture in a thin stream to temper the egg yolks, then add the remaining custard and mix until well combined. (Or mix the two together with a hand mixer or whisk, incorporating a little of the hot mixture at first while beating constantly so the eggs don't curdle.) Remove the bowl from the stand mixer and mix in the whipped egg whites by hand until just incorporated. Pour the custard into a large measuring cup with a pour spout and fill each muffin cup to the top of the crusts, stirring occasionally, if needed, to keep the custard from separating. (It's fine if the custard spills over the edges of the pastry slightly.)

Bake the tarts, rotating the pan front to back halfway through, until the custard is golden brown on the edges, 10 to 12 minutes. Immediately run a small knife around the edges of each tart to loosen the sides of the pastry from the muffin cups.

In a small bowl, mix together the powdered sugar and cinnamon and use a fine mesh strainer or sifter to sprinkle the sugar on top of the tarts. Serve warm.

Tips
- You can line the muffin tins with the pastry dough several hours before baking the tarts (or freeze the dough-lined tins to use another day).
- Frozen puff pastry is typically sold by weight in various sizes; trim any larger sheets and refreeze the scraps for another use.

Lisbon in a Can

One of the great things I took back from Lisbon was the love and elevation of the sardine. When we eat canned food here, it's out of convenience. In Portugal, even just the process of canning the fish is an art. They're packed in beautiful olive oil; some have flavors like hot pepper, garlic, tomato sauce. Even the packaging itself is beautiful. I now order them online so I always have some around.

Find some good bread. Open a can of really good sardines and put them on the bread. Eat that. You don't even need the bread. Now you're there.

Helen: What's that? Oh, you have sardines.

Phil: Should we open one and see?

Helen: No, you're gonna get olive oil all over the place.

Phil: We're gonna live dangerously. What do you think? I like to show you what I'm eating, because I know you worry that I don't eat enough.

Helen: Oh, it's dripping!

Phil: Oy! Someone call 911!

Max: Without bread?

Phil: Without bread I do it!

Dinner and a show.

Growing up my mom used to play opera all the time in the house. And as a ten-year-old, I have to say, there was nothing I hated more. It sounded to me like a lot of yelling, and we had enough of that in our house.

This dinner at Belcanto was so incredible. I got to eat in the kitchen, but to sit down with José Avillez and eat his food with him, that was really special. You don't see that much on the show. Chefs cook for you and watch while you enjoy it. What you see in that scene is José enjoying every single bite as much as I am. It's like when you watch a musician and they are still completely taken by the music they're making. Here the food even looks like works of art, but it's also absolutely delicious. José compared the meal to an opera, and for me, this was my favorite opera.

What we have now in Portuguese cuisine is completely different than five hundred years ago. What I say is even tradition, it is evolution. But the soul is completely Portuguese. —**José Avillez**

Lisbon is the number one place people have told me they go from this series. And Ponto Final is the number one restaurant people say they visit from the series.

All the guys on the crew told me we had to go eat at this place. Ivo, our fixer who became my good friend, picked me up from the airport and we instantly bonded because of his tattoo of Bruce Springsteen. I knew I had to go with him.

You're on this little concrete slab so small you couldn't even call it a pier. You're looking out over the huge, wide river. This place has no railing. I asked Ivo how many people have fallen in. Nobody. Why? Because when people see they don't have a guardrail, they're extra careful. Hm. Something to think about.

We had grilled sardines, my favorite fish, on that bread soaking up the oil, then that gorgeous stew of monkfish and rice and tomato sauce. That stew wouldn't be the same anywhere else, even if you could get seafood that good. The whole setting was perfect. Even the sounds of the water, the ocean. It's all you need. It really was the perfect soundtrack for eating. (By the way, Ivo is also a great musician.)

This is the perfect time to talk about my number one pet peeve in restaurants: volume. If I want to go to a restaurant with you, I want to talk to you. When they crank loud music at a restaurant, you can't hear yourself think. Is this to create atmosphere? No. You know the reason? It's to get you out faster. It's so cynical, that reason. That place in Tel Aviv where they yell at you to get out does that, but at least they're upfront about it. No one likes being bamboozled. Look, I understand how hard it is to make a profit in the restaurant business. But the price of your dinner should not include you going deaf. You want the restaurant experience to be transporting.

Here's what I do. I sit down, and if the music is too loud, I very nicely ask the server if they could turn it down a bit because I have a bit of a hearing problem. And that's true. I can't hear you talking to me if the music is too loud. They're always nice. But sometimes the volume goes back up, so I ask nicely again. It's up to all of us to be vigilant in this battle, people! Because if we demand it, if everyone demands it, things will change.

Go to Ponto Final, get the sardines and the stew. Listen to the water.

Here was my come-to-Jesus moment. And here it is, your new communion wafer. There's so many flavors going on, Jesus thought it would feel like a boxing fight in my mouth, but to me, it was more like sexy-time.

The Holy Burger

Serves 10 to 12 as an appetizer

Whenever I eat the food at my restaurant, like this, I'm back in Goa.

These burgers you need to make into little balls, fry them up in very hot oil in a pan, and then put the poached egg yolk on top. —**Jesuslee Fernandes**

1 pound (450g) ground beef	2 tablespoons finely chopped fresh ginger
1½ teaspoons ground turmeric	3 garlic cloves, minced
½ teaspoon ground cinnamon	1½ tablespoons freshly squeezed lime juice
½ teaspoon ground cloves	1 medium bunch fresh cilantro, both tender top stems and leaves, finely chopped
½ teaspoon fine sea salt	
Generous pinch light or dark brown sugar	
1 teaspoon tamarind pulp (page 13, optional)	3 tablespoons vegetable oil, divided
1 serrano or other small hot chile pepper, seeds removed and finely chopped	18 large eggs, well chilled
	3 to 4 pickled cherry peppers, such as Mezzetta, or ½ roasted red bell pepper, finely chopped

In a large bowl, break up the ground beef gently with your hands. In a small bowl, mix together the turmeric, cinnamon, cloves, salt, and brown sugar. Sprinkle the spices over the beef and use your hands to loosely incorporate the spices into the meat.

Rehydrate the tamarind pulp, if using, in 1 teaspoon of hot water, set aside for 5 minutes, then smash the pulp with a spoon or between your fingers until softened. (Discard any hard seeds, if needed.) Mix together the tamarind, serrano or other chile pepper, ginger, garlic, and lime juice in the same bowl used for the dried spices. Stir in the cilantro and use your hands to mix the spices into the meat. Cover and refrigerate the beef for at least 3 hours or overnight.

Shape the beef into eighteen small meatballs about 1 ounce (30g) each. Heat 1 tablespoon of the oil in a large sauté pan over medium-high heat. Add half the meatballs and use a spatula to flatten each into a patty so it is slightly larger than an egg yolk (about ½ inch or 3.5cm wide). Cook the patties until golden brown on the bottom, about 2 minutes; flip and brown the opposite sides briefly until the meat is rare, or still very red in the center and feels soft when pressed with your finger, 10 to 15 seconds (the patties will continue to cook off the heat and when rewarmed). Transfer the patties to a plate. Wipe out the pan with paper towels, add another tablespoon of the oil, and fry the remaining burger patties the same way, wiping out the pan as needed.

Preheat the oven to 350°F (180°C) and arrange a rack in the top and bottom of the oven. Arrange eighteen soup spoons (each should be big enough to fit 1 burger patty) on a serving tray.

Fill three 6-cup muffin tins or two 12-cup muffin tins about halfway with water, carefully transfer the tins to the oven, and bake until the water is very hot, about 5 minutes.

Meanwhile, crack the eggs over a medium bowl and carefully add the egg yolks so they do not break (save the whites for another use).

Remove one muffin tin from the oven and use your fingers to gently scoop up 1 egg yolk at a time and drop each into a muffin cup. When the tin is full, return the muffin tin to the oven and set a timer for 5 minutes. Fill the remaining muffin tins the same way (make note of the time each went into the oven), and bake the yolks until most have set on the edges (they will appear lighter in color) but the centers are still runny, typically about 5 minutes but up to 8 minutes. (The yolks will be cooked to slightly different stages, depending on where they are in the tin, the size of the tins, and how cold they were when they went in the tins.)

Meanwhile, heat the remaining 1 tablespoon of oil in the sauté pan over medium heat and return the burger patties to the pan. Cook the burgers, flipping each patty once, until medium rare, or pink in the center (the meat should feel firmer when you press down on a patty with your finger), about 30 seconds per side. Remove the pan from the heat and loosely cover the pan.

When the eggs are almost ready, arrange 1 burger patty on each serving spoon. Use a small spoon to gently scoop up each poached yolk from the muffin cups, starting with any that are noticeably firmer around the edges (typically those around the sides of the muffin tins will cook most quickly). Gently hold the yolk on the spoon with one finger, pour off any hot water, then lay the yolk on top of a burger patty and repeat with the remaining yolks, working your way from the most firm to the least. Sprinkle the burgers lightly with sea salt, top each with a small dollop of the pickled cherry or roasted bell peppers, and serve.

Tips

- These cocktail-size burgers are a little larger than those at the restaurant to account for the size of most commercial egg yolks; for a spicier kick, top them with pickled cherry peppers, or use roasted red peppers for a sweeter flavor.
- The oven poaching method for the egg yolks makes serving a large number of burgers at once easier. Watch the yolks closely in the final minute or two as they bake; they will continue to cook outside the oven. (Or, you could poach the eggs in a hot water bath on the stovetop, if preferred.)
- The patties also work well as sliders: shape the meat into 8 patties and cook them for a few minutes longer until medium rare. Serve the burgers on slider buns or small dinner rolls with a poached or fried egg.

I think if you're really watching the show, you've picked up on the fact that it's not really about the food.

The food and my stupid sense of humor is just the way in, to get you to travel. And to get you to the best part of travel: the people. And if you're really lucky, you can actually make wonderful new friends. It only happens to me every trip.

It's like when you stay at a bed and breakfast. You eat breakfast, and you see people you met the day before again. Remember *Room with a View*? In that dinner scene, where they are having a communal dinner and the whole thing starts. They not only became friends, they got married. I'm not saying you'll get married. But travel is a much better way to meet someone than online.

I already had a wife, so I took Monica back to Lisbon with me the year after we shot the episode. I wanted her to meet everyone I got to know there.

Of course, I made sure I took Monica to Ginjinha Sem Rival. Célia met us at the shop. I like the specificity of those kinds of things. People walk up to these shops. They get a shot glass, drink that beautiful sour cherry liqueur, and life is good. Before dinner, after dinner, whenever they want. These people aren't just having a drink, they're having *that* drink at *that* place.

And you can take a bottle home, to take you back to that place in your mind. I told you the story about the expensive bottle of port I'd gotten that we were going to save for our fiftieth anniversary. I now buy Monica ginja.

Ginja Ice Cream

You can't not like this stuff. Pour ginja over ice cream, and you're gonna like it even more.

Hide 1 bottle of ginja somewhere your wife can't find it. Scoop a lot of vanilla ice cream into a bowl and pour the ginja on top. Hide the bottle again. Eat the ice cream, fast.

I don't think I talked about Ramiro so much in the episode.

Some of the places we go on the show there's way too much to fit in, so some things have to get edited. But if I were to go back to one place in Lisbon, it would be Ramiro. You need to go with people. Some places are like that. Miguel Pires took us; he said it was his favorite seafood place in Lisbon, so we took our producer, Abbie Harper, and our production manager, Andrew Wiesner.

There's a line outside it's so popular. They have a keg of beer for people, and so you're having fun already. Then you go inside and it's just fresh, crazy delicious seafood, twenty kinds of prawns and shrimp that you've never seen before. And then they have the most brilliant dessert in the world: a prego, which is a steak sandwich.

Why doesn't everyone do this? When the sandwich comes, it's so satisfying. You're in heaven. And you may be already full, but it's such a great idea, your stomach makes room.

The Prego

In Lisbon these steak sandwiches are everywhere. Here's mine.

Call up your favorite Philly cheesesteak shop and order 2 steak sandwiches. Tell them you don't want anything on them. No cheese, no onions, no sauce. Just the steak (sliced up), the juices, and the hoagie roll. (Let them get upset, then ask nicely again.) If you want, melt a good chunk of butter in a skillet. I'm going to add some garlic because I like garlic, and this is my sandwich. Maybe a few sliced onions, cook those up a little. Open up the sandwiches and take out the meat

and dip the insides of the roll in the garlicky butter. Now add the meat to the skillet to warm it up, and put the meat along with the onions and garlic back inside the rolls. Eat one with spicy mustard and that spicy peri peri sauce. Have the second one for dessert.

What makes a great neighborhood? Great people.

The Lisbon episode was really a turning point. We met with people who weren't part of the scene originally who completely changed what we were doing next. Even when a location and guest is prearranged, every little thing you see and hear on the show is spontaneous and improvised. We leave room in the shoot schedule for discoveries, but Lisbon was an example of serendipity upon serendipity.

We went to film at Nannarella, the gelato shop owned by Costanza, who's from Rome. I meet Sergio, her wonderful and funny friend who works there. And then while we're filming, a giant ball of energy enters. This is Allesandro, their friend from Rome who has the pizza shop next door. That would have been enough for any scene, but then Sergio told me about the Austrian sausage place across the street, Wurst. He told me he was in love with the owner and chef, Maria. As soon as I heard that, I knew I had to take him with me across the street. None of that was planned. All of it was spontaneous, all of it was great. When you are making a documentary, you have to have structure. But you also have to have luck, or it's boring. We could have never written a scene like this.

When I took Monica back to Lisbon the next year, we met up with Allesandro's family to go down the coast with Sergio and Costanza (and of course we got sausages from Maria). By chance, the first day we went to pick up something from a pharmacy, and we also ran into our local fixer from the show, Rute Avelar. She was the one sitting with Ivo and me at the very last fado scene in the episode. So then we said, "You've got to come with us!" What a fantastic day with my friends.

Serendipity.

Lisbon is probably the city I've talked about the most here, but every place in Portugal is fantastic.

Even just that detail in the cobblestones everywhere. It's nicer than any floor in my house, the public sidewalks. What that does to your psyche, seeing these works of art on the ground beneath you. It's so worth knowing that sensibility, understanding that level of detail. It says, "We care about you, the person who walks the street. We care about the everyday person."

The little town, Sintra, with that little bakery, Casa Piriquita, is also so beautiful (get the travesseiros, the local puff pastries filled with almond cream). The castle, Palácio da Pena, is well worth seeing, by the way. You can take a tour of the inside, too. We just didn't have the time.

Then go to Alma, where you're going to have the most amazing meal by Henrique Sá Pessoa. Maybe you will have literally just taken a photo of the cobblestone streets outside, like I did. I had just taken that picture on my phone when Henrique brought out his most famous dish, that "cobbled street" cod. You'll see his genius, taking a classic dish and turning it into an artwork, both the flavors and the pure physical beauty of it. You also need to get the chocolate bomb. Whenever I have things like that I think of Monica. "When she sees this, she's going to kill me." And when she does see them on the show, she doesn't kill me, but she does say that I can never complain about anything again.

Still the most ridiculous question I've ever gotten from a chef was when Henrique asked me, "How come you like chocolate so much?" I didn't have a good answer other than "Because I'm a human being."

. . . .

You need to be a pastry chef to make Alma's chocolate bomb, so Henrique is giving us the really fantastic dark chocolate mousse that makes up more than half of the center of this thing. It's got enough chocolate to be its own dessert, and it has those delicious candied hazelnuts he serves with the bomb. You can put it in fancy little cups like here, but I'd just put it in a giant bowl with a lot of spoons. Invite over a bunch of friends. Make sure they're really good friends. They're going to want to go with you on that trip to Portugal.

Dark Chocolate Mousse
with Caramelized Hazelnuts
Serves 8

This is the chocolate mousse component inside our chocolate bomb and the caramelized hazelnuts that are sprinkled on top. Together you get the key flavors—chocolate, hazelnut, caramel—and different textures, without all of the work. (Even the keenest home cook could have difficulties with all the steps required to make the bomb and accompaniments.)

When making the mousse, it is important not to let the chocolate cream cool down too much before adding it to the cold whipped cream or the chocolate will seize.
—Henrique Sá Pessoa

1¼ cups (300ml) heavy whipping cream, well chilled

1 cup (160g) roughly chopped 63 percent to 66 percent chocolate or good-quality dark chocolate chips, such as Guittard Extra Dark

2 large egg yolks, room temperature

1 tablespoon granulated sugar

2 teaspoons corn syrup

⅔ cup (150ml) whole milk

Caramelized Hazelnuts, recipe follows

In a stand mixer fitted with the whisk attachment, whip the heavy cream on medium high-speed to soft peaks (the cream should be pillowy but not stiff), about 2 minutes. Transfer the whipped cream to a bowl and put it in the refrigerator while you make the chocolate custard.

Put the chocolate in a large bowl and set a fine mesh strainer over the bowl.

In a small bowl, whisk together the egg yolks, sugar, and corn syrup and set the bowl on a kitchen towel.

In a small saucepan, heat the milk over low heat just until tiny bubbles form (do not boil). Very slowly pour about a quarter of the hot milk into the egg mixture, whisking constantly to prevent the eggs from curdling, then slowly whisk in the remaining milk. Pour the milk mixture back into the saucepan and cook over low heat, stirring constantly with a rubber spatula, until slightly thickened, 3 to 4 minutes. (Do not let the custard boil.) The custard is ready when your finger leaves a clean path when you run it across the spatula.

Pour the hot custard through the strainer into the bowl with the chocolate. Let the chocolate melt, undisturbed, for about 1 minute, then stir until the chocolate is completely melted.

Wipe out the stand mixer with a paper towel. Add the warm chocolate custard and whip on low speed until glossy but still warm to the touch, or between 105° to 115°F (40° to 45°C) on a digital thermometer, 1 to 1½ minutes. Remove the stand mixer bowl and scrape most of the chocolate custard off the whisk attachment. Add half of the whipped cream to the stand mixer bowl. Use a rubber spatula to fold the whipped cream into the chocolate custard until just combined (there should still be streaks of whipped cream). Add the remaining whipped cream and gently fold the cream into the mousse until just combined.

Divide the mousse among eight ½-cup (4-ounce/ 120ml) ramekins, tap the ramekins lightly on the counter a few times to settle the mousse, and use your finger or the back of a small spoon to smooth the top. Cover the ramekins with plastic wrap (do not let the plastic wrap touch the mousse) and refrigerate at least 2 hours or up to 3 days.

Serve the chocolate mousse chilled with a few hazelnuts on the top of each and any remaining hazelnuts on the side.

Caramelized Hazelnuts
Makes about ¾ cup (120g)

¾ cup (100g) whole blanched unsalted hazelnuts, lightly toasted

3½ tablespoons granulated sugar

2 generous pinches fine sea salt

2 tablespoons finely chopped cocoa butter or 2 teaspoons coconut oil

Line a baking pan with a nonstick baking mat or parchment paper.

Use a serrated knife to cut the hazelnuts in half along the seam. (It's fine if some break into smaller pieces.)

In a medium saucepan, combine the sugar, salt, and 2 tablespoons of water (do not stir). Bring to a boil over medium-high heat and boil, swirling the pan occasionally, just until the sugar begins to caramelize and turn golden brown around the edges of the pan, 3 to 4 minutes. Immediately add the hazelnuts to the sugar syrup and use a metal spoon or rubber spatula to stir the nuts until they are well coated in the syrup and just begin to turn light golden brown, 30 to 45 seconds. Stir in the cocoa butter or coconut oil and continue to stir until the cocoa butter has melted or the nuts are evenly coated with the oil, about 10 seconds, then scrape the hazelnuts onto the prepared baking pan. Use two spoons to begin to immediately break the hot nuts apart, then when the nuts are cool enough to handle, use your fingers to separate the nuts into individual pieces. Let the nuts cool completely, transfer to an airtight container, and store at room temperature for up to 5 days.

Tips
- For a cocktail party, divide the mousse among sixteen espresso or demitasse cups.
- Many unsalted and blanched (skinless) hazelnuts are sold pre-roasted and don't need to be toasted again. If using raw nuts, toast them in the oven at 375°F (190°C) for a few minutes until just beginning to brown.
- Pure cocoa butter, available at specialty bakeshops and health food stores, is the primary ingredient in white chocolate. Do not substitute prepared white chocolate, which has added sweeteners and does not melt properly. (Coconut oil is a good substitute.)

People always ask me what I've learned by traveling around the world.

It still comes down to two things. There's not going to be enough time to visit all the friends you make in life. And you're never going to be younger than you are right now. Someone asked Woody Allen once, "Are you worried you're going to run out of ideas?" And he said, "No, I'm worried I'm going to run out of time."

What if you love a place, what if you love the people—and maybe even fall in love? You're going to hate yourself for not having gone before. Discover what you love in the world. And go. Now.

5

New Orleans

There's a lot to love in New Orleans: all the great food and music, the incredible melting pot of French, Spanish, the old South, the new South, everything mixing together in this gumbo of fun.

I FELL IN LOVE WITH NEW ORLEANS THE FIRST TIME I came here with Monica more than twenty-five years ago. Is there a better place?

For a lot of us in the US, it's an easy place to get to in a few hours, and you don't need a passport to be transported to this whole other world. But what I love most is the spirit of New Orleans. Since Katrina, everybody helped everybody to rebuild this beautiful city, and people moved here from all over to start new lives here. Everything is beyond what it was before—especially the people.

The first thing I want to do when I get off a plane is find something to eat.

In New Orleans, there are so many iconic foods and places, the hardest part is picking where to start. Luckily, I had an invitation from a fantastic chef and his equally fantastic wife.

Going to Alon and Emily Shaya's house for their weekly gathering with friends was the perfect welcome. I got to see a different side of this city that's known more for its late-night street parties than its dinner parties in someone's home. Bourbon Street is all well and good, but like every other place I've been, the best thing about this city is when you connect with the people who live here (and they're not careening down the street, drunk).

A lot of the folks in this episode appear again later in the series because we really connected. Alon and Emily met me up at Blue Hill at Stone Barns in the New York episode; Julia Reed was another instant friend—and the whole reason we went to the Mississippi Delta in the fourth season.

Then you've got that final dinner at Mosca's, which was probably one of my top three favorite dinners we shot in the entire series because of the fun I had with my new friends. I'm still in touch with most of them.

If Bourbon Street and Mardi Gras are what get you to come to this great city, I'm happy for you, you're young. Just be sure to save room for some Monday night red beans and rice at the Shayas' house. (They won't mind that I just invited you all over there.)

. . . .

Turns out not long after we were in New Orleans, Emily won a city-wide competition for her red beans and rice, beating out local diners, chefs, and home cooks. That's because she's the best!

Emily's Red Beans and Rice

Serves 10 to 12

Red beans and rice is a dish that is enjoyed all over New Orleans each and every Monday. You can find it served in every school lunchroom, on restaurant lunch menus all over town, and on dinner tables. Each Monday, we invite a close group of friends, along with any friends that happen to be passing through town, to join in our "cajun shabbat" where we all dine on a steaming plate of red beans and rice accompanied with a fresh salad and cornbread. —**Emily Shaya**

2 pounds (900g) dried red beans

¼ cup (60ml) extra-virgin olive oil

6 ounces (170g) slab or thick-cut bacon, finely chopped

1 medium yellow onion, roughly chopped

2 stalks celery, roughly chopped

1 medium green bell pepper, deveined and roughly chopped

1 bay leaf

1 tablespoon sweet paprika

½ teaspoon cayenne pepper

1 meaty smoked ham hock or shank (about 24 ounces/680g)

1½ quarts (1.4L) chicken stock, homemade or low-sodium store-bought

1 pound (450g) smoked sausage, preferably andouille

1 tablespoon vinegar-based hot sauce, preferably Tabasco, plus more as needed

2 teaspoons granulated sugar

2 teaspoons kosher salt, plus more as needed

1 bunch green onions, thinly sliced

Seasoned Rice, recipe follows

Soak the beans in cold water at least 6 hours or overnight and drain.

In a large Dutch oven or stockpot, heat the olive oil over medium heat. Add the bacon and cook, stirring occasionally, until the fat renders and the bacon is golden brown, 8 to 10 minutes. Add the onions, celery, bell pepper, and bay leaf. Stir to coat the vegetables in the fat and cook, stirring occasionally, until the onions are translucent, 8 to 10 minutes. Add the paprika and cayenne pepper and cook, stirring occasionally, until the spices are fragrant, 1½ to 2 minutes. Add the beans, ham hock, and chicken stock, scraping any brown bits off the bottom of the pot, and bring to a boil. Skim off and discard any foam that rises to the top of the liquid. Reduce to a simmer, cover the pot, and cook, stirring occasionally, until the beans are falling apart, 3 to 3½ hours. If the cooking liquid ever falls below the level of the beans, add just enough water to fully cover the beans.

Remove the ham hock and set aside until cool enough to handle, then roughly chop the meat (discard the bone). Return the ham to the pot.

Slice the sausage into bite-size pieces and add them to the pot with the hot sauce, sugar, and salt. Cover the pot and continue to cook the beans, stirring occasionally, over low heat for at least 30 minutes or up to 2 hours. Season the beans with additional Tabasco and salt, if needed, and remove the bay leaf.

Just before serving, scatter the green onions on top of the beans and serve the beans family-style with the Seasoned Rice and additional hot sauce.

Seasoned Rice

Serves 10 to 12

½ cup (120ml) vegetable oil	1 bay leaf
2 ounces (½ stick, 55g) unsalted butter, quartered	2 teaspoons kosher salt
1 medium yellow onion, finely chopped	2 cups (16 ounces/450g) long grain white rice, preferably jasmine

In a large saucepan with a lid, heat the oil and butter over medium heat and stir the butter until melted. Add the onions, bay leaf, and salt and cook, stirring occasionally, until the onions are translucent, about 5 minutes. Add 3 cups (720ml) of water, bring to a boil, add the rice, reduce the heat to low, cover the pan, and steam the rice until tender, about 15 minutes (or according to the package instructions). Remove the pan from the heat and let the rice rest for 10 minutes (do not remove the lid). Discard the bay leaf, fluff the rice with a fork, and serve immediately, or cover the pot to keep the rice warm for up to 30 minutes.

Tip   The beans can be left largely unattended while they slowly cook in the pot and can be kept warm on the stove for several hours.

· · · ·

Everything that Alon brought out when we were at Shaya was incredible. Now I want you to know, if you're going to New Orleans, Alon's not at Shaya anymore. It's a long story. But if you want the real Alon Shaya, he opened the phenomenal Saba down the street. That's where he is. Go there. Or his house.

His pita, hot from the oven, I could eat that every day. You don't need a single thing on it. But if you are gonna make something to put on it, this would be it. Your choice.

Lutenitsa

Serves 6 to 8 as an appetizer

The aroma of peppers and eggplant charring over an open flame, a technique that creates an intense flavor without hiding the qualities of the summer vegetables, is what made me fall in love with food. I remember my grandmother making this dish throughout my childhood, and it always stuck out as my favorite bites in the world.

When you cook the eggplant especially, it will be ugly and you'll think you overcooked them, but this is what gives the lutenitsa a ton of flavor and a creamy texture. Resist the urge to rinse the peppers under running water after charring as it also rinses away the smoky flavor you just built. Serve the lutenitsa with pita bread or crudités alongside, or spread leftovers on a sandwich or toast. I hope you will taste this and know that I share Phil's deep love of all food—and cherish the times we have dashed around LA in his electric car eating at his favorite spots (and learning lots of new dad jokes).
—Alon Shaya

4 medium red bell peppers

1 medium eggplant

4 tablespoon extra-virgin olive oil, divided

¼ cup (55g) tomato paste

1 garlic clove, minced

¾ cup (225g) canned whole tomatoes, with juice

1 teaspoon kosher salt

2 tablespoons finely chopped fresh parsley leaves

Good-quality pita bread, for serving

Prepare a grill for direct cooking over high heat or line two burner plates on a gas stove with foil (to make cleanup easier) and put a baking rack over the burners. Arrange the peppers on their sides on the grill or baking rack so they are exposed directly to the flames (if using a gas stove, turn both burners to high). Char the peppers until completely blackened on one side, 3 to 4 minutes. Use tongs to flip the peppers, char the opposite side, and set aside to cool.

Use a fork to prick the flesh of the eggplant several times on all sides. Lay the eggplant on its side directly on the grill or over one gas burner, as you did with the peppers (if using a gas stove, reduce the heat to medium-high). Cook the eggplant, flipping it occasionally to char each side, until the flesh is blackened and has bits of papery-white ash and a skewer easily pierces the center, about 45 minutes. When cool enough to handle, slice the eggplant in half lengthwise and use a spoon to scoop out the flesh (discard the skin). Set aside.

Moisten your fingers with water and rub the papery skin off the cooled peppers, pull out the stems and scrape out the seeds, and roughly chop the flesh.

In a large sauté pan, heat 2 tablespoons of the olive oil over medium heat. Add the tomato paste, stir to break up the paste, and cook until slightly darkened, 3 to 4 minutes. Add the garlic and stir until fragrant, about 1 minute, then add the roasted peppers and eggplant. Crush the tomatoes between your fingers as you add them to the pan along with the tomato juices, then add the salt. Reduce the heat to low and slowly cook the vegetables, stirring and scraping the bottom of the pan occasionally, until most of the moisture has evaporated and the vegetables have a deeply caramelized flavor, about 1 hour. Let the lutenitsa cool completely and use immediately, or cover and refrigerate for up to 3 days. (Let the lutenitsa come to room temperature before serving.)

Spoon the lutenitsa into a wide, shallow serving bowl, drizzle the remaining 2 tablespoons of oil over the entire surface of the dip, sprinkle the parsley on top, and serve with the pita bread.

Tip The eggplant can take up to 45 minutes to thoroughly cook. If the center still is not creamy when you take it off the flame, preheat the oven to 375°F (190°C), slice the eggplant in half lengthwise, and roast, flesh side down, on a sheet pan until soft, about 10 minutes.

Running into someone you know when you're traveling is the greatest feeling.

That was a true story about my friend Wendell Pierce. I was getting on the plane to go to New Orleans, he was getting off the flight to spend a few days in LA, so I asked when he was coming back to New Orleans. And that's how we ended up having lunch at Cochon Butcher. The same serendipity happened with Nikky, when I was in Saigon. She said she was going to get married in New Orleans, so I asked her when, and she says, "April."

"April? That's when we're filming there!" Every great romantic comedy ends with a wedding.

You don't need a TV show to make these things happen. All you need is an airport.

Monica Don't Be Hysterical

At Turkey at the Wolf, the drink is called Ma'am Don't Be Hysterical, but this is my book, so I'm dedicating this to my lovely, sweet, hysterical wife.

Fill a glass with ice. Pour in a lot of Campari. Keep going. Now top it off with a splash of club soda and an orange peel, if you have one. Hand it to Monica. Run away.

. . . .

The main attraction for me at Turkey and the Wolf is the best vegetarian sandwich I've ever had in my whole meat-eating life.

The Collard Green Melt

Serves 6

Sometimes, when I stop at a corner store in New Orleans for some Funyuns and a cold drink or beer, I'll ask the person at the register how it's going, and we'll sit there and talk and laugh for fifteen minutes. Neighbors whose paths I'd otherwise never have crossed have become some of my closest comrades just because we shared an interest in looking out for each other and drinking beer on the sidewalk. And if I'm really lucky, when I walk my dog, Darla, I'll hear the next generation of musicians grooving in marching band practice as they're getting ready for parade season. Other times, and this is no exaggeration, a brass band and a Second Line parade will dance by my front door. I've spent my entire adult life here, so perhaps I don't have a ton of other places for comparison, but this has got to be some New Orleans shit. Plus, Popeye's tastes better down here. I ain't leavin'.

—Mason Hereford

Collard Greens, with pot likker (pan juices), recipe follows

9 large slices good-quality caraway-rye sandwich bread

3 ounces (¾ stick/85g) unsalted butter, room temperature

16 slices deli-style Swiss cheese (16 ounces/450g)

Cherry Pepper Russian Dressing, recipe follows

Coleslaw, recipe follows strained

Preheat the oven to 375°F (190°C).

Rewarm the Collard Greens, if needed, over low heat, stirring occasionally.

Cut the bread slices in half crosswise, and spread the butter on both sides of each piece. Arrange the slices on one or two sheet pans and bake until lightly toasted, about 5 minutes. Set aside 6 slices of toast to cool. Lay the Swiss cheese on the remaining 12 slices, and bake until the cheese has melted, about 5 minutes.

Meanwhile, spread about 1½ tablespoons of the Cherry Pepper Russian Dressing on one side of the reserved 6 slices of toast.

Top 6 of the hot cheese toasts with a small handful of the Coleslaw and stack the other cheese toasts on top, cheese side up. Use tongs to stir the Collard Greens in the pot likker so the greens are moist, then pile a generous handful of the greens on top of the cheese toasts. Top the sandwiches with the reserved toasts, Russian dressing side facing down, press down gently to close the sandwiches, cut each in half, and serve.

Collard Greens

Makes about 3½ cups (450g)

4 large bunches (about 2½ pounds/1.2kg) collard greens, rinsed

1 ounce (¼ stick/28g) unsalted butter

6 garlic cloves, minced

¼ cup (60ml) rice vinegar

¼ cup (60ml) red wine vinegar

3 tablespoons granulated sugar

1½ teaspoons Creole seasoning, preferably Zatarain's

1 to 1½ teaspoons gochugaru or crushed red pepper flakes

Kosher salt and freshly ground black pepper

Soak the collard greens in cold water to remove any grit and shake off the excess water. Holding the stem end, run your hand down the length of each stem to remove the leaves (discard the stems) and roughly chop the leaves. You should have 12 cups/3L of greens, packed.

In a large Dutch oven or stockpot, melt the butter over medium heat. Stir in the garlic and cook until fragrant, about 30 seconds. Add the vinegars, sugar, Creole seasoning, gochugaru or crushed red pepper flakes, salt, pepper, and ⅓ cup (80ml) of water. Bring to a boil and cook until the liquid is reduced by about half, about 5 minutes. Add about half the collards, cover the pot, and cook until the greens have wilted, 1 to 2 minutes. Stir in the remaining collards, cover the pot, reduce the heat to low, and cook, stirring every 30 minutes, until the collards have broken down into the pot likker, about 2 hours. If the greens ever appear dry or begin to stick to the bottom of the pot, add another ¼ cup (60ml) of water. Season the collards with salt and pepper. Use the collards immediately or let cool, cover, and refrigerate (with the pot likker) for up to 5 days.

Coleslaw

Makes about 4 cups (450g)

½ medium green cabbage, cored and thinly sliced

2 tablespoons grated white onion

⅓ cup (80ml) mayonnaise, preferably Duke's

1 to 1½ tablespoon distilled white vinegar

½ teaspoon freshly ground black pepper

Pinch kosher salt

In a large bowl, combine the cabbage, onions, mayonnaise, vinegar, pepper, and salt and use your hands to massage the seasonings into the cabbage until the leaves soften, 2 to 3 minutes. Cover and refrigerate the slaw for at least 2 hours or overnight. (Strain off any accumulated juices before using.)

Cherry Pepper Russian Dressing

Makes about ½ cup (120ml)

½ cup (120ml) mayonnaise, preferably Duke's

2 to 3 pickled cherry peppers, such as Mezzetta, finely chopped

1 teaspoon ketchup

2 dashes vinegar-based hot sauce, preferably Crystal

½ teaspoon gochugaru or crushed red pepper flakes

Generous pinch smoked paprika

Generous pinch kosher salt

In a small bowl, combine the mayonnaise, pickled cherry peppers, ketchup, hot sauce, gochugaru or red pepper flakes, paprika, and salt and whisk until well incorporated. Use the dressing immediately, or cover and refrigerate for up to 5 days.

Tips

- You can make all the sandwich components ahead and rewarm the collards just before assembling the sandwiches.
- Hot pickled cherry peppers are available at many well-stocked grocery stores or online.
- Many good delis sell their own rye bread, or use store bought caraway-rye bread (often called "light rye"), such as Oroweat Jewish Rye.

If you hear music in New Orleans, you best start dancing.

That should be our motto in life, even if you're a buffoon like me who can't dance. One of the things that I love about this city is all the great jazz. You can go see a show every night of the week, and even just walking down the street you're probably gonna get a concert. When we heard about Roots of Music in the heart of the Treme, we knew we had to go.

That whole scene of the kids marching down the street was incredible. Watching Butter, the drummer, was amazing. There was also that gorgeous little girl that happened to be marching next to me, and I kept saying to get a camera over here so we could get her on-screen, and I'm so happy we did.

The reason the band goes through the streets is that they're actually recruiting the next generation. When kids look out the window, they start marching behind the band, and they can't wait to be part of the action. Little kids are inspired; they want to be part of this civic pride. Of course, after Nikky's wedding we went out into the street with the band, and people started coming out of their houses and dancing.

Will never forget that.

I don't ever want
to live in a world
without the
diners and the
coffee shops, the
mom and pop
places.

So many eateries in New Orleans are like walking into a time capsule. Camellia Grill is like that, it's been around since the 1940s, it's a local institution. I've been going there for years. I love to eat at counters because you get to talk to the people. What's great about this one is that the counter curves around, so not only are you sitting next to somebody, you're also sitting across from someone. And before you know it, you're all having a conversation.

Every once in a while in my stupidly lucky life, I get to meet a legend.

People like Leah Chase, who had an impact on the world. Leah was more than a legend, she was part of our country's history. Martin Luther King, the Freedom Riders, the Voting Rights Act. Dooky Chase's was The Restaurant where everybody met and hung out during that time, where they got things done, and it was all around the table, eating her food.

By the way, her fried chicken is the best I've ever had. If you search it up, you'll find the recipe from her cookbook from a long time ago. There was something special about it. The crust is integrated into the skin. It's not a separate shell.

Remember Leah's rule: no hot sauce, or she'll slap your hand. Just ask President Obama.

You've got to talk it over and come to some kind of agreement over something. It can be all done over some food. That's what we do in New Orleans. We'd have a bowl of gumbo and it would change the whole world.
—Leah Chase

Fluffy Omelet

You don't go places like Camellia Grill to get a salad. Omelets are one thing I actually do make at home. These are the lightest and fluffiest. You can have a three-egg omelet and not feel like you ate a three-egg omelet. And the secret weapon of the Camellia Grill omelet? The blender.

Throw 3 eggs and a pinch of salt in a blender and blend them on high until they are very frothy. You want to get a lot of air in there. Heat up a pan, melt some butter, add the eggs, then move the pan around a little so the eggs spread out. Cook the eggs until they start to set. Now throw a handful of grated cheese in the middle, fold the whole thing up, and eat it. Take your pulse. You know what the best follow up is to the omelet? The Camellia Grill bacon cheeseburger. Sorry, doctor.

Mosca's would be one of the first places in New Orleans I'd go back to. There are places we all go back to because you can get the same dish you loved the last time. You wouldn't think to go there, it's forty minutes out of town. It doesn't look like much. But then you eat. The menu is a mashup of New Orleans and Italian food. Simple food. That spaghetti bordelaise may not be something you'd remember on its own, but when you do the Alon Shaya hack and put their oysters on top, that's what I'm talkin' about! And that's why you go to places with the locals.

By the way, April and November are the only times of year I'd recommend traveling somewhere surrounded by swamplands. The weather in New Orleans is beautiful then, and it's oyster season.

Almost Oysters Mosca

You're going to have to go to Mosca's to try their oysters. (The recipe is a family secret.) But I do know a great local chef who helped me out on this one.

Shuck some fresh oysters and save the juices (or buy some fresh oysters in a jar, you need the ones from a really good seafood place), and chop up a little onion and a lot of garlic. Heat a lot of butter in a pan and cook the vegetables, add some salt and other seasonings (dried oregano, maybe New Orleans' favorite Creole seasoning like Zatarain's, probably some cayenne?). Put the oyster juices you saved into the pan and cook that for a little while. Now add the oysters and put the whole thing in a baking dish. Mix together a lot of bread crumbs, melted butter, (maybe?) some grated parmesan, and season that how you like it. Put the bread crumbs over the oysters and broil it until it looks like it does at Mosca's, delicious and dark brown on the edges. Get a cocktail, pile this Pasta Bordelaise on your plate, and throw the oysters on top.

Pasta Bordelaise

Serves 4 to 6

Mosca's was originally founded around 1921 in Chicago Heights, Illinois, by my grandparents Provino and Lisa Mosca, both Italian immigrants. They had three children: Nicholas, Mary, and the youngest, John (my father). Nicholas and my father were drafted to fight in World War II; meanwhile, Mary moved to New Orleans where she married an oyster fisherman, Vincent. My grandfather, enamored by the culture of New Orleans and the availability of fresh seafood, followed suit in 1946 and moved to a little shack on Highway 90 in Jefferson Parish so he and my grandmother could be closer to their daughter. It was here that they reopened their restaurant, Mosca's; after my father returned from the war, he and my mother joined them in the family business. This is where Mosca's still stands to this day.

Mosca's Pasta Bordelaise is our version of the classic Italian dish aglio e olio (pasta with garlic and oil garnished with fresh parsley). Because of the strong French influence in New Orleans, my aunt Mary added butter to

the mix, and the "Bordelaise" was born. (No parsley! My grandmother hated parsley garnish.) —**Lisa Mosca**

½ cup (120ml) extra-virgin olive oil	Pinch kosher salt
1 ounce (¼ stick/28g) unsalted butter	16 ounces (450g) dried vermicelli or spaghetti
3 to 4 garlic cloves, minced	Pecorino Romano cheese, grated, for serving (optional)

In a small saucepan, combine the olive oil, butter, and garlic. Turn the heat to low and gently cook the garlic, swirling the pan occasionally, until just beginning to brown, 6 to 8 minutes. Remove the pan from the heat and add the salt.

Bring a large pot of water to a boil. Cook the pasta according to the package directions until al dente, 7 to 8 minutes for vermicelli and 10 to 11 minutes for spaghetti. Let the pasta cook 30 seconds longer, strain, and transfer to a large serving bowl. Add the garlic sauce and use tongs or two large forks to toss the pasta in the sauce until well combined. Serve the pasta immediately with the Pecorino Romano, if using.

Tips
- Cooking the garlic slowly over low heat intensifies the garlicky flavor.
- The pasta is cooked just beyond al dente so it's no longer chewy in the center but also not too soft.

Diversity is America's superpower.

I love that quote from Will Smith. If that's so, then New Orleans is a leading source of energy.

It's seen some hard times, but who hasn't? The lesson New Orleans has for us is how you get up from those times. You see that in the spirit that's on the street, in the good times to be had, and mostly, in the people.

And once you get up, you may as well go to the party.

Helen: Hi there, what's doing?

Phil: I love New Orleans, it's a very happy place. Everybody's out in the street, everybody's, you know . . . it really came back. And the tourism is fantastic. I'm telling everybody. If you can't travel outside the country, this seems to be the most European of American cities.

(sound of sirens in New York)

Helen: What?

Phil: They're coming to get you. I hear the sirens.

Max: Would you like the audience to see where we live out our window?

Phil: You want everybody knowing where you live? You want them knowing where your apartment is? Do you know how many fans you have? They'll be screaming outside your window like you're Justin Bieber.

Helen: What does that mean?

Max: Monica said you're going to a wedding today.

Phil: It's true. People I met in Saigon. And she's a chef, and she's cooking for us, but we're part of the wedding party.

Helen: When is that? Today?

Phil: Yeah, in a couple of hours. Just so happens.

Max: That's unbelievable. Everybody's getting married all of a sudden.

Phil: You recommend it, right?

Max: No.

(phil laughs)

Max: Marriage is a good institution. But who wants to live in an institution?

>6<

Mexico City

Mexico City is a lively modern city filled with innovation and a lot of soul. A city of openness, laughter, and friendship.

THIS WAS MY FIRST TIME IN MEXICO CITY BUT NOT my first time to Mexico. A lot of us think of the resorts when we think about going to Mexico, and those are easy places to start if you've never been outside the country. But you can't really see a country if all you do is sit by the pool.

Mexico City has more museums than any other city in the world; the buildings are more modern than what we have in Los Angeles; the subway is nicer, smoother, and cleaner than New York's. It's amazing. And then there are all these parks, these beautiful parks. It's massive with a population of more than 21 million, yet it feels so familiar, so comforting. And the food was as good as or beyond any I'd ever had anywhere else.

But as always, these people, that's why we're here. Every person I met was so warm, so wonderful. So many have built something, pursued their dreams that mean something not only to them, but is vital to the community. The high-end restaurants, the tortilla places, everybody at the markets selling cheese or pottery. It's life.

You need to be free, and think, and to be crazy. Mexico is in many ways the American dream, but like in Mad Max. *You can be anything you want to be, but if you don't do it, nobody will take care of it. You're on your own.* —**Jair Téllez**

You don't turn the taco, you turn your head. That's a philosophy of life. Maybe you bend a little, maybe you adjust.

I always say, if you like something, go to the source.

Those tacos on the street at that place, El Huequito, where I was trying to get everyone to stop and try it, it was just meat in a tortilla. But it was crazy. We've all had tacos, many, many times, but here, at the source, where tacos are from, it can blow the top of your head off.

That's not to say that any particular taco is "authentic." Authentic is a very overrated phrase. A grandma in a little town in Mexico can make a dish, and so can the one next door. Which one is more "authentic"? The only thing that matters to me: Is it delicious?

That's why I always say, "This is the best." Is it absolutely, without question, the best in the world? It is for me, at that moment.

. . . .

My favorite part of the scene with Elena is when we go to her kitchen and a piece of equipment started to fill the place with smoke. She's so sweet, apologizing, so I tell her that true story about my friend burning her kitchen down.

Elena really is brilliant. She starts with classic Mexican dishes and then takes them to a whole other level. Here she turns mole into a dessert . . . or if you're me filming in the morning, breakfast.

Pink Mole

Serves 6

*This dessert is a derivation of the mole rosa we origi-
nally served with suckling pig. Mole sauces contain so
many seeds and spices that it's easy to imagine them as
desserts. This one includes beets and pink pepper, and
we increased the amount of white chocolate. Unlike in
the savory version, we use yogurt instead of pulque and
added hibiscus flowers. We serve this at the restaurant
with a yogurt foam; this version uses enriched yogurt
that's easier to make.*

*The mole is meant to be served at room tempera-
ture, even a little cool. With Mexico's weather, we just
take it out of the refrigerator. If you live in a cold place,
you could rewarm it on the stove gently for a minute or
two. Pink pine nuts are the native Mexican piñon, but
they can be perfectly substituted with the Italian variety.*
—**Elena Reygadas**

½ cup (20g) whole dried hibiscus flowers

2 teaspoons pink peppercorns, smashed

1 whole clove

1 small dried chipotle pepper, seeded and torn into small pieces

Pinch dried thyme leaves

1 small red beet, peeled and roughly chopped

2½ tablespoons granulated sugar

1⅓ cups (320ml) whole milk

1 ounce (¼ stick/28g) unsalted butter

1 tablespoon vegetable oil, preferably sunflower

¼ cup (25g) whole blanched, unsalted almonds

3 tablespoons Mexican (pink) or Italian pine nuts

3 tablespoons untoasted sesame seeds

1 cup (160g) roughly chopped white chocolate or good-quality white chocolate chips, such as Guittard

⅓ cup (95g) full-fat plain Greek yogurt

2 cups (8 ounces/225g) strawberries, trimmed and halved

1½ cups (6 ounces/170g) raspberries

1½ cups (6 ounces/170g) blackberries (optional)

Yogurt Cream, chilled, recipe follows

4 generous pinches Hibiscus Flower Powder, recipe follows

Tie up the hibiscus flowers in cheese cloth or put the flowers in a coffee filter and seal the top with kitchen twine.
Put the hibiscus flower sachet, peppercorns, clove, chipotle, thyme, beets, sugar, and milk in a medium saucepan.
Bring to boil, reduce to a simmer, and cook until the beets
are tender but still slightly firm when pierced with a fork,
about 5 minutes. Use the back of a spoon to gently press
on the sachet of hibiscus flowers to squeeze out the juices
(discard the flowers) and let cool. Transfer the infused milk
to a blender and blend until smooth.

In a small sauté pan over medium heat, melt the butter
and vegetable oil. Add the almonds and toast the nuts, stirring constantly, until just beginning to brown, 1 to 1½ minutes, then add the pine nuts and sesame seeds and stir
until both are lightly toasted, about 30 seconds. Transfer
the nuts to the blender with the steeped milk and blend,
scraping down the sides of the container if needed, until
smooth (the mixture should be the consistency of a thick,
somewhat grainy sauce).

Gently melt the white chocolate in a small saucepan
over very low heat, stirring constantly with a rubber spatula, until just beginning to melt. Remove the pan from the
heat and stir until the chocolate fully melts. Transfer the
chocolate to the blender, add the yogurt, and blend until
well combined. Or, if the blender is too small to accommodate the chocolate and yogurt, mix everything together
in a large bowl. Let the mole cool completely, cover, and
refrigerate overnight or for up to 5 days.

Take the mole out of the refrigerator about 2 hours
before serving to allow it to come to room temperature. If
the mole is still too thick to easily spread, rewarm it gently
in a saucepan over low heat, stirring constantly, and add
1 tablespoon of water, if needed.

Divide the mole among six shallow serving bowls and
arrange the strawberries, raspberries, and blackberries,
if using, in the center of each. Spoon the Yogurt Cream
over the berries (or serve the Yogurt Cream on the side),
sprinkle a pinch of Hibiscus Flower Powder on top of each,
and serve.

Yogurt Cream

Makes about 1¼ cups (300ml)

¼ cup (60ml) heavy whipping cream

2 tablespoons granulated sugar

1 cup (280g) full-fat plain Greek yogurt

In a small saucepan over low heat, warm the cream and sugar, stirring occasionally, just until the sugar dissolves, 10 to 15 seconds. (Do not let the milk boil.) Transfer the cream to a medium bowl, add the yogurt, and whisk until smooth. Cover and refrigerate the yogurt at least 3 hours or for up to 5 days.

Hibiscus Flower Powder

Makes about 3 tablespoons

½ cup (20g) whole dried hibiscus flowers

Break up any large hibiscus flowers into small pieces. Arrange the flowers in a dehydrator and dehydrate the flowers according to the manufacturer's instructions.

Or, use the oven: Preheat the oven to 175°F (80°C). Scatter the flowers on a sheet pan or in a metal baking dish so the petals do not touch one another and bake, stirring occasionally and rotating the pan front to back halfway through, until the petals begin to darken around the edges, about 20 to 25 minutes. (Be careful not to burn the flowers; some may still be slightly soft in the center; they will dry out more as they cool.) Turn off the oven and let the flowers cool for 30 minutes in the oven.

Transfer the flowers to a blender, blend into a fine powder, and store in an air-tight jar for up to 1 month.

Tips

- Whole dried hibiscus flowers are available at many Latin markets and tea shops.
- Pink peppercorns, the berries of the Brazilian pepper tree (a relative of cashews, unlike white and black peppercorns), have a fruity and mildly peppery flavor; look for them at spice shops.
- Save the remaining Hibiscus Flower Powder to sprinkle over ice cream or cocktails.

You don't need to research this. There is one place you absolutely must go when you're in Mexico City: Xochimilco.

This place is on the outskirts of the city. It looks like a bunch of canals, but it's really these tiny man-made islands called *chinampas*, which means "floating gardens." It's where Mexico City started. People put stakes in the ground and filled it in with dirt, so the water that surrounds these islands becomes the perfect place to grow food. The Aztecs grew food here; Enrique Olvera gets a lot of his produce here. Today it's run by a non-profit that supports farmers taking back the land. It's unbelievable. You're not looking at the ruins of something while somebody tells you what you're supposed to know about it. You're *witnessing* how they did it because it's still happening right now.

· · · ·

To those of you who think I seem to like everything, may I direct your attention to the cow udder taco. I got to experience this at the market in Tepito, and I did not get the recipe for you. Many people love this, but for me, it tasted like there was still a little old milk in there.

That scene was also the one time we went somewhere that we'd heard could be a little dangerous, and I'm not just talking about that taco. Tepito is known as

And now a little something for the ladies . . . here's Antonio the farmer, who looks like Tom Cruise got a shovel.

Barrio Bravo, which means "the fierce neighborhood." It's also one of the biggest markets in the world. It's miles and miles long. It's no secret that there are some things of dubious legality there. For example, they sell video cassettes of movies that not only haven't been released yet, they haven't been made yet. But this was Bill Esparza's favorite neighborhood to eat street food, so we wanted to go. Did we go at night? No. You go there during the day to get the migas, the tacos. Do that. My one piece of advice is maybe don't take a camera crew. You're attracting a different kind of attention when you're filming something. At one point, some guys came up to our crew and said, "You will be leaving now." And we said, "But we're still filming."

And they said, "You will be leaving now, or you will be leaving without your cameras."

I just wished they'd approached us before I had the cow udder taco.

Max: I see the photos you're sending us, I think you're having more fun there than all the other places you've been to. Is that true?

Helen: No, I don't think so.

Phil: Why don't you think so, Ma?

Helen: I think you enjoy every place you are.

Max: But I think this is a little more.

Helen: No.

Max: They seem to be . . . the people seem to be very friendly or something. I don't know.

Helen: Max, you said the same thing when they were in Israel. Now you're saying he's happier here. He's happy wherever he is.

Max: As long as he's not here.

Phil: You guys, just take it away. It's your show now, I'm giving you the show. I'm gonna add, hang on . . .

(Another caller joins the screen.)

Monica: Hello!

Phil: Yes, you're here, too! So we have Max and Helen sitting in Manhattan, and we have Selma and this pretty girl, I think her name is Monica, in Pennsylvania. In Selma Horan's house. And I've spent many a nice evening on your grandmother's old bed, where she died.

Selma: Weren't you the lucky boy?

Phil: Yes. Selma, you're the new one that people don't really know. Should we do a show in Philadelphia? Philadelphia has amazing food.

Monica: She's a very good cook herself.

Phil: She is, just like my mom.

Monica: I think this finally, Helen, is your redemption. I've always loved my mother-in-law's cooking.

Helen: Thank you, Monica.

Phil: When I had the unspeakable part of the cow in a taco yesterday, I actually said, "I miss my mother's cooking."

Helen: Well, you should be ashamed of yourself.

Phil: Goodbye, everybody!

Max: Goodbye, it was a pleasure.

When you taste the history of a place, it can be incredible.

I just happen to prefer my local history lesson in the form of tacos, sandwiches, gelato . . . Before the show, I thought I'll never eat a bug, I'm not interested in that. And then I ate those ants in the Tokyo episode of *I'll Have What Phil's Having*. They tasted lemony, like someone put a Lemon Drop on my tongue. Am I looking for ants now everywhere I go? No. But it was very interesting. Maybe I was a little braver because the cameras were on me. You almost feel like it's not real life, you're on a TV show, so that makes you a little braver.

By the time I went to Mexico, I'd done the ants. At Pujol, you've got one of the greatest chefs in the world, Enrique Olvera, taking these things that are part of the culture and turning them into something brilliant, like the flying ants that locals toast up and eat like popcorn. Enrique grinds them up and puts them in that mayonnaise that goes on the baby corn and it is really great. The crushed ants are the salt of the dish.

I loved when we went to Enrique's house for lunch, and the star dish is not Enrique's, it's the quesadilla his son and his daughter make. It's the thing they eat the most, at the home of probably the most famous chef in all of Latin America.

Aldo's Quesadilla

Aldo was eight when we filmed this. I'm a terrible cook but even I can make this. I learned from the best.

Get a comal, the flat Mexican griddle without any sides. Get some good corn tortillas. You want the fresh ones, from a tortilleria or Latin market. Pull apart some Oaxacan cheese (quesillo cheese) or if you can't find that, people say a stick of mozzarella string cheese works. Heat your comal—that one Aldo's used was very hot—throw the cheese right in the middle, and put a

corn tortilla on top. Let the cheese cook until it looks really good and brown on the edges. Now lift up the whole thing with a spatula and flip it. (If you used a pan with sides, now you know why you need a comal.) Toast the other side, hand it over, and squeeze a little lemon juice on top. The kid's a genius.

Quesadillas with Epazote and Salsa Verde

Makes 4 quesadillas

I'm sharing with you the classic quesadilla recipe. My kids came up with the other version you saw where the cheese goes on the hot griddle first so it gets brown, then you flip the quesadilla and put some lemon on it. It's one of the things we eat the most at home. Either way you make them, it's best to make your own tortillas. If you buy tortillas, the only ingredients should be corn, limestone, salt, and water. —**Enrique Olvera**

5 ounces (140g) Oaxacan string cheese (quesillo) or 5 mozzarella string cheese sticks

4 good-quality corn tortillas, preferably freshly made

8 to 12 fresh epazote leaves (optional)

Salsa Verde, recipe follows

Use your fingers to pull the cheese apart into long strings.

Heat a cast iron comal or griddle over medium-high heat until hot and rewarm each tortilla, one at a time, until lightly toasted, about 10 seconds on each side.

Lay the tortillas on a work surface and divide the cheese among each so the cheese covers one half of each tortilla. Lay 2 to 3 epazote leaves, if using, on top of the cheese and fold the tortillas in half to cover the filling. Cook the quesadillas, one at a time, on the preheated comal or griddle until the cheese is melted, 30 to 45 seconds. Flip the quesadilla and cook until the opposite side of the corn tortilla is lightly browned, 5 to 10 seconds longer. Serve the quesadillas hot, as they come off the grill, with the Salsa Verde.

Salsa Verde

Makes about ¾ cup (180ml)

5 large tomatillos (8 ounces/225g)

1 garlic clove

¼ large white onion, roughly chopped

1 to 2 serrano or other small, hot chiles, stems removed

½ medium bunch fresh cilantro, both tender top stems and leaves

Sea salt

Remove the papery husks from the tomatillos, rinse the tomatillos well to remove any debris, and cut each in half.

Use tongs to hold the garlic clove directly over the flame of a gas burner and cook until charred on all sides, about 10 seconds. Or, toast the garlic in a hot comal or cast iron skillet.

Put the tomatillos, garlic, onions, serrano or other chiles, and cilantro in a blender, blend until almost smooth, and season the salsa with salt. Serve the salsa immediately or cover and refrigerate for up to 3 days.

Tip   Oaxacan string cheese, or quesillo, and fresh epazote, an herb native to Mexico, are available at most Latin markets.

Growing up in the US, you think you know what Mexico's like, because it's so close.

There are those who want to steer the conversation about Mexico for their own reasons, but I hope you don't let them. Because I thought I knew what Mexico City was like, and I wasn't prepared to have it take my breath away.

7

Venice

There are no special effects here.
Venice is the special effect.

I STARTED THE VENICE EPISODE WITH MY FAVORITE quote from baseball legend Yogi Berra: "Nobody goes there anymore, it's too crowded."

Venice has been touristy for generations. Nobody denies that. This city relies on tourism, it's what enables everything and everyone, from the gondoliers and mask craftsmen to the gelato makers and great chefs, to continue offering not just their community, but all of us, these wonderful things for so many generations. Sure, there are some places I don't ever want to go, the tourist traps, but there are also plenty of really good artisanal restaurants, mom and pop places. You just have to seek them out. This is another very good reason to make friends with locals.

And if you have young kids, Venice is the first place overseas I would recommend taking the family. It's the "It's a Small World" ride, only everyone waving to you is Italian. You know how hard it is to get kids to walk around? When we took our kids to Venice, they would walk anywhere as long as the walk ended in pizza or gelato. And in Italy, it usually does.

Another reason to go? Because it looks like this.

Some people are in the happiness business.

And there's probably no happier business than a gelato shop. Right after we got to Venice, Richard and I were walking around, not filming, and we see Alessandra's place, Boutique del Gelato. It really is about the size of a closet. We go in, get gelato, and it was great. Alessandra was great, too. So we asked if we could come back and shoot there.

The reason we knew she doesn't give out tastes is because Richard and I asked for one that first time. When we went back, she gave me a taste of the passion fruit, and I knew I was in.

. . . .

The first time I went to Da Arturo, I didn't think it could be as great as many friends of mine had told me. First, it's legendary with Hollywood types, so I thought it was

more famous for the scene than for the food. And it's in Venice, and the place doesn't even serve fish. How good could it be? Turns out, very, very good.

We don't show a lot of cooking on the show, it's not a cooking show. But of every dish we've ever featured on the show, the making of that pork chop was the one thing I wanted to make sure we filmed so you could try it at home. It's so simple, but it's the best pork chop I've ever had. And sure enough, it's the most requested recipe from the show.

So you can either watch the episode, or here's the recipe in perfect detail. You're gonna need to make two: one to eat now, so you can try it the way Ernesto likes it; and one for leftovers, so you can taste it how Hani prefers. One note: We say "white vinegar" in the show, but in Italy, that means white *wine* vinegar. There's a difference. You're welcome.

Braciola all'Arturo

Serves 2 (1 for today, 1 for tomorrow)

When I opened this restaurant in 1968, people said I was crazy in Venice to have only meat, no fish. This is one of our most popular dishes. You need to pound the pork chop very thin.—**Ernesto Ballarin**

2 8- to 10-ounce (225 to 280g) pork chops, preferably bone-in

½ cup (60g) all-purpose flour

1½ cups (165g) fine bread crumbs

3 large eggs, lightly beaten

Fine sea salt

Vegetable oil, for frying

1 cup (240ml) white wine vinegar, divided

Use the smooth side of a meat mallet to pound the pork chops as thin as possible without tearing the meat (about ¼ inch/6mm thick). If using pork chops with the bone, pound the meat up to the bone but leave the bone in place.

Put the pork chops on a sheet pan, sprinkle the flour evenly over both, and toss the pork chops in the flour until well coated.

Put the bread crumbs in a mound on another sheet pan and put the eggs in a large bowl.

Dip 1 floured pork chop into the eggs, shake off the excess, then lay the pork chop on top of the bread crumbs and flip the pork chop in the bread crumbs until evenly coated. Dip the pork chop again in the eggs, coat it a second time in the bread crumbs, and sprinkle both sides with the salt, to taste. Bread the remaining pork chop the same way.

Heat about 1 inch (2.5cm) of oil over medium-high heat in a large cast iron skillet or sauté pan (large enough for 1 pork chop to lay flat) until very hot. Test the oil by adding a few bread crumbs; they should sizzle. Add 1 pork chop to the skillet and fry until golden brown, 2 to 3 minutes, flip, then brown the other side, about 2 minutes longer. Transfer the pork chop to a plate.

Carefully pour the hot oil from the skillet into a saucepan or metal bowl (save the oil for the second pork chop).

Return the pork chop to the skillet, pour ½ cup (120ml) of the vinegar evenly over the surface of the meat, and cook over medium heat, flipping the pork chop occasionally, until the vinegar has mostly evaporated, about 5 minutes. Transfer the pork chop to a plate, let rest for 5 minutes, and serve.

When ready to cook the second chop, pat the skillet dry with paper towels, pour the reserved oil through a strainer into the skillet, and add more vegetable oil, if needed, to fill the skillet by about 1 inch (2.5cm). Fry the remaining pork chop the same way, let cool completely, cover, and refrigerate overnight. Serve the second pork chop at room temperature.

Tip Use the smooth side of a meat mallet, not the textured (tenderizer) side to pound the pork chops to avoid tearing the meat.

Phil: Oh, hi!

Helen: Hi, hello.

Max: Venice must be the most beautiful country in the world.

Helen: A beautiful *city*.

Phil: It used to be a big empire.

Phil: Listen, listen, listen.

(*man singing in Italian outside Phil's window*)

Max: I hear nothing.

Helen: I do.

Phil: What do you hear?

Helen: Birds? Birds.

Phil: I have to ask you, what kind of birds you have around your house?

Helen: Well, it could be from the outside.

Phil: It's definitely from the outside. It's a gondolier who's going by singing.

Max: You mean there's somebody walking on the street singing?

Phil: Gondolier! You know the streets are water, right? Because I'm in Venice.

Max: Oh, that's right. Did you hear about the street walker in Venice?

Phil: No.

Max: She . . . she drowned.

(*Phil and the crew laugh*)

Helen: So?

Max: That's, that's the joke.

Phil: I'm glad the people got to hear it.

(*Richard laughs*)

Phil: Did you hear I got to take a gondola lesson?

Helen: Oh?

Phil: Really, the tension just to stay balanced, and the oar doesn't stay in the thing, it keeps slipping out, and I'm gonna fall into the water I'm thinking . . .

Helen: Why didn't you stop?

Phil: Because I'm on television.

(*Max laughs*)

The problem with the rest of the world is that it's not Italy.

Venice is like a movie that's been art directed. Every single place you turn is another stunning visual. At one point, Richard looked at me and said it looked like I'd been green screened. The whole place is a masterpiece. You can't create these kind of places today.

I love that story Luca Marchiori, the food writer and historian, told me. There were these laws hundreds of years ago that you couldn't spend money on fancy clothes, so people spent money on what was around them: paintings, churches, buildings. Coffee beans were brought over from Istanbul, then you've got the wine, the incredible food. The rest of the world is still trying to catch up.

Today the city is sinking, being destroyed by the very tourists it relies on. When we were filming the episode, I saw it. The massive cruise ships get too close to the buildings and the water rises. You could actually feel the vibrations. And then, thousands of people get off the boat only to sightsee for a few hours, buy a tchotchke, then go back and eat on the boat. They're not supporting the local hotels or restaurants or businesses. It's just another kind of invasion. You probably remember when I was at Ristorante al Covo, Cesare and Diane's son, Lorenzo, said people ask him what time Venice closes, like it really is a theme park.

We don't need another theme park in this world. We need Venice.

When you lose the people, you lose the culture, you lose everything. —**Lorenzo Benelli**

. . . .

Monica and I have been going to Ristorante Al Covo for years. Cesare and Diane have become friends, and their food is glorious. You're going to love Cesare's linguine with clams. It's on the next page.

Linguine alle Vongole

Serves 4

This is a mythical, historical Venetian dish. With just enough patience in the preparation, the celebrity status is immediately justified.

If you have Mediterranean vongole veraci clams, they are the best, but fresh Palourde ("carpet shell"), littleneck, or Manila clams could be substituted. You need to put the clams in a basin of fresh, salted water, or better, sea water, for about one hour, in order to flush out any residual sand. It helps to use a fork to "twirl" the pasta and put a ladle underneath to move and place it nicely on each plate. My wine suggestion is Malvasia di Carso (a dry white) with mineral and aromatic hints.
—**Cesare Benelli**

1½ pounds (680g) small clams, such as vongole veraci, littleneck, or Manila, scrubbed

1½ tablespoons plus 1 teaspoon fine sea salt, divided

4 tablespoons extra-virgin olive oil

2 garlic cloves, "in their shirts" (unpeeled)

12 cherry tomatoes, roughly chopped

12 ounces (340g) good-quality artisan linguine, preferably Pastificio Gentile or Benedetto Cavalieri

8 fresh zucchini blossoms, thinly sliced (optional)

1 tablespoon finely chopped basil leaves

1 tablespoon finely chopped fresh parsley leaves

Freshly ground pepper, preferably white

Zest of ½ small lemon

1 small pepperoncini or similar small hot chile pepper, seeds removed and finely chopped (optional)

Gently place the clams in a strainer (be careful not to break the shells), rinse well under cold running water, and transfer to a large bowl. Put 2 cups (480ml) of cold water in a large measuring cup, add 1½ tablespoons of the salt, and stir well to partially dissolve the salt. Pour the salt water over the clams and add another 4 cups (950ml) of cold water. (Or, use fresh sea water, if available.) Add a handful of ice cubes to the bowl, let the clams rest in the salt water for about 1 hour, strain, and rinse well. Use the clams right away, or cover with a damp cloth and refrigerate for up to 12 hours.

Fill a large stockpot with water. Add the remaining 1 teaspoon of salt, and bring to a boil.

Meanwhile, heat a large, deep sauté pan with a lid or Dutch oven over medium heat. Add the olive oil and garlic and cook until the garlic skins just begin to color, 3 to 4 minutes. Add the tomatoes and clams, cover the pan, and steam the clams until most have opened, about 2 minutes. Turn off the heat and use a spider or slotted spoon to transfer the clams to a bowl. (Discard the garlic cloves and any clams that do not open.)

Add the linguine to the boiling water and cook according to the package directions until barely al dente, about half the suggested cooking time, about 5 minutes, depending on the brand. Scoop out and reserve about ¼ cup (60ml) of the cooking water, strain the pasta, and transfer the pasta to the pan with the tomatoes.

Return the heat to medium and gently stir the pasta until the pan juices are mostly absorbed, 2 to 3 minutes. If the pasta appears dry, add 2 to 3 tablespoons of the reserved pasta cooking water. Increase the heat to high, add the steamed clams and any accumulated juices, then scatter the zucchini blossoms, if using, basil, and parsley on top. Gently stir the pasta until the clams are just warm, about 45 seconds, and season the pasta with the pepper.

Transfer the pasta to four shallow bowls, divide the clams and any cooking juices among each, sprinkle the lemon zest and pepperoncini on top, if using, and serve.

One of my favorite scenes in the whole show was when we went down to Modena, to the Mercato Albinelli.

Caterina Schenetti handed me the very special six-year-old cheese and I accidentally dropped it. Before I could get it, Richard picked it up off the floor and ate it. This is how I'll be feeding him from now on.

Parmesan and Champagne

Good parmesan is one thing I always bring back when I go to Italy. It comes in those vacuum-sealed bags so you can throw it in your suitcase under the socks.

Oh, I have a great pairing for you: parmesan and Champagne. It's my little hack. It blew me away the first time I tasted them together. I love showing this to chefs and watching their faces when they try it. It's my one contribution to the culinary arts.

Get out a really big piece of Parmigiano Reggiano (it's got to be the good stuff). Open a bottle of Champagne. Say, "Phil was right!"

. . . .

I didn't know what to expect when I met Massimo. I'm going to the home of a chef whose restaurant, Osteria Francescana, was voted number one in the world, and I'm some guy filming a TV show. But he and his wife, Lara Gilmore, couldn't have been more gracious or genuine. We've been good friends ever since.

Massimo actually never told us if we would be able to film at the restaurant, he just said, "Spend the day with me." And so I did. And as much fun as I had with him, and all the places he took me, I have to admit, in the back of my mind was, "Am I going to get to eat in the best restaurant in the world today?" And if you've seen the show, you know what happened.

I really did feel so special being in the Francescana kitchen. Massimo told me no one had been allowed to eat or film in the kitchen before. I felt like some bum who snuck in somehow and was now eating their profits. In the episode, he wanted to show me his world-famous dish, the Five Ages of Parmigiano-Reggiano in Different Temperatures and Textures, and he wanted to share it here with you exactly as he wrote it. Now remember, this recipe is by Massimo Bottura, one of the world's great chefs. Good luck to you.

Five Ages of Parmigiano Reggiano
in Different Temperatures and Textures

Serves 1

This is the only recipe that I have never been able to take off the menu since opening Osteria Francescana in the spring of 1995. "Five Ages" is like a Jazz Standard. One ingredient—Parmigiano Reggiano—which we know well and use often in our kitchens (at least in Italy), played out in five different ways by changing the temperature and texture, the shape and form, while still remaining true to the flavor and essence of the cheese. The techniques are complicated but not impossible. The real trick is finding really great Parmigiano Reggiano cheese, and even tougher, five different ages to understand just how different they can be.

If you are as obsessive as Phil, or at least as curious, give this recipe a try. Even if you only make three of the different textures and temperatures, you are off to a great start and will not be disappointed. —**Massimo Bottura**

P.S. Serve with hot dogs (hahaha).

2 quenelles of Demi Soufflé (recipe follows)	Parmigiano Foam (recipe follows)
2 spoonfuls Parmigiano Sauce (recipe follows)	1 Parmigiano Wafer (recipe follows)

Place 2 quenelles of the Demi Soufflé at the base of each plate and add 2 spoonfuls of Parmigiano Sauce around the soufflé. Place the Parmigiano Foam on top, add the Parmigiano Wafer at a diagonal slant, and finally a cloud of Parmigiano Air covering one quarter of the plate. Serve.

Demi Soufflé

200g organic ricotta	40g double (heavy) cream
60g egg white	1 gram sea salt
100g 24-month Parmigiano Reggiano, grated	0.5g white pepper

Grease some 8x4cm (3x1-inch) aluminum timbales. Smoke the ricotta lightly over cherry wood chips in a sealed oven for 3 minutes.

Whip the ricotta. Whisk the egg white to stiff peaks.

Mix the Parmigiano with the cream, fold in the ricotta, and season the mixture with the salt and pepper. Fold in the whisked egg white and steam the soufflés in the timbales for 45 minutes, remove from the timbales, and shape the soufflé into quenelles.

Parmigiano Sauce

20g capon stock, not strained	100g 30-month Parmigiano Reggiano, grated

Bring the stock to 60°C (140°F) at medium speed in a thermal mixer. Add the Parmigiano and bring it to 85°C (185°F), then increase the speed and process to create a smooth, velvety sauce. Pass the sauce through a fine chinois. (Refrigerate if not using right away.)

Parmigiano Foam

125g capon stock	100g double (heavy) cream
250g 36-month Parmigiano Reggiano, grated	

Put the capon stock in a thermal mixer and bring to a boil at setting 3. Add the Parmigiano a spoonful at a time. Increase the speed for 1 more minute, then add the cream. Cool the mixture to 4 to 8°C (39 to 46°F), place it in a siphon, shake it, charge it with a double cartridge, and shake again. Let the foam rest in the refrigerator for at least 1 hour at 4 to 8°C (39 to 46°F) before serving.

Parmigiano Wafer

100g 40-month Parmigiano Reggiano, grated	100g mineral water

Put the Parmigiano and water in a saucepan and slowly bring it to a boil until the cheese becomes stringy. Remove the pan from the heat, let the cheese rest at room temperature for 2 hours, then drain off the liquid and put the cheese in the fridge overnight.

Preheat the oven to 170°C (325°F). Roll out the cold cheese dough very thin to a thickness of 1mm (.03 inch) and lay it out flat on a silicone baking mat. Bake for 12 minutes until it is a thin wafer. Let the wafer cool at room temperature, then crack it into 4 parts and break the wafers into imperfect triangular shapes, about 5cm (2 inches) each. (Store tightly sealed at room temperature.)

Parmigiano Air

200g 50-month Parmigiano Reggiano crusts	200g 50-month Parmigiano Reggiano, grated
	2g lecithin

Place the Parmigiano crusts in a pan with 500g of water and simmer for 3 hours over low heat. Strain and cool the liquid. Blend the chilled liquid and the grated Parmigiano for 30 minutes, then cover and let it rest in the refrigerator overnight. Strain it through a tamis sieve and transfer the strained liquid to a large bowl. Just before serving, add the lecithin and whisk the liquid with a handheld blender until it rises into a cloud of air.

Someone said to me once, "Phil, you seem to have friends all over the world." I said, "My god, that's right, I have friends all over the world now. Shouldn't we be friends with people from all over the world?"

Who doesn't want to go to Italy? The history, the art, the food, the citizens, the sheer beauty of this place is incredible.

That final dinner was made up of friends from the first version of the show, the Florence episode in *I'll Have What Phil's Having*. It was our first Italy episode in the series, Florence and Umbria, which was probably my favorite episode I've shot because it's so personal. From Florence we had Silvana Vivoli, who makes the best gelato in the world, and from Panzano, Dario Cecchini, the world's most famous butcher, and his wife, Kim. Dario is maybe the only person who gets more excited about food than me. Jim Lahey from Sullivan Street Bakery in New York, one of the great bakers, happened to be in town; he's a friend of Dario and Kim's. The food was incredible. The views weren't bad, either. But I would have been happy in the basement, just to see their faces.

Funiculì, Funiculà!

8

Dublin

It's hard not to feel good when you're in Ireland. One reason is the incredible beauty. But it's mostly the Irish: their warmth, their spirit, their sense of fun.

I'D NEVER BEEN TO IRELAND BEFORE THIS EPISODE. I said on the show that Ireland is a part of my life because I married an Irish girl. I'd always wanted to go there with Monica. She counts as a local.

And what a place. Dublin is the capital of Ireland, famous for literature but also famous for good times. They say Ireland is the birthplace of comedy, and you get that immediately when you're here. I do think that's one reason Ireland feels a little like home to me. Folks used to say the food here wasn't so great, but I can tell you, Irish food has finally caught up with the drink. Everything I had was fantastic. I'm so happy I went.

What I will always remember most is that the whole place is filled with people like Monica: sweet, positive, warm, and telling me I don't drink enough.

. . . .

I couldn't wait to try a "Full Irish Breakfast." The first place we filmed in Ireland was a breakfast place, and the one thing they didn't have was a Full Irish Breakfast.

Kale–Sunflower Seed Irish Butter

Makes about 1½ cups (335g)

When Phil visited, we treated him to possibly the last kind of breakfast he was expecting to have in Dublin: our version of a delightful Turkish dish called eggs menemen. Giving an American tourist anything but the classic "Full Irish" for his first breakfast in Dublin was always going to be controversial, and it was great to see him lost for words (though he soon made up for that). The unfortunate side effect of feeding this to Phil was the popularity of this already popular dish soared, to the extent that it came to dominate our menu. It was time for a change (any chef will tell you that they can fall out of love with even the greatest dish if it is too popular). We reinvented it into a version we call "eggs baba bida"

with an eggplant baba ghanoush, but the original will be back.

As for our Irish breakfast, that's also actually Phil's fault somehow. After the episode, we started getting a lot more tourists coming in, which has been amazing of course and we are so grateful. We'd often be their first or last stop in Ireland, so we felt it was so very important to give them the best possible experience, for Ireland. And honestly, there was a limit to the number of times I could see that "look" of disappointment wash over people's eyes when I had to tell them that we didn't do a "Full Irish." We compromised with what we call "The Full Hubbard," inspired by the classic but very much our version with homemade pork kofta (a Middle Eastern–style meatball), maple-glazed bacon, our spiced baked beans, along with a fried egg, roasted baby tomatoes, and the best black pudding we could find. One thing that's always required to make an Irish breakfast complete is homemade soda bread. We serve ours with this toasty kale–sunflower seed butter. The butter has unlimited uses; use it on grilled fish or meats, or toss it into pasta with a pinch of chile pepper. But be sure to use good traditional Irish butter—good and creamy and salty—for the base. —**Garrett Fitzgerald**

8 ounces (2 sticks/225g) good-quality salted butter, such as Kerrygold	1 cup (140g) raw unsalted sunflower seeds
	1 garlic clove, roughly chopped (optional)
1 small bunch kale, any variety (6 ounces/180g), stems removed	Coarse sea salt
	Freshly ground black pepper

Let the butter sit at room temperature very soft, at least 1 hour.

Bring a medium pot of water to a boil. Add the kale and blanch until wilted and bright green, about 45 seconds, then strain and immediately rinse the kale under cold running water until cool. Use your hands to squeeze out any excess water, then roll the kale in a kitchen towel to fully dry the leaves.

If you're going out in Ireland, you're going for a pint.

Put the kale, about ⅔ of the sunflower seeds, and the garlic, if using, in a food processor, and pulse until the mixture is coarsely ground into a paste (small flecks of kale and sunflower seeds should still visible). Transfer the kale mixture to a bowl, stir in the softened butter and remaining sunflower seeds until well incorporated, and season the butter with salt and pepper, to taste. Turn out the butter into a crock or container, cover, and refrigerate for at least 2 hours or up to 1 week.

. . . .

The great thing about the Guinness Storehouse is you don't even have to like beer or even drink the beer to go (although you should). It's the most visited tourist spot in not just Dublin, but all of Ireland. It's like a pilgrimage site. When you take the elevator to the bar at the very top, you're greeted with a 360-degree view of the city and beyond. That alone is worth the trip. And you can swap bad bar stories with somebody who will actually appreciate it. Here's mine:

I worked as a bartender after college and lasted about a month. I was terrible. The very first drink somebody asked me for was a Pink Squirrel. I had no idea. Below the bar, I looked in my *Mr. Boston's* under P for "Pink," then under S for "Squirrel," then under R for "Rodent Drinks." Couldn't find it. I looked back at the lady and said, "Can ya help me? It's my first day. Can I get you something simple?" She asked for a gin and tonic. An act of kindness.

Pink Squirrel

Today there's this new thing called the Internet. If you want a very sweet, creamy, and, yes, pink, cocktail from the 1940s, this is for you. I'm sticking with Irish whiskey.

Put a couple cubes of ice in a cocktail shaker. Now add equal parts white crème de cacao and crème de noyaux (or amaretto) and some heavy whipping cream. Shake that for a couple seconds and strain it into a martini glass. Taste, hand it to someone else. Open your whiskey.

There are some places where you think this just couldn't get any prettier. And then it does.

In less than an hour from Dublin, you're in a whole other world. You hear the name Greystones and it doesn't sound like a place you need to go. Then you get there and it's on the sea, these rocky cliffs, it's so beautiful. The drive itself is out of a storybook.

But when we got there, it was early morning, and we saw a bunch of mental cases with bathing suits on. They're jumping in the freezing cold water. No wet suits. And they do this every day, like they're vacationing on an island in the Caribbean. They're grinning and laughing through chattering teeth and telling me that I am now in the best town in the world. I didn't believe it at first. But I was.

. . . .

Of all the people I've met traveling, Steven and David are still tops on the happy scale. They remind me of the character in Frank Capra's 1936 movie *Mr. Deeds Goes to Town*. Gary Cooper plays this guy who is so happy and positive they say he's pixelated. It's not supposed to be a compliment, but I love that idea. By the way, it turns out the whole town is pixelated, and so is Greystones.

When the twins opened The Happy Pear, they gave anybody who stopped by the shop a bowl of porridge, or what we call oatmeal. They put out fresh fruit, nuts, and their homemade jams and syrups. All free. With that bowl of oatmeal, they built something special. People would come by every day to say hello, take home some produce for later. Most people would have charged for that kind of breakfast when the business got going. They didn't. You can still get a free bowl of

oatmeal every morning. When you do something like that, you engender not only loyalty, but community. It's why I support and even invest in restaurants. Selfishly, they make where I live better. Steven and David made their town better.

This is my book, so I'm renaming their porridge. Maybe they'll keep the name. I did jump into that freezing cold water with them.

Pixelated Porridge

Serves 1 health nut or 2 people with a normal appetite

We eat so much porridge in Ireland that we joke our blood is half oatmeal. The Irish love a thicker-style porridge, but that doesn't mean you have to use steel-cut oats. We actually prefer smaller rolled oats, but use whatever size you like (a coarser steel-cut will take longer to cook). Non-dairy milk is our secret weapon as it's very flavorful so you don't need sugar. Rice and almond milk are naturally quite sweet and make a very creamy porridge. For a more indulgent porridge, try coconut milk diluted with half water, or half hazelnut milk, half water for a subtle Nutella-like flavor.

When topping and decorating your porridge, think of texture and color: crunchy (granola), nutty (peanut or almond butter, toasted seeds or nuts), fruity (compotes, jams, fresh fruit), creamy (caramelized bananas, yogurt), and even savory. Our good friend Mark likes avocado and seaweed in his porridge, and miso and mushrooms find their way into the rice-based breakfast porridges in Japan. —**Steven and David Flynn**

1 cup (100g) rolled oats (not instant)	3 to 4 tablespoons Berry-Chia Jam, recipe follows
1¼ cups (300ml) rice or almond milk	Toppings: Fresh fruit, nuts, granola, and yogurt, or whatever you'd like

In a medium saucepan, combine the oats, milk, and 1 cup (240ml) of water. Bring to a boil, stirring occasionally, and cook until slightly thickened, about 5 minutes. (For a thicker porridge, continue to boil the oats until the liquid is slightly reduced.) Serve the porridge hot with the Berry-Chia Jam and your favorite toppings.

Berry-Chia Jam

Makes about 1⅓ cups (320ml)

10 ounces (280g) mixed berries, such as fresh or frozen blackberries, raspberries, and/or blueberries	⅓ cup (80ml) apple juice
	⅓ cup (80ml) maple syrup
	⅓ cup (45g) ground chia seeds

In a medium saucepan, combine the berries, apple juice, maple syrup, and chia seeds and bring to a boil. Reduce to a simmer and cook, stirring occasionally, until slightly thickened, about 5 minutes. Use a fork to smash any large berries and let the jam cool completely. Use the jam immediately, or cover and refrigerate for up to 2 weeks.

Tips
- Chia seeds act as a natural thickening agent in the jam.
- For a smoother texture, purée the finished jam in a food processor or blender.

. . . .

Everywhere we went, we had people telling stories about traveling somewhere and never wanting to leave. Some fell in love. Caitlin at Deasy's was one. She was from Dublin, New Hampshire, and moved to Dublin, Ireland, after she met an Irish fellow in Belgium. (I'll say it again: better than online dating, people!) That whole area is out of a storybook; all of the Irish countryside is like that. Why wouldn't you move here? At Caitlin's place, the fish was brought in by the local fishermen and the produce was dropped off by the guy next door, even the butcher in town owns his own cattle. And you get nice little beverages like this one.

Rhubarb Martini

Makes 1 cocktail

This martini was the most popular cocktail that we served at Deasy's. Luckily, rhubarb has a long growing season in Ireland. It came to life while I was creating a wedding menu for a bride who wanted a lemony sorbet course and wanted the main ingredients of the menu to be Irish (lemons aren't). Each version I made with cooked rhubarb seemed muddy and didn't have the required zing. The idea to use raw rhubarb came to me in the middle of the night, as most of the best ideas do.

It's unusual to use rhubarb raw, but the resulting cocktail is more tangy and gin-y (and delicious) than sweet. The fizzing beetroot "sherbet" that rims the glass makes the cocktail extra special (it's also delicious sprinkled on desserts). For those who don't drink cocktails, the rhubarb juice mix freezes into that wedding sorbet (if you have an ice cream maker) or a granita (put the juice directly into the freezer and scrape off the icy bits into a bowl), or use it to make a sparkling tonic water.
—**Caitlin Ruth**

1 teaspoon Beetroot Sherbet, well stirred, recipe follows	2 ounces (60ml) London dry gin, such as Tanqueray
3 ounces (90ml) Rhubarb Juice, recipe follows	Dash Angostura bitters

Spread out the Beetroot Sherbet in a circle on a small plate roughly the size of the mouth of a martini glass. Wipe the rim of the glass with a damp paper towel, turn the glass upside down, and twist the glass into the Sherbet to lightly coat the rim.

Fill a cocktail shaker with ice, add the Rhubarb Juice, gin, and bitters, and shake vigorously for 10 to 15 seconds. Strain the cocktail into the martini glass and serve.

Beetroot Sherbet

Makes about 4 tablespoons (enough for 12 cocktails)

¼ cup (50g) granulated sugar	½ teaspoon beet powder
1 teaspoon citric acid	¼ teaspoon baking soda

In a small bowl, whisk together the sugar, citric acid, beetroot powder, and baking soda until well combined. Store the beetroot sherbet in an airtight container at room temperature for up to 1 month.

Rhubarb Juice

Makes about 2½ cups (600ml)

3 cups (12 ounces/340g) roughly chopped fresh rhubarb (4 to 5 medium stalks)

½ cup (120ml) freshly squeezed lemon juice (about 3 medium lemons), or to taste

½ cup (100g) granulated sugar

Pinch sea salt

Put the rhubarb and ¾ cup (180ml) of water in a blender and blend to a smooth paste. (Do this in batches if needed.) Set a fine mesh strainer over a large bowl and use your hands to firmly press on and squeeze out the rhubarb solids to release as much of the juice as possible; you should have about 1¾ cups/420ml of juice.

Rinse out the blender, add the lemon juice, sugar, and salt, and blend until the sugar is well incorporated, about 10 seconds. Transfer the lemon juice mixture to a pitcher, add the rhubarb juice, stir to combine, and add more lemon juice, if needed. Use the cocktail base immediately, or cover and refrigerate for up to 1 week. (Stir the cocktail base well before using.)

Tips

- Fresh rhubarb stalks range from almost green to rosy pink; the color won't affect the flavor of the cocktail. Frozen rhubarb is not a good substitute; the root absorbs excess water when frozen, diluting the flavor and affecting the ratio of liquid to sugar ingredients in recipes.
- Beet powder, available at health and specialty food stores, is made from dehydrated, finely ground beets. Citric acid, found naturally in citrus fruits, is used as a preservative in home canning. If you can't find the beet powder and citric acid, swipe the cocktail glass rims with a cut lemon wedge and dip the rims in granulated sugar.

It all makes sense now.

A couple of the guys driving our vans kept saying that I had to stop by The Oval Bar when we got down to Cork. You'll remember these three guys—Des, Tom, and Owen—were there, and after a few drinks the conversation shifted to my lovely wife. Turns out Monica and Tom share the same last name. Like any good husband, I asked if the Horans were famous in Ireland. Des comes back with that great line, "Oh, the Horans *are* famous, but I can't tell ya why 'cause you said it's 'yer wife." Gotta love these people. My wife's people.

Here's another Irish love story that you may remember. Takashi Miyazaki was working at an Irish pub in Japan, fell in love with an Irish girl, moved to Ireland, and opened a couple of restaurants, including Miyazaki. (I've still never had anything like that seaweed tempura.) My favorite part in that scene was when he finds out I married an Irish girl. You can tell he's excited. This guy is a chef, so of course he wants to know what she cooks. I was being nice when I said, "Chicken."

By the way, the name Horan comes from the Gaelic term *Ó hUghróin*, or "descendant of Ughrón." Guess what that means? Warlike.

Seaweed Tempura

This couldn't be simpler. Seaweed, battered and fried. Why aren't people doing this? Here's why. You need fresh seaweed. For that you need an expert like Sally McKenna. By the way, if you do go to Ireland and go seaweed foraging, know this: as soon as you walk into the water in those knee-high rubber boots, all of the freezing cold water pours right into your boots. I'll be at Miyazaki.

Have somebody get some fresh seaweed for you. Order some dashi from your favorite Japanese place. Get some other stuff to eat in case this recipe doesn't work. (I'm gonna guess making this tempura is like slicing fish for sushi: it looks easy but there's a reason a chef is doing it.) Make some tempura batter. Heat up some oil in a pot, dip the seaweed in the batter, and fry that until it's crispy. Now make more. You want a bag of this stuff. Sit in front of the TV and eat it with the dashi.

- *If you go seaweed foraging, I recommend buying a tide table or investing in an App to check the tides in your area. Visit when the tide is low, when the full goodness of the shore is exposed.*
- *A good place to start is channeled wrack, one of the easiest seaweeds to spot that's found on rocks at the high tide mark. Look for the little "channels" in its fronds, there to catch the surf.*
- *Be mindful of the tides! Water comes back in fast. If you're visiting the shore, go with friends and tell someone you are going. Rocks are slippery!*
- *Always use a knife or scissors, never pull. And only forage for small amounts of seaweed; a little goes a long way.*
- *Back home, use the seaweed for a salad, raw or cooked, to bring umami to your food.* —**Sally McKenna**

I finally got my Full Irish Breakfast. Darina cooked the whole thing in fifteen minutes: blood sausage, regular sausage, ham, and bacon from the pigs; fried eggs from the chickens; and a few fresh tomato slices from the farm "for good measure." Oh boy.

And because that's not enough, here you also get delicious breads: scones, classic Irish soda bread, and this recipe that's a little sweeter. And the best homemade butter you've ever had in your life! Oh, and fresh honeycomb…that I had to go get from the bees.

Stupid Richard.

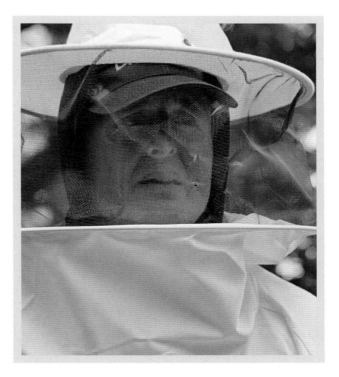

Mary Walsh's Currant Cake

Serves 8

A wonderful home baker named Mary Walsh lived in the little village of Cullohill in County Laois, where I grew up as a child. She's famous for her currant "cake," which falls somewhere between a very rich, citrus-scented Irish soda bread and a cake. She usually made it on Sunday mornings, and as children we used to fight about who would collect the milk from their farm that morning so we could have a slice fresh from the oven.

One of the secrets of why it tastes so good is that she uses sultanas (golden raisins) not currants, despite the name. Mary suggests plumping up the dried fruit for a minute or two in the oven or in a saucepan with some fresh orange juice if you don't have tender sultanas. And you must let the fairies out, a very important Irish tradition! (Before baking, make small pricks where the "cross" you make on the top of the dough meets.) —**Darina Allen**

2 ounces (½ stick/55g) unsalted butter (room temperature), plus more for the pan

3¼ cups (450g) all-purpose flour, plus more for dusting

2 tablespoons (25g) castor or light or dark brown sugar

½ teaspoon baking soda

½ teaspoon kosher salt

1 large organic lemon

3 medium organic oranges

1 cup (150g) sultanas (golden raisins)

1 large egg

1¼ cups (300ml) buttermilk

2 tablespoons (30ml) buttermilk cream or heavy whipping cream

1 tablespoon demerara or turbinado sugar

Good-quality salted Irish butter, for serving

Preheat the oven to 425°F (220°C) and place a baking rack in the lower third of the oven. Lightly butter an 8-inch (20cm) iron skillet or round cake pan.

In a large bowl, mix the flour, castor or brown sugar, baking soda, and salt together bowl. Use your fingers to rub the butter into the dry ingredients.

Use a citrus peeler to remove the peel from the lemon and 2 of the oranges in large strips, avoiding the white pith, and finely chop the peels; you should have about 4 tablespoons of chopped peel. Finely zest the remaining orange.

Add all of the finely chopped peels and citrus zest and the sultanas or golden raisins to the bowl with the flour mixture and stir until well combined.

Put the egg in a medium bowl and whisk in the buttermilk and cream. Set aside 2 tablespoons of the buttermilk mixture. Make a well in the center of the dry ingredients and pour in the remaining buttermilk, stirring with a wooden spoon to make a very moist, shaggy dough. Or, use your hands: grip the edge of the bowl with one hand, stir with a broad circular motion with the other.

Turn the dough out onto a well-floured work surface and dust your hands lightly with flour. Gently shape the dough into a thick, roughly 6-inch (15cm) round and use a bench scraper or large spatula to transfer the dough to the center of the iron skillet or cake pan. Dust a knife blade with flour and make an X across the dough round, then use the tip of the knife to make a small prick in each of the four corners where the X or "cross" intersects at the center of the dough round. Brush the top and sides of the dough with the reserved buttermilk mixture and sprinkle the demerara or turbinado sugar on top.

Put the cake pan in the oven, reduce the temperature to 400°F (180°C), and bake until the bread is lightly golden brown on top and sounds hollow when you tap the bottom with a wood spoon, about 40 minutes. (To test, flip the cake pan upside down to pop out the loaf. If it's not ready, use a hot pad to put the cake back in the pan and bake for another 5 to 10 minutes.) Transfer the bread to a wire rack and let cool for about 20 minutes. Cut the bread into thick slices and serve it warm with the butter.

Tip
- Demerara and turbinado sugar, available at well-stocked grocery stores, have a coarse sea salt–like texture and subtle molasses flavor.

Phil: Faith and Begorrah!

Helen: Hello, how are you?

Phil: Very nice . . . Dad, are you playing bridge?

Max: I played yesterday.

Phil: How'd you do?

Max: Not so good. This woman I didn't want to play with, she asked me to play with her because she didn't have anybody, so I said, "Okay."

Helen: Max, I'd prefer if you didn't talk about the fact that you didn't want to play with her. This will be on the show.

Phil: Yeah, and what's her name? Do you have an address maybe?

Max: No, no, no.

Helen: He likes these two other women.

Phil: Oh, really? Ma, you all right with this? Your husband playing with other ladies?

Helen: Oh, I'm perfectly fine. I'd even pay them.

Max: You were in Dublin, and you went somewhere else?

Phil: I went down the East Coast. I went to this place that's a working farm, it's called Ballymaloe.

Helen: How were the pigs?

Phil: Delicious.

Helen: Oh, no!

Phil: I forget, have you been to Ireland? It's so beautiful, so lush and green. All the food, I have to say, has been fantastic. My favorite thing . . . (*holding up bread*) this is sourdough bread, it's actually hot out of the oven. The other thing, Dad, that you would love, is there is nothing like this. (*holding up butter*) You see how yellow it is? I'm telling you I'll

put this butter up against any butter anywhere. This is like a paradise.

Helen: You know we haven't had breakfast yet.

Max: You've also been to the pig farm there, where you feed the pigs?

Phil: That's right.

Helen: We went through that already.

Max: When was that?

Helen: A few minutes ago.

Phil: Maybe it's not the lady at bridge's fault.

Max: Enjoy the rest of your stay there. You can't have it any better really.

Phil: I think you're right.

Helen: Would you like to be in his place?

Max: No. I enjoy it here.

Phil: Maybe you couldn't have it any better.

Max: Right.

Phil: Did you think of that?

(*Max looks at his wife, then makes a face as if to say, "What choice do I have?"*)

Phil: Thank you for the good ending. Goodbye.

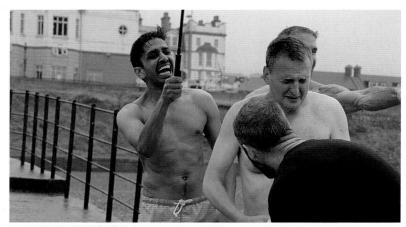

It's hard not to feel good and eat well when you're in Ireland.

I love the food, the spectacular scenery. I was knocked out by how lush and green Ireland is and how kind and generous, and, yes, funny these people are.

But to me, the best part of traveling is always gonna be, you know this by now, the folks you meet. Sometimes you meet people whose attitude about life is so wonderful that even if it seems crazy, you'd be crazy to forget about it.

I didn't like jumping into that freezing water, but I'm glad I did it. (I am very sorry everybody had to see me half naked. I apologize.) Even to this day, when I take a shower, the last thirty seconds I put it on cold. (I started with ten seconds, and then worked my way up.) More than waking me up, it absolutely reminds me of this experience. And that's beautiful.

Sometimes you just gotta jump in.

9

Buenos Aires

Buenos Aires. Even the name sounds so mysterious and exotic, but once you're there, you instantly recognize the people as kindred spirits.

I'M OFTEN ASKED HOW WE CHOOSE A LOCATION TO feature on the show. We've only done twenty-eight shows so far, including the PBS series, so I've only scratched the surface of the earth. If my mission is to get you to travel, I thought I'd start with Earth's Greatest Hits. Buenos Aires fits that.

It's always somewhere I had wanted to go but I knew very little about—other than I'd heard there's a lot of great steak. Definitely an incentive. My preconception was that the streets would be filled with people tango-ing, and sure enough, people really do dance everywhere there. We saw people doing the tango in a shopping center. That's a nice society.

There's a lot of similarities between all of us in the Americas. The first Spanish explorers landed here in the sixteenth century, then European immigrants and later people from all over the world have fed this city ever since. You feel like you're in Europe with the incredible architecture, the beautiful parks and mature trees that line the sidewalks, and the grand, wide avenues. It's spectacular. Why aren't we all going here?

When a local recommends something, you have to be open to trying it.

I've told you that I always rely on locals for the best advice. I wouldn't have necessarily ordered that dulce de leche pancake at El Obrero, the bodegón, if Soledad Nardelli hadn't told me I had to try it. I'm in Argentina, so I would have gotten the steak. (By the way, I did manage to take that jar of dulce de leche home. We wrapped it like it was an antique glass sculpture with bubble wrap. It survived. Until I got it home and it met my family.)

Being open to something when you travel also applies to going somewhere that might be outside your comfort zone, or even just a place you're not usually all that interested in going. I've probably met people at a bar three times in my life. I want to go someplace where you can actually hear the person you're talking to. But I went to that bar Julián Diaz restored, Los Galgos, because I'd heard how great it was. It's like going back to a different time period in Buenos Aires . . . and you can drink a negroni while you sit through your history lesson.

Negroni

One thing I'm not open to is losing sleep. In Buenos Aires, the locals go out dancing after they have dinner, and they usually don't start dinner until ten o'clock. Very impressive. Here's a cocktail for those of you who want to stay up late. Enjoy. If you need me, I'll be in bed.

Put a coupla ice cubes in a cocktail glass. Add equal parts gin, Campari, and vermouth, stir, and throw in an orange or lemon peel.

Enthusiasm goes a long way.

When you're meeting people, there's also got to be chemistry. I've done enough of this type of show in smaller versions to know what I didn't want to do. I'm not a chef, I'm not an expert. I'm a tourist like you. I think one reason that works is how we shot the show. The one thing I did insist on was to have two cameras. If we had just brought one camera, you'd see me talking, then the camera would have to turn around and we'd get the other person talking afterwards, and the conversation would be constructed in editing. You lose the honest reactions. And real human interaction is the most important part of the show.

Another thing I've learned is that sitting in the kitchen or at a bar or diner counter with the chef, owner, waiter, or whoever you're there to see is way better than sitting at a formal table. At a table, the meal has to be so amazing, or the conversation has to be so scintillating, that it carries the scene. A lot more spontaneity and interaction happens when you're at the counter or the bar.

Gonzalo Alderete at Perón Perón gave us the perfect example of that, of what you hope happens on a show. It was a quintessential scene for me. In that moment, you have such great material that's so entertaining and fun and provocative. You meet a real character. But when you get there, you have no idea if you're going to click. Gonzalo could have taken great offense at my Perón comment. By the end of the scene, he's so comfortable, he turns and looks right at the camera and talks to you. I loved it. You get a little history, a tiny bit of conflict, a little risqué material, just a great buddy feeling—and spectacular food.

Chemistry.

How to Eat an Empanada

"Have some wine. You have to shake the empanada first, move the juice. Then bite, and give it a long, big kiss, like your girlfriend. It's juicy, spicy, like a woman. All things lead to the woman . . . and to wine, and to friendship, and to enjoying your life. Yes! Do it. Now. Go!" — **Courtesy of the great philosopher Gonzalo Alderete**

. . . .

The recipe on the next page is from the wonderful chef Narda Lepes, and it may change your life. It's not just a fruit salad. She hates fruit salad. It's fruit with a delicious lime curd *and* white chocolate cream. Now you know what made it a "F*** You" fruit salad.

Summer Explosion
(aka F*** You Fruit Salad)

Serves 6

At the restaurant we serve this salad in bowls with layers of the curd and white chocolate cream beneath the fruit, but you can serve the curd and cream on the side. Play around with different creams, curds, ganaches, and toppings. And of course, have fun with different fruits of the season or region. No apples or bananas!
—**Narda Lepes**

3 cups (110g) loosely packed unsweetened coconut chips

1 tablespoon coconut oil

1 tablespoon honey

1 tablespoon light or dark brown sugar, lightly packed

Pinch fine sea salt

A mix of your favorite summer fruits, such as:

4 cups (16 ounces/450g) strawberries

1½ cups (6 ounces/170g) blackberries or raspberries

1½ cups (8 ounces/225g) cherries, pitted if desired

6 to 8 figs, halved

2 medium peaches or nectarines, cut into wedges

Lime Curd, recipe follows

White Chocolate Cream, recipe follows

Preheat the oven to 325°F (165°C). Line a sheet pan with a baking mat or parchment paper and pile the coconut chips in the middle of the pan.

In a small saucepan, combine the coconut oil, honey, brown sugar, and salt. Bring to a simmer over medium heat, stir to dissolve the sugar, and let cool completely.

Use a rubber spatula or spoon to scrape out the coconut oil mixture over the coconut flakes, then use your hands to evenly coat the flakes in the oil. Arrange the flakes evenly throughout the sheet pan and bake, stirring every few minutes to redistribute any that are browning, until golden brown on the edges, 10 to 12 minutes. (Watch the pan closely the last few minutes as the coconut burns easily.) Use the coconut flakes immediately, or set aside for up to 2 hours.

Use a rubber spatula or the back of a large spoon to spread about 3 tablespoons of the Lime Curd on the bottom and halfway up the sides of six shallow bowls, then spread about 3 tablespoons of the White Chocolate Cream over the curd. Divide the fruit among each bowl, scatter the toasted coconut on top, and serve. Or arrange the fruit on a large serving platter and scatter the toasted coconut on top, and serve the Lime Curd and White Chocolate Cream in bowls on the side for dipping.

Lime Curd

Makes about 1¼ cups (300ml)

3 to 4 medium limes

½ cup (100g) granulated sugar

1 large egg plus 1 egg yolk

4 ounces (1 stick/110g) unsalted butter, chilled, cut into ½-inch (12 mm) cubes

Set a fine mesh strainer over a small bowl.

Zest and juice 1 lime; you should have about 1 tablespoon of zest. Juice enough remaining limes to equal ⅓ cup (80ml) of juice. In a small saucepan, combine the lime zest and juice, sugar, egg, and egg yolk and gently cook over medium-low heat, whisking constantly, until the curd thickens to the consistency of a thin pudding, 3 to 4 minutes. (Do not boil.) Pour the curd through the fine mesh strainer into the bowl and use a rubber spatula to gently press the curd through the strainer, if needed.

Gradually add the butter, 3 to 4 pieces at a time, to the hot curd, and whisk until the butter has melted. Continue to gradually add the remaining butter in batches until fully incorporated. Press a piece of plastic on the surface of the curd and refrigerate for at least 3 hours or up to 5 days.

White Chocolate Cream

Makes about 1½ cups (360ml)

¾ cup (120g) roughly chopped white chocolate or good-quality white chocolate chips, such as Guittard

¼ cup (60ml) whole milk

1 large egg yolk

1½ tablespoons granulated sugar

½ cup (120ml) heavy whipping cream, well chilled

Put the white chocolate in a medium bowl.

In a small saucepan, whisk together the milk, egg yolk, and sugar and gently cook over medium-low heat, whisking constantly, until the custard thickens to the consistency of a thin pudding, 3 to 4 minutes. (Do not boil.) Pour the hot custard into the bowl with the chocolate and whisk until the chocolate has melted. (If the chocolate does not completely melt, set the bowl on the warm stovetop for a minute or two.) Transfer the chocolate custard to the refrigerator to cool for 10 to 15 minutes.

In a stand mixer fitted with the whisk attachment, whip the heavy cream on medium high-speed until soft peaks form, about 2 minutes. (Do not overbeat or the cream will separate.) Add the chocolate custard to the whipped cream and whip on low speed until just combined, about 10 seconds. Remove the mixer bowl from the stand and use a rubber spatula to mix the custard and cream until fully incorporated. Transfer the white chocolate cream to a bowl, cover, and refrigerate at least 3 hours or up to 5 days.

Tip Unsweetened coconut chips, which are large, thin strips of shaved coconut, are available at well-stocked grocery stores, such as Trader Joe's and bakeshops.

If you put yourself out there a bit, you never know what you can do.

Probably the single scariest thing for me on the entire show was learning the tango in front of you. Even more than jumping into the water in Ireland. There are no expectations of your performance when you're jumping into cold water. I am not a dancer. I've never taken a dance lesson in my life. And at my ripe old age, I was completely nervous, anxiety ridden, shy, and scared of embarrassment.

Luckily, my instructor was the lovely and very kind Cecilia Piccinni. She is a professional dancer with years of experience who would now be dancing with a putz. We had about an hour-long lesson where we practiced some rudimentary things. I think at the end of the show, we looked nice. And when I say "we," I mean she looked nice.

By the way, the single best thing I ate in Buenos Aires was a steak sandwich down the street from the hotel. It's not something I'd think to order. The meat isn't usually the best cut in our steak sandwiches. What we get in the United States can be tough and chewy, but there, you bite it and your teeth melt through it like a cloud. And the flavor is so delicious, the sweet and hot peppers. That was the one thing in Buenos Aires we ate that all of us wanted again. That's why you see it the show. Some of the food in those calls with my parents came from places we went with the crew when we weren't filming.

Those pastrami ribs at Tomás's restaurant, Mishiguene, are what happens when you put a brilliant Jewish chef in the middle of beef country. You wouldn't believe the size of the ribs in Argentina. I'd never seen anything like it. It's like pot roast on a stick. You can't get ribs like that most places in the United States, but right here, you can make Tomás's recipe. Tell me if that's not the best pastrami you've ever had. L'chaim!

Pastrami Ribs

Serves 6

We serve two kinds of pastrami at Mishiguene. A grano de pecho (under the neck of the cow), that we serve with a very special pasta my grandmother Olga used to make. The other, this one, is very Argentinian, with the whole rib that we serve with a homemade spaetzle. You get two very different flavors. —**Tomás Kalika**

¾ cup Diamond Crystal or ½ cup (105g) Morton kosher salt (see Tip page 282)

½ cup (110g) light or dark brown sugar, packed

1 tablespoon Prague powder #1

2 tablespoons coriander seeds

1 tablespoon whole black peppercorns

1 tablespoon red pepper flakes

2 teaspoons mustard seeds

1 teaspoon whole cloves

1 star anise

1 cinnamon stick

1 5- to 6-pound (2.3 to 2.7kg) whole beef plate bone-in short ribs

In a medium saucepan, combine the salt, brown sugar, Prague powder, and 1 quart (950ml) of water. Bring to a boil, stir to dissolve the sugar and salt, and remove the pot from the heat.

In a small bowl, mix together the coriander seeds, black peppercorns, red pepper, mustard seeds, cloves, and star anise. Heat a small skillet over medium heat, add the spices, and toast, stirring occasionally, until fragrant, about 2 minutes. Add the spices and cinnamon stick to the pot with the salt cure and let the brine cool completely.

Fill a turkey brining bag or a large, deep roasting pan with 2 quarts (about 2L) of water. Add the cooled salt cure and submerge the ribs in the brine. Remove the air and seal the bag, or place a pot lid or other weight on top of the ribs in the pan before covering the pan. Refrigerate the ribs for 6 days.

Put a colander in the sink (to prevent the spices from clogging the drain), pour off the brining liquid, and brush the excess spices off the meat. (Discard the spices.) If you aren't smoking the ribs immediately, wrap them in plastic wrap and refrigerate for up to 24 hours.

Set up a smoker to smoke at 250° to 275°F (120° to 135°C) according to the manufacturer's instructions. Or, prepare a charcoal grill for indirect cooking over medium to medium-low heat and add enough charcoal to smoke or grill the ribs for up to 6 hours. Put the ribs in the smoker or on the grill, fat side up. Close the lid and smoke until blackened on the outside and the meat is tender and has shrunk back from the ends of the bones by about 2 inches (5cm), 5 to 6 hours.

Phil: Hello!

Max: Can you move over this way?

(*Max helping Helen move her chair*)

Helen: I'm trying. I can't just . . . Okay.

Phil: Are you good? Dad, come in the picture.

(*Max scooting over chair*)

Helen: How are you? I loved to see you dancing the tango. That was my favorite.

Phil: That was the most frightening thing I've done on the show so far.

Helen: You looked terrific.

Max: Yeah, but you danced a little bit . . . klutzy.

Helen: No he didn't!

Max: Stick to what you do best, your gab . . . your gift for gab. Forget the dancing.

Helen: No, don't forget it. I think you did very well. I don't agree with him.

Max: (*whispering*) Okay, because she's not a good dancer. Anyway, are you having a good time?

Use tongs to transfer the ribs to a sheet pan, tent the ribs loosely with foil, and let rest at room temperature for 30 to 45 minutes. Slice the rack into individual bones and trim off and chop any meat alongside the ribs so each rib is easy to pick up and eat. Arrange the ribs and chopped beef on a large platter and serve.

Tips

- Here, more widely available plate short ribs (uncut slabs with 3 to 4 roughly 12-inch [30cm] long bones), stand in for the full rack the restaurant smokes.
- When curing the meat, you can double the recipe and freeze the extra cured rack of ribs (drain the brine first) for up to 3 months.
- Prague powder #1, also called pink curing salt #1 or Insta Cure #1, is available at many spice shops. It is a sodium nitrate and salt-based curing mix that gives cured meat its pinkish hue and inhibits bacteria growth during the long brining process. (Do not substitute regular pink, or Himalayan, table salt.)

Good napkins. Never realized how important they were until I was without them.

That scene at the pizza place Donato de Santis took me to, La Mezzetta, is the one of the few times you see something from me that's not completely positive. Not the fugazzeta, the local style of pizza, that was great. (By the way, Donato's restaurant, Cucina Paradiso, was also fantastic; we ended up going there again for our final crew dinner the night before we left.) What happens in the pizza scene is I'm holding this grease bomb and the first thing I'm thinking is, "I need a napkin." So I get a napkin, and it's as if someone took one of those old black-and-white notebooks and tore a page out of it.

Usually I'm open to the local culture; we have a lot to learn in America. Not so with these napkins. I've accumulated a certain set of rules. For example, a hotel is only as good as the water pressure. And now I feel this way about napkins. Turns out a lot of Argentinians

told me later that they feel the exact same way about those napkins. They really related to that scene. Consider it a public service.

In case you're wondering, the toilet paper in Argentina is way better than the napkins. I almost went into the bathroom to get something that might be more absorbent.

The bottom of the world is now right side up.

That last scene at Julián's house, when we're having that traditional asado, really shows how genuine the connections and friendships can be that you make when you travel. The greatest hits of the episodes were all there: Gonzalo, Rodolfo, Donato, Allie, even my saint of a tango teacher, Cecilia. And the food kept coming—meat, and meat, and more meat. (I'm still convinced they feed the cows something different here.) Then Donato hands over that present, the napkins from La Mezzetta. I love him, but that's the most useless gift I've ever received. I made some new friends from the other side of the world.

Argentinians are warm, generous, and so funny—kindred spirits. They will get you right away . . . and that makes you feel like you can do anything.

10

Copenhagen

The Danish love of style and creativity is alive and well. I've got to say I'm a little in love with wonderful, wonderful Copenhagen.

COPENHAGEN IS IN MY TOP THREE PLACES I'D want to live if I had to live somewhere else. The theme song for this place is straight out of the Hans Christian Andersen movie-musical starring Danny Kaye. It's a utopian society. Yes, half your money goes to taxes, but look what you get: universal health care, free school through college, and the cleanest air, food, and water in the world.

From the design to the architecture to the food, everything is on a whole other level. We could have done three episodes in Copenhagen there was so much incredible food. The other thing you notice? The people here seem genuinely happy.

The one time in Copenhagen I was not happy was in that first scene, schlepping up the tower of the Church of Our Savior. The camera crew was right behind me with forty pounds of equipment. One of our guys had a real fear of heights. And it really was a terrifying height with the thinnest of guardrails. Richard enjoyed it.

. . . .

Adam Aamann has taken the smørrebrød, a traditional open-faced sandwich that had basically become the bologna on white bread of Denmark, and turned it into something incredible. When he's in charge of the picnic, the rye bread becomes the canvas for the art.

And in this scene, Phil was short for Philistine because you're supposed to use a knife and fork on these beautiful creations. I admit, that if no one was looking, I'd probably go back to eating with my hands.

Pork Smørrebrød with Rhubarb Relish

Serves 10 to 12

It's no secret that I love smørrebrød, and most of all, I love the gastronomic treasure of good ingredients and ways of cooking them. In my work to combine the different types of smørrebrød, my starting point is always to focus on seasonal ingredients of vegetables, berries, and

fruits. Not because the vegetables always play the main role, but because it is largely the green preparations and all the ways you can work with them that define the expression of the finished smørrebrød. This is where Danish cuisine is completely unique. **—Adam Aamann**

Rhubarb-Braised Pork Belly, chilled, as needed, recipe follows	Soured Milk Mayonnaise, recipe follows
6 ounces (170g) slab or thick-cut bacon, finely chopped	1 small head butter lettuce, such as Bibb, Boston, or Little Gem
4 ounces (1 stick/110g) unsalted butter, softened	Rhubarb Relish, strained, recipe follows
10 to 12 slices Scandinavian or German-style whole grain rye bread	3 sprigs fresh thyme

Remove the Rhubarb-Braised Pork Belly from the refrigerator at least 30 minutes before serving, and use your hand or a paper towel to brush off the congealed braise (do not rinse the pork). Use a sharp knife to slice off the skin, if needed, and thinly slice the meat about ¼ inch (6mm) thick.

Meanwhile, in a cast iron skillet or sauté pan, fry the bacon over medium heat, stirring occasionally, until golden brown, 6 to 8 minutes. Transfer to a paper towel.

Spread the butter on both sides of each slice of bread, arrange 2 to 3 slices of the pork belly on top of each, and spread about 1 tablespoon of the Soured Milk Mayonnaise over the pork. Lay a few lettuce leaves on top of each open-faced sandwich, dollop small spoonfuls of relish evenly all over the lettuce, then sprinkle the crumbled bacon and a few thyme leaves on top, and serve.

Rhubarb-Braised Pork Belly

2 to 2½ pounds (900 to 1.2kg) boneless pork belly, preferably with the skin still attached	1½ cups (6 ounces/170g) roughly chopped fresh rhubarb (about 2 medium stalks)
3 tablespoons coarse sea salt	1½ cups (360ml) chicken stock, homemade or low-sodium store-bought
1 tablespoon vegetable oil	

¼ cup (85g) honey	1 5-inch (12.5cm) sprig rosemary	Pinch freshly ground black pepper	3 tablespoons Scandinavian-style soured milk, buttermilk, or heavy whipping cream
¼ cup (60ml) apple cider vinegar	2 bay leaves	½ cup (120ml) vegetable oil	
	2 whole black peppercorns	1 medium organic lemon	

Rinse the pork belly, pat dry with paper towels, and rub the salt evenly over all sides of the meat. Wrap the pork belly well in plastic wrap or put it in a large zip-top bag and refrigerate overnight.

Preheat the oven to 300ºF (150ºC). Pat the pork belly dry with paper towels. Heat the oil in a large iron skillet or sauté pan over medium-high heat until very hot. Add the pork belly, skin or fat cap side down, and cook until golden brown, about 10 minutes. Flip the pork belly (lay a heavy pot on top of the meat if it doesn't lay flat in the pan) and cook the bottom side until golden brown, about 10 minutes.

Transfer the pork belly, fat side up, to a baking dish slightly larger than the pork; the dish should be just large enough to snugly fit the pork belly, rhubarb, and braising liquid so the meat is mostly submerged while it cooks. Scatter the rhubarb alongside the pork and put the baking dish on a sheet pan.

Pour off and discard the fat in the skillet. Add the chicken stock, honey, apple cider vinegar, rosemary, bay leaves, and peppercorns and bring to a simmer. Remove the pan from the heat, pour the hot braising liquid over the pork, and transfer the pork to the oven.

Bake the pork belly, flipping the meat every 30 minutes, until the meat can be easily pierced with a knife and a digital thermometer reads 165ºF (75ºC) when inserted in the middle, about 1½ hours. Let the pork cool completely in the braising liquid, cover, and refrigerate overnight or for up to 5 days.

Soured Milk Mayonnaise

Makes about 1 cup (240ml)

2 large egg yolks, room temperature	2 teaspoons apple cider vinegar
2 teaspoons Dijon mustard	¼ teaspoon fine sea salt

Put the egg yolks, mustard, vinegar, salt, pepper, and 3 to 4 drops of water in a blender and blend on low speed until the yolks turn pale yellow, about 5 seconds. With the blender running, drizzle in the oil a few drops at a time until the mixture emulsifies, then slowly pour in the remaining oil in a steady stream.

Zest half the lemon; you should have about 1 teaspoon of zest. Add the lemon zest, 1½ tablespoon of freshly squeezed lemon juice, and the soured milk, buttermilk, or heavy cream (if using heavy cream, add about 2 teaspoons of lemon juice) and blend until well combined. Transfer mayonnaise to a jar, cover, and refrigerate at least 2 hours or for up to 3 days.

Rhubarb Relish

Makes about 1 cup (240ml)

⅓ cup (80g) granulated sugar	1½ cups (6 ounces/170g) finely chopped fresh rhubarb (about 2 medium stalks)
3 tablespoons apple cider vinegar	

In a medium saucepan, combine the sugar, vinegar, and ⅓ cup (80ml) of water. Bring to a boil and stir to dissolve the sugar. Remove the pan from the heat, stir in the rhubarb, and let cool completely. Transfer the relish to a jar, cover, and refrigerate at least 2 hours or up to 1 week.

Tips

- Frozen rhubarb is not a good substitute for fresh, especially in the relish; the root absorbs excess water when frozen, diluting the flavor and affecting the ratio of liquid to sugar ingredients in recipes.
- A denser Scandinavian or German-style rye (not a whole grain America-style sandwich bread), such as Mestemacher, is needed to accommodate the toppings; look for them at specialty grocers.

It must be human nature that we don't appreciate what's right around us.

One reason I love architecture is that it's the urban environment. It's very easy to learn to appreciate the art of it.

The park that Bjarke Ingles designed, Superkilen Park, is really about the diversity of Copenhagen and how much it's changed. He talked to the local community and asked residents what they missed from their former hometowns. That's why you see things like that Moroccan fountain, the fiberglass octopus from Tokyo, and the Mexican love seat. It's the architecture of inclusion. Some people are blessed with this way of seeing the world, imprinting onto the world in a way that helps.

Why don't we look at ethnic diversity, cultural diversity, as a positive? Then we could actually maybe do something good. —**Bjarke Ingles**

. . . .

Everything Rosio Sanchez makes is incredible. If you're in Copenhagen in the summer, go to her taco stand like we did in the episode. She also opened a full-service Mexican restaurant, Sanchez, that you don't see in the show. I've been to a lot of Mexican places since I moved to California. Hers is the best I've *ever* been to outside of Mexico. Rosio shared the recipe for those cod skin tacos on the next page. If you have the patience to find, and actually dehydrate, fish skins yourself, maybe you should open up a restaurant, too.

Cod Skin Tacos with Mussel-Tomatillo Salsa

Serves 4 as a main course, or 6 to 8 as an appetizer

This dish is about using what you have locally, so we dry and fry up cod skin for the tacos and blanch local green gooseberries instead of tomatillos. —**Rosio Sanchez**

4 ounces (110g) tomatillos (about 3 large)

½ medium beefsteak or similar tomato

½ medium white onion, roughly chopped

½ medium jalapeño, roughly chopped

½ garlic clove

¾ cup (180ml) Mussel Stock, recipe follows

1 small bunch fresh cilantro, divided

3 sprigs fresh parsley

Sea salt and freshly ground black pepper

Vegetable oil, for frying

Dried Fish Skins, recipe follows

8 good-quality corn tortillas

4 tablespoons Mexican crema or sour cream

2 limes, cut into wedges

Jalapeño Salt, recipe follows

Husk, wash, and quarter the tomatillos and put them in a blender. Add the tomato, onions, jalapeño, garlic, and Mussel Stock and blend until almost smooth. Transfer the salsa to a medium saucepan and cook over low heat until thickened and reduced by about one-third, about 20 minutes. Put 6 whole sprigs of cilantro and the parsley sprigs in the blender, add a few spoonfuls of the hot salsa, and blend until smooth. Stir the puréed cilantro and parsley into the salsa, season with salt and pepper, and keep the salsa warm over very low heat while you make the tacos.

Remove the leaves from the remaining cilantro sprigs and set aside (discard or reserve the stems for another use).

Line a plate with paper towels. Heat about 1 inch (2.5cm) of vegetable oil in a medium cast iron skillet or frying pan over medium-high heat until very hot. (Test the oil by adding a small piece of fish skin; it should curl up when it hits the oil.) Add about half the fish skins to the skillet (do not crowd the pan) and fry, turning the pieces with tongs once or twice, until puffed and crispy, about 30 seconds. Transfer the fish skins to the paper towel–lined plate and fry the remaining fish skins the same way.

Pour off and discard the oil from the skillet and wipe out the skillet with paper towels. Heat the skillet over medium-high heat until hot and rewarm each tortilla, one at a time, for about 5 seconds per side.

Arrange the tortillas on a serving platter or individual plates and spread out about 2 tablespoons of the warm tomatillo salsa in the middle of each. Lay 2 to 3 pieces of fried fish skin on top of the salsa, drizzle about ½ tablespoon of crema over the fish, and scatter a few cilantro leaves on top. Sprinkle a generous pinch of Jalapeño Salt over each taco and serve with the lime wedges and any remaining tomatillo salsa on the side.

Dried Fish Skins

Makes about 24 3-inch (7.5cm) pieces

3 to 4 pounds (1.4 to 1.8 kg) skin-on cod or wild-caught salmon fillets (see Tips)

Use a sharp knife to carefully remove the fish skins from the meat in strips. Try to remove as much of the flesh as possible, but a thin layer of flesh attached to the skin is fine. Or, have your butcher remove the skins for you. (Reserve the fish flesh for another use.)

Bring a medium pot of water to a low boil. Add the skins, boil for 5 minutes, and use a spider or slotted spoon to carefully transfer the skins to a paper towel. (Do not use tongs to remove the skins from the water as they tear easily.) When the skins are cool enough to handle, use your fingers to gently pull off and discard any larger pieces of flesh still attached, and cut the skins into 3- to 4-inch (7.5-10cm) pieces. (Don't discard any smaller, torn pieces of skin; they can still be used.)

Arrange the skins on a silicon mat in a dehydrator so none are touching and dehydrate at 165°F (75°C) for 2 hours. Flip each skin and continue to dehydrate until crispy, 2 to 3 hours longer (for a total of 4 to 5 hours), or according to the manufacturer's instructions. Line a zip-top bag or airtight container with a paper towel and store the dried fish skins at cool room temperature for up to 2 days.

Phil: Do you want to say hi to Ben?

Ben: Hi, Grandpa!

Max: You look great, Ben. Are you enjoying your time there?

Ben: Yeah it's great here. Hi, Grandma!

Phil: We went for fried chicken on Ben's birthday.

Max: How is the fried chicken over there?

Ben: Good. It was special fried chicken, it's not like normal.

Max: It's not like New York?

Ben: No.

Helen: How was it different?

Ben: It had vinegar on it. Vinegar powder, like a spice.

Helen: Forget that. That's the end of that chicken.

Mussel Stock

Makes about 1½ cups (360ml)

4 ounces (110g) mussels, scrubbed and beards removed

¼ small white onion

1 garlic clove

In a medium saucepan, combine the mussels, onion, garlic, and 3 cups (720ml) of water. Bring to a boil, reduce to a simmer, and boil until the broth is reduced by half, about 30 minutes. Let the stock cool completely, strain, cover, and refrigerate half the stock for up to 3 days. Freeze the remaining stock (about ¾ cup/180ml each) for up to 2 months for more tacos or fish stew.

Jalapeño Salt

Makes about 2 tablespoons

2 large jalapeños, thinly sliced

2 to 3 teaspoons flaky sea salt, preferably Maldon

Put the jalapeños in a dehydrator and dehydrate according to the manufacturer's instructions.

Transfer the dried jalapeños to a mortar and grind with a pestle into a powder. Stir in the salt. Store the Jalapeño Salt in a jar or spice container, tightly covered, for up to 1 month.

Tips

- If you can't find fresh fish skins from your fishmonger, slice off and freeze any raw cod or salmon skins whenever you buy fillets and store them in the freezer until you have enough skins for the recipe.
- The Mussel Stock can also be made ahead and frozen (this recipe makes twice as much as you need).
- Oven-drying the fish skins is not recommended; the temperature consistency of a dehydrator is key to both the texture of the fish skins and to ensure they are safe to eat.

· · · ·

That scene at Balderdash exemplifies what happens in so many big cities: there are all of these small communities within the larger community. It's like any business. Everybody who works in the local bars and restaurants gets to know each other. They become friends, and you start to see how they influence each other, like in this cocktail that Geoffrey Canilao created because of his friends Rosio Sanchez and her co-chef, Laura Cabrera.

It's basically a milkshake with booze. Who doesn't like a milkshake? I hear that the avocado ice cream is good on its own, maybe even your kids would like it. Don't know. Never tried it. My kids are now old enough to make it themselves, with the booze.

The Rosio and Laura

Serves 1

The flavors of The Rosio and Laura were influenced by one of the first paletas Hija De Sanchez did when they opened. As food immigrants in Denmark, Rosio Sanchez, Laura Cabrera, and I naturally gravitated toward each other as friends, encouraging each other. I was always inspired by how they integrated their food culture into the Nordic food scene respectfully, but with a pride in their Mexican heritage. In a sense, the cocktail goes beyond that flavor inspiration and into a friendship in a foreign land that we all came to love and call home.

For the avocado ice cream, we use a natural powdered acid instead of lemon juice as the acid because the flavor is more concentrated and stable in an ice cream. You could also use citric acid (made from citrus), but I prefer malic acid (from apples) with the avocado. We make our own cricket salt (equal parts toasted, ground dried crickets and sea salt) or you can buy the premade salt. **—Geoffrey Canilao**

⅔ cup (100g) Avocado Ice Cream, or to taste, recipe follows

1 ounce (30ml) white crème de cacao

1 ounce (30ml) mezcal or tequila

Generous pinch cricket salt or sea salt (optional)

1 freeze-dried raspberry, crumbled, or 1 teaspoon dried raspberry flakes

If the ice cream is very firm, let it rest at room temperature until scoopable, about 10 minutes.

Put the Avocado Ice Cream, crème de cacao, mezcal or tequila, and ¼ cup (30g) of crushed ice in a blender and blend until smooth. Add more Avocado Ice Cream or ice, if needed, and blend again. Pour the cocktail into a cocktail glass, sprinkle the cricket or sea salt on top, if using, garnish with the freeze-dried raspberries, and serve.

Avocado Ice Cream

Makes about 1 quart (940g)

2 cups (480ml) smashed avocado (about 4 medium)	½ cup (120ml) whole milk
	1 teaspoon coconut oil
1 14-ounce (400g) can sweetened condensed milk	1 teaspoon malic or citric acid dissolved in 2 teaspoons of warm water
½ cup (120ml) heavy whipping cream	

Put the avocados and condensed milk in a blender and blend until smooth. Add the heavy cream, milk, coconut oil, and malic or citric acid mixture and blend until well combined.

Freeze the ice cream base in an ice cream maker according to the manufacturer's instructions. Transfer the ice cream to a storage container, cover, and freeze for at least 3 hours or up to 5 days.

Tips

- Like lemon juice, both malic (available at many health food stores) and citric acid (available at well-stocked grocery stores) help keep the avocado from browning.
- Freeze-dried raspberries and cricket salt are available online and at some specialty food stores.

. . . .

Copenhagen was one place I wanted to bring my kids. Since we filmed the episode, I've been back a few times with my family. The first time I brought my daughter, after two days she said, "I want to live here." My son and I always go back to get a burger at the Gasoline Grill. That's our thing. We go insane, split the regular cheeseburger and the Butter Burger. He'll look back one day and say, "I used to go here with my dad." This is the one recipe in the book I wanted here for Ben.

Butter Burger

Makes 4 burgers

When I was sixteen years old, I went to the United States as an exchange student. On the trip from the airport and back to my host parents' house, we stopped for a bite to eat at an all-American diner. At the time a standard burger in Denmark was a frozen patty, Chinese cabbage, and crème fraiche dressing in a sad version of a bun. The closest we could get to the American version was a Big Mac at McDonald's, and only when visiting one of the bigger cities in Denmark. At that diner I had my first authentic American burger: a bacon cheeseburger, served open-faced with a big pickle on the side, self-service mustard and ketchup at the table, and a side of fries. I still remember biting into the soft bun and tasting the meat, seared to perfection. I was hooked. I had to develop the perfect burger myself.

The secret to cooking a great burger is great ingredients—and not just the meat. Denmark is dairy country and known for its high-quality butter. We use an organic artisanal butter with flaky sea salt from the island of Læsø ("butter burgers" are something I was also introduced to in the Midwest). Go for a really fluffy bun, either potato or brioche (we make our own potato buns). As for the meat, ours is fresh, never-frozen, organic beef that we grind at each location every morning. We use around 50 percent chuck and 50 percent boneless short rib meat, but find the cuts you like. What is most important is you want at least 25 percent fat. Since the beef has such a high fat content, no additional fat is needed for cooking, but you'll want a good, even, dark brown sear on the patties. And don't press down on the patties (or the bun) after the initial smash! You will lose all of the delicious juices you worked so hard to create. —**Klaus Wittrup**

(the meat should be light pink in the center), 1½ to 2 minutes longer.

Lay the burger patties on the bottom buns and top each patty with a slice of the butter, 4 to 5 onion slices, and 3 to 4 dill pickle slices. Return the top buns to the griddle, buttered side down, to rewarm for a few seconds, then gently place the buns on top of the burgers, and serve.

Tip   If you don't have a meat grinder to grind your own beef, ask your butcher to coarsely grind good-quality beef with a high fat content (at least 25 percent rather than the standard 20 percent fat).

There's this thing called vacation magic.

You think something's not going to work out, and then it works out better than you could have imagined.

When we went to Copenhagen to film, I was so disappointed because the world-famous Noma was closed. They were in between locations. I'd never been. The whole reason we all know about modern Nordic food is because of René Redzepi. Almost every chef we talked to in town had a connection to René or Noma at some point. Rosio Sanchez used to be the head pastry chef at Noma; Thorsten Schmidt partnered with Rene at Barr, where we had that incredible cod that he glazes fourteen times as it cooks; Matt Orlando out at Amass was the head chef at Noma for a few years. Even Anders Selmer, the owner of Fiskebar, the great seafood place in the meatpacking district, used to be Noma's sommelier.

You can see in the show how excited I was when we got a surprise: the night before we were supposed to leave, we heard that the Noma chefs were going to do a pop-up barbecue out by the water the next day. We get our Noma! So we rearranged our schedule to fit that scene in.

When I went back to Copenhagen with my family a year or two later, I heard that René liked our show. But more important, that we could get into Noma! We were gonna go to the actual restaurant. We had five people but you had to book for an even number, so I invited

1¼ pounds (560g) good-quality coarsely ground beef (25 percent fat), preferably freshly ground

3 ounces (¾ stick/85g) good-quality salted butter, at room temperature, divided

4 potato or brioche buns

Coarse sea salt and freshly ground black pepper

½ medium red onion, thinly sliced

12 to 16 sliced dill pickles

Gently shape the beef into four 5-ounce (140g) balls; do not smash the meat.

Slice 4 tablespoons (½ stick/55g) of the butter into four equal pieces and set aside. Lightly butter the inside of the buns with the remaining 2 tablespoons of butter.

Heat a griddle top or large sauté pan over medium-high heat. Add the buns, buttered side down, and toast until light golden brown. Set aside.

Add the beef balls to the griddle or pan, leaving at least 2 inches (5cm) between each. (If using a pan, fry the burgers in batches to avoid overcrowding the pan, if needed.) Use a spatula to gently smash the balls into patties about ⅔ inch (16mm) thick, then lightly sprinkle the patties with the salt and pepper. Cook the patties until the bottom of each is nicely charred and dark brown in spots, about 1½ minutes. Gently flip the patties and cook to medium my friend Klaus from the Gasoline Grill. Then René invites us to come over early so he can give us a tour. What? We got a tour from René Redzepi! We got to see the gardens, and he introduced us to the fermentation specialist, David Zilber.

The other thing about Noma is you eat what is on the tasting menu, you don't have a choice. What is the theme of the tasting menu when we are going? Mold.

The art of fermentation is about the sweet spot between "it's not ready yet" and "this has gone bad." It has to do with everything: aged meat, the acceptable amount of mold you want in your cheese. Now, on this menu, they're going to take that to a whole different level.

We had moldy barley; it was soft like felt, and it tasted like a truffle ice cream taco. We had moldy asparagus that was completely white. Then there was the moldy yolk of an egg. It took a little courage to eat it. Then they move on to the "non-mold" dishes. It was all just as spectacular. The artistry, the science, the flavors. They were pushing things to the extent they could go. I loved it.

My daughter's review? "This is the worst meal I've ever had in my life."

Hedonistic sustainability.

Maybe that's it. Maybe the secret to Copenhagen is what Bjarke calls "hedonistic sustainability." Why can't environmentalism be sexy? Why can't healthy food actually be the *more* delicious choice?

It just seems like everybody here is looking out for everybody else. And that feeling's all around. I would go if I were you.

11

Cape Town

How we enjoy life, how we live in it, eat it in it, dance in it—how we enjoy each other— that's what makes life worth living. And that's something you can feel in South Africa.

THE PHYSICAL SETTING OF CAPE TOWN AND ALL of South Africa is so beautiful, but so is the whole spirit of this country. The wine country scene at Babylonstoren at the end of the episode sums up how it felt to be in South Africa. It's this stunning winery from 1692 with vineyards and gardens that was set up to supply passing Dutch ships as they rounded the tip of Africa on the way to India and the Far East. You've got the history, you've got the beauty, and you've got the incredible food. To eat breakfast in that dining room while looking out at the farm where all the food came from was magical. I was sitting there thinking how lucky I was to be there, while realizing this was probably the only time in my life I was going to be in that place, eating that breakfast. There's a lesson.

I only wish it didn't take a day and a half to fly here. Is it worth the trip? Take a look for yourself.

Sharing is the real test of compatibility.

I don't think I could be friends with somebody if they didn't want to share. Sharing food, but also sharing what someone finds special, even just a local place they like.

When I asked our local production assistant, Shaheen Sydow, what he recommended, he said we had to get a Gatsby at The Golden Dish. This is a sandwich named after extravagance, after *The Great Gatsby* in fact. Other than the thirty-foot hero at Manganaro's on Ninth Avenue in New York, this was the biggest sandwich I've ever tried to take down myself. So maybe share this, or you may not make it to your next meal.

My Great Gatsby, or How to Ruin a Sweater

A Gatsby is the local specialty. It's basically a giant sub filled with as many things as you can fit: steak, chicken, bologna, eggs, American cheese, and, why not, French fries. No polony!

Order some French fries from your favorite place or get some frozen ones. (You want the thicker ones, like you get at a diner.) Season them however you like (you get them with salt and vinegar most places here). Get a giant sub or Philly steak roll and put some iceberg lettuce on it. Fry up some meat—steak, bologna, ham, chicken, whatever you've got—and put that on the sandwich. Now fry a couple eggs, put some American cheese on top and that piri piri sauce, and stuff the fries in the sandwich. Eat that, then order a new sweater.

Helen: Hi.

Phil: Oh, hi.

Helen (*to Max*): No, that's still low . . .

Max: Wait!

(*Max adjusts the computer volume.*)

Helen: Now you did it all wrong.

Phil: We've got this down to a science, haven't we?

Helen: (*to Max*): Oh, now it's too loud.

Phil: Now I hear the echo.

Max: How are you enjoying . . .

Helen (*to Max*): He gets an echo.

Max: How are you enjoying your trip?

Helen: He says he gets an echo!

(*Phil laughs*)

Helen: He's turning you off altogether now.

Max: Okay.

Phil: Probably the rest of the world is doing that as we speak.

(*Helen puts her hand in front of Max to tell him to be quiet.*)

Helen (*to Phil*): Now, how is the sound now?

Phil: It's good, now it's good.

Helen: Philip, how do you like Cape Town?

Phil: Boy it's beautiful. This city has these giant, beautiful mountains very close to the ocean, and the city just kind of filled in between the mountains. And I fed the ducks in the park! I've decided I'm going to be an old man who feeds the ducks.

Helen: Well, it suits you very well.

Phil: You know, they eat cuts of meat here we don't have, things on nature shows like impala.

Helen: Ohhh, they're so beautiful.

Phil: Sorry. Then there's kudu . . .

Helen: That's all you say? "Sorry"? They're just so beautiful.

Phil: Listen, do you want to stop eating all animals? Then you can do that, but we can't be hypocritical.

Helen: But impalas are just so beautiful.

Max: So are chickens.

Phil: You hit it, Dad. Dad is right.

You can't talk about South Africa without talking about Nelson Mandela.

This country has a long history of colonialism and conflict, but it's also got a future of restoration. That's something so many of us around the world can relate to.

That scene where I'm having breakfast with Nelson's grandson Zondwa and his lovely wife, Lindo, at their favorite spot, Jarryds, shows how much we're all the same in so many other ways, too. To Zondwa, Nelson Mandela wasn't a political figure who got out of prison after twenty-seven years for standing up for civil rights; he was his grandpa. He was family. And to

a seven-year-old, the day Nelson Mandela got out of prison was just a very long day. Zondwa was about the same age, it turned out, that Zondwa and Lindo's two kids were when we filmed.

If you don't know how to get a conversation going with a stranger, here's a little tip: Start by asking someone about their family. There's an instant connection.

It also works with food. Or humor.

We're not living with the assumption that things are the way they should be. But the point is now we need to be grateful for what we had. That should be celebrated before anything else. —**Zondwa Mandela**

Do as the locals do.

I say that a lot, but that's because I believe it's so important when you're traveling.

That's not how I grew up. My dad was the guy who would go someplace and never try the one thing that place is famous for. He'd already decided he didn't like it. That's a choice.

People like their fries soft and floppy instead of crispy here. They call them "slap" chips, based on an Afrikaans word that actually means "limp" or "flabby." (No jokes.) We all know what those are like. I prefer crispy fries, but I understood those floppy fries. If that's how they eat fries here with their local fried fish, then I go with it. And I enjoyed it. Would those fries go as well with my burger back home on La Brea Boulevard? Probably not. But in South Africa, at Fish on the Rocks, this shack surrounded by the water, they're the best. When in Rome . . . eat the floppy fries.

. . . .

That raw chocolate at Honest Chocolate was the purest chocolate I've ever had. I'm sure some people love it. But for me, raw chocolate is like eating a building material. Call me when the house is finished. Everything else there that I tried was incredible, especially this, the single best brownie I've ever eaten. Am I wrong?

Phil's Brownies!

Makes 8 brownies

We are a small bean-to-bar chocolate company in Cape Town with a chocolate café in the heart of the city. When Phil was here, the funny thing was he wasn't a big fan of the dark chocolate, but luckily the brownies came to the rescue. Since the episode aired, we always have American tourists coming in asking for "Phil's Brownies," so we've started affectionately calling them that, too.

These brownies are all about the quality of the chocolate. We use single origin cacao beans from Kakao Kamili in Tanzania to make our 70 percent chocolate bars. Look for good-quality, ethically sourced chocolate. The farmers and fermenters must get a lot of the credit as it all starts there. Be sure the melted chocolate is warm, not hot, or the butter will cook the eggs. (That's breakfast.) And resist temptation! Let your brownies cool for at least thirty minutes in the pan. It needs this short beauty nap for the chewy textures and chocolatey flavors to come together. **—Anthony Gird**

2½ ounces (5 tablespoons/70g) unsalted butter, plus more for the pan	½ teaspoon baking powder
	¼ teaspoon fine sea salt
¼ cup plus 1 tablespoon (30g) Dutch-processed cocoa powder	2 ounces (55g) bittersweet chocolate, preferably 70 percent or higher, roughly chopped
¾ cup (150g) granulated sugar	
⅓ cup plus 1 tablespoon (45g) cake flour	¼ cup (30g) roughly chopped unsalted almonds, toasted1 large egg, lightly beaten

Preheat the oven to 350°F (180°C) and put a baking rack in the top third of the oven. Lightly butter the bottom and sides of a standard (8½x4½-inch/21.5x11.5cm) loaf pan. Cut a piece of parchment paper about 4 inches (10cm) longer than the loaf pan and trim the sides so the paper lays flat in the pan but overhangs at either (these parchment paper "handles" will make it easier to remove the brownies). Lightly butter the parchment paper.

In a small saucepan over low heat, melt the butter, stirring occasionally. Set aside to cool.

In a large bowl, mix together the cocoa powder, sugar, flour, baking powder, and salt until well combined, then stir in the chocolate and almonds. Add the cooled butter and egg, and use a rubber spatula to mix until well combined. (The batter will be very thick.) Spread the batter in the prepared loaf pan so it fills the pan evenly. Bake, rotating the pan front to back halfway through, until the brownies are dark brown about 1 inch (2.5cm) along the edges (the center will still be soft), 30 to 32 minutes. Transfer the brownies to a baking rack to cool for 30 to 45 minutes.

Run a knife along the inside of the pan to loosen the brownies and use the parchment paper to lift the brownies out of the pan. Cut the brownies into eight squares and serve warm. Or let the brownies cool completely, cover, and store at room temperature for up to 3 days.

. . . .

I loved the cute grandkids in that scene at Faeeza's place in the Bo-Kaap neighborhood, which is the oldest Muslim community here. We instantly bonded. Faeeza, too. You're not gonna meet sweeter people than this.

That's why we sit down at the table, to make that connection. You see it happening right there, in someone's home where you can go in and learn to cook and then eat together. Faeeza says that some people who have come to her home are surprised to learn that she is so nice—simply because of her religion. If you haven't heard me say this before, I promise you'll hear me say it again: I find that most people in the world are so much nicer than their governments.

And now, here's her curry! I want you to make Faeeza's Cape-Malay curry and invite some people over for dinner that you're not sure you're gonna like. Do what Faeeza does: give them a hug when they walk in the door.

Butter Bean–Eggplant Curry
Serves 4

I had a mom who was an excellent cook. I loved all of her food growing up with four siblings. I definitely have her taste buds and also her cooking style—quick, easy, wholesome food. I am happy to pass that on to all of my guests. And we always have lots of fun. When you are warm, people warm toward you. When they come into my home, I give them a hug. And then they leave, and they hug me.

There are as many different versions of masala and curry powder as there are curries in the world. You choose the one that suits your tastes. I use roasted masala, which has warm spices like cinnamon and cloves (the spices are toasted for an even deeper flavor), but you can also use a spicy Madras curry powder (fenugreek and mustard as usually the main ingredients). I work with so many different taste buds from all over the world; a dish like this is enjoyable every time no matter what you may choose. I look forward to meeting all of you and your families in Cape Town. —**Faeeza Abrahams**

1 medium or 2 to 3 small eggplants (about 10 ounces/280g), any variety

2 Roma or other firm tomatoes

3 tablespoons vegetable oil

2 medium white or yellow onions, finely chopped

½ green bell pepper, roughly chopped

3 garlic cloves, smashed

1 teaspoon roasted garam masala or your favorite curry powder

1 teaspoon ground cumin

1 teaspoon ground coriander

½ teaspoon ground turmeric

½ teaspoon chili powder

2 cardamom pods

1 cinnamon stick

1 teaspoon fine sea salt

2 15-ounce (425g) cans Lima (butter) beans, drained

½ bunch fresh cilantro, roughly chopped

Trim the ends off the eggplant, slice it in half lengthwise, and use a spoon to scrape out the seedy core, if needed. Cut the eggplant into roughly ½-inch (12mm) cubes. Peel the tomatoes and use a cheese or box grater to grate the flesh.

In a Dutch oven or other large pot with lid, heat the vegetable oil over medium heat. Add the onions and cook, stirring occasionally, until softened and beginning to brown, 8 to 10 minutes. Add the eggplant, bell pepper, and garlic and reduce the heat to medium-low.

In a small bowl, mix together the garam masala or curry powder, cumin, coriander, turmeric, chili powder, cardamom pods, cinnamon stick, and salt. Stir the spices into the vegetables and cook, stirring constantly, until the mixture is fragrant, 2 to 3 minutes. Add the Lima beans and tomatoes, cover the pot, and cook the curry for 10 minutes. Stir in ½ cup (120ml) of water and use a wooden spoon to scrape any caramelized bits off the bottom of the pot. Cover the pot again and cook until the eggplant is tender when pierced with a fork, 5 to 10 minutes. Season the curry with salt, sprinkle the cilantro on top, and serve.

Tip The widely available, larger purple globe eggplants typically have bitter seeds that need to be scraped out for this dish; smaller Asian an Indian varieties do not need to be de-seeded.

When you hit it just right, the world comes.

Mzoli's was one of my favorite kinds of places. It's in Gugulethu, a neighborhood outside of Cape Town that was created by the unfortunate racial segregation policies of apartheid. Mzoli Ngcawuzele built a place where all walks of life could meet, eat, have fun, and help the local economy. It's a butcher shop, barbecue restaurant, dance club, and your best friend's living room, all in one place. A true community that helps the whole community. That's a very good reason to support restaurants. They have such a huge impact beyond providing good things to eat. You've got the cooks, the dishwashers, the waiters and waitresses. But when you start figuring in the farmers, the butchers, even the guy who delivers the drinks, you're talking about a much bigger impact. If you need another reason to travel, or just another reason to go out to eat in your neighborhood, find a Mzoli's.

I'm always looking for great people to talk to, and sometimes you get lucky.

The scene with Leah Ashanti is one of my favorite scenes we did in the whole series. Melissa's, which is now called PepperTree Café, was near where I was staying. We walked into the shop and there was Leah. She was so naturally funny and charming. That scene has the serendipity that you want when you travel, at least if you're me and you want to meet fantastic people. That's even better than discovering something great to eat.

. . . .

Nature doesn't discriminate. The land, the sea, the sky, and of course, the food that comes from it: these are everyone's pleasures in life.

Travel gives you perspective. *That's* what you can take home with you.

Even though I was in Africa, I kept thinking of "This Land Is Your Land, This Land Is My Land."

Serving
FRANKFURTERS
Since 1916.

OPEN ALL YEAR

SEAFOOD

FROG LEGS • SOFTSHELL CRABS • LOBSTER ROLLS

FRIED SHRIMP & CLAMS • CLAM CHOWDER

SERVED INSIDE

OLD FASHIONED
HEESEBURGERS

CHOW MEIN-ON-A-BUN

KRISPY CHICKEN TENDERS

burgers are 100% BEEF

12

New York

The center of the known universe. New York is the very definition of a city: bustling, loud, nonstop with buildings stacked on top of each other into the distance. For me, it's exhilarating. And it will always be where I'm from.

I REALLY WAS NERVOUS ABOUT DOING THE NEW York episode. Everyone's done something on this city. How can you do a definitive episode? And then it hit me. You can't. You can only do "your" New York.

And sure enough, just like everything else I've ever learned about writing, the more specific something is, the more universal it becomes. If the New York episode was going to be true to me, it might be true to someone else. This is the New York I lived in for the whole first half of my life. The New York I keep coming back to. This is the New York I love.

How can you keep eating when you're full? Some things can only be explained by the fact that dessert is a separate room.

If you need proof, go to Peter Luger. After you've just eaten more calories than ever before and your arteries are closed, here comes a hot fudge sundae, and a cheesecake, and a pecan pie, and, because that's not enough, a giant bowl of their famous whipped cream: schlag! And you eat them all anyway.

My favorite moment here is when Massimo Bottura goes over to the table next to us and asks if he can try that woman's salmon. To them, here's a crazy Italian guy they don't know. They have no idea he's one of the greatest chefs in the world. And that nice lady said yes,

he could have a piece of her fish! Then Massimo came back to our table and I asked him how it was, and he says, "A little overcooked."

You really get to know Massimo, as an individual, in that scene. And guess what? Chefs are just like us. You can't stereotype anybody. I love chefs in general because of what they do. Yes, these people are artists. And yes, some chefs are annoying, a pain in the ass, a diva. But then you've got chefs who are also the greatest people, like Massimo and my dear friend Nancy Silverton. For me, the more open and loving chefs are as people, the better their food tastes.

Schlag

Schlag (short for the German schlagsahne, *or whipped cream) is sweet, creamy, cold, and makes everything you put it on a party.*

Pour a carton of heavy whipping cream into a mixer and throw in a few spoonfuls of powdered (confectioner's) sugar. There might be some vanilla extract in there, you'll have to ask (another reason to go to Peter Luger's). Whip the cream until it turns into giant peaks and then put it on your head.

The BEST.

I know I say that phrase a lot in the show. I even get notes from people, from friends, the network that I say it a lot. For me, something is "the best" because I'm having this great thing at *that* moment. That's how I feel. It's not a fact, it's a feeling. You forget what was objectively the *very* best, so this new thing that's in front of you is now the best. That's called living in the moment. It's like your favorite movie. You can't compare *Mary Poppins* and *Jaws* and *The Godfather*, but they're all "the best" movies for certain reasons. There's certainly no better movie than that "one." I could say that about a hundred movies, and about a hundred pizzas.

That pizza crawl I went on with Ed Levine is another great example. Every place you saw was the best because of what and where it is. There's Totonno's on Coney Island, where sisters Antoinette Balzano and Cookie Ciminieri are part of the delicious experience. There's a photo on the wall of Anthony Pero at Lombardi's, the birthplace of American pizza, and they're telling you Anthony was the pizzaiola. He was *the* guy who made *the* first pizzas in New York. The creator. Will we ever never know if Anthony really was the one, or if he just got some flour on his shoes that day? But that's the story. And that's New York.

Then you've got "Dom" De Marco at Di Fara in Brooklyn. He's a legend. He's the only guy who's ever made the pizza there, since 1965, after he immigrated to New York from Italy. He understands there are people willing to wait three hours just to taste his pizza, so he's there every day. *He's* become the destination. And for good reason.

Then you meet Dan Richer at Razza in Jersey City, New Jersey. That's the state-of-the-art version of pizza. You realize when people say, "I like old-school," they only want one thing. Who says that something new can't also be fantastic? He's obsessed. We should all be as good at our jobs as Michael Jordan is at basketball. That's Dan Richer. And that's what I love, when chefs care about every bite of every dish.

· · · ·

When we shot the New York episode there was this new place called White Gold on the Upper West Side run by two world-class butchers, Erika Nakamura and Jocelyn Guest. These women can slug 150-pound slabs of meat on their shoulders effortlessly. Their S.E.C., which was my staple diet in the 1980s, was the best I've ever had (turn the page). But don't just take it from me: *They had the best version of an S.E.C., ever, at White Gold.* —**Richard**

S.E.C. (Sausage, Egg, and Cheese)

Makes 4 sandwiches

White Gold Butchers was a fleeting Upper West Side fixture that lasted but a heartbeat, but incredible things came of it. (We've since moved on to our own endeavors with J&E SmallGoods and Butcher Girls.) Many of the daytime offerings at the sandwich counter were inspired by the cultural phenomenon of the New York City bodega, or corner store, offerings. In what is now classic highbrow/lowbrow food industry fashion, our aim was to take something that New Yorkers took for granted and offer it with exceptional ingredients. For years, we aimed to educate people on the true value of food, especially the labor it takes from every hand that touches it to make it possible to exist on your plate. A simple sausage, egg, and cheese sandwich is elevated with well-sourced and thoughtful ingredients in order to highlight every subtle nuance. The salty, fatty, crispy sausage patty coupled with the hot and gooey melted American cheese and the smashed, sunny fried egg oozing onto the plate from the back of the bun. Like White Gold, that sandwich may be gone in a New York minute, but it lingers on in your memories for you to visit over and over again.

We like to fry the eggs in beef tallow, which has a high smoke point and pure flavor, but you can use the leftover sausage fat. You'll have a few extra sausage patties for later in the week. —**Erika Nakamura and Jocelyn Guest**

4 poppy seed Kaiser rolls	8 large eggs
6 tablespoons mayonnaise, preferably Duke's	Kosher salt and freshly ground black pepper
4 Sausage Patties, recipe follows	8 slices American cheese
Beef tallow, for frying (optional)	

Slice the Kaiser rolls in half lengthwise and spread about 1½ tablespoons of mayonnaise inside each.

Heat a large griddle or cast iron skillet over medium heat until very hot. Add the Sausage Patties and cook until golden brown, about 2 minutes. Flip the patties and cook until the meat is no longer pink in the center, 2 to 3 minutes longer, and transfer to a plate.

Pour off all but a thin layer of the pork fat from the griddle or skillet (reserve the remaining fat). Or, if using beef tallow, discard all the pork fat and add enough tallow to lightly coat the bottom of the griddle or skillet. Add half the Kaiser rolls, mayonnaise side down, and sear the buns until lightly toasted, about 2 minutes. Repeat with the remaining rolls and set aside.

Use a paper towel to wipe any crumbs off the cooking surface and add another thin layer of the reserved pork fat or beef tallow. Reheat the griddle over low heat and crack 2 eggs, side by side, onto the griddle. (If using a skillet, crack the eggs off to one side to allow room for the sausage and Kaiser roll.) Put 1 sausage patty and 1 Kaiser roll, mayonnaise side down, on the griddle or skillet to rewarm.

When the egg whites are almost set (they should be white everywhere except around the yolks), use a spatula to pop the yolks and smear them over the surface of the whites. Sprinkle the eggs with a pinch of salt and pepper. Lay 1 slice of cheese on top of 1 egg and use the spatula to flip the other egg on top of the cheese like you are closing a book. Lay the second slice of cheese on top of the eggs.

Transfer the bottom half of the Kaiser roll to a serving plate and put the Sausage Patty on top. Lay the top half of the Kaiser roll over the egg stack, slide the spatula underneath the eggs, and use one hand to hold on to the Kaiser roll to help transfer it to the bottom roll. Serve the S.E.C. as it comes off the griddle, then add more pork fat or beef tallow, if needed, to the griddle and cook the remaining sandwiches the same way.

Sausage Patties

Makes 6 large patties

1 pound (450g) coarsely ground pork (30 percent fat), preferably freshly ground

¼ cup (30g) fine bread crumbs or panko

1½ teaspoons lightly packed light or dark brown sugar

1½ teaspoons freshly ground black pepper

1 teaspoon kosher salt

¼ teaspoon ground nutmeg

¼ teaspoon red pepper flakes

Use your hands to gently break up the pork into the bowl of a stand mixer fitted with the paddle attachment.

In a small bowl, mix together the bread crumbs or panko, brown sugar, black pepper, salt, nutmeg, and red pepper flakes and sprinkle the bread crumb mixture over the pork. Mix the pork on low speed just until the bread crumbs are incorporated, 3 to 4 seconds. Drizzle 2 tablespoons of ice-cold water over the meat, increase the speed to medium, and continue to mix until the sausage just begins to bind together, 8 to 10 seconds. (Do not overmix.)

Shape the sausage into six 3-inch (7.5cm) patties. Use immediately or cover and refrigerate for up to 3 days.

Tip   Unless you have a very large griddle top, it's easiest to fry up the sausages first, then cook the sandwiches to order (one at a time). Ask your butcher for coarsely ground pork with a high fat content (30 percent rather than the standard 20 percent), or look for good-quality ground pork. (Prepackaged ground pork is typically finely ground which results in a gummy sausage mixture.)

The very best thing about New York? New Yorkers.

That scene at Zabar's with my longtime friend Judy Gold is all about New Yorkers. It's a city full of characters, and Judy may be my favorite.

By the way, we found out later what that woman at Zabar's said wasn't true. If you get Fox's U-bet syrup during Passover, it still has corn syrup in it. But what I love is that New York certainty.

Chocolate Egg Cream

Other than my parmesan and Champagne hack (page 109), this may be the one recipe that I can truly offer. Wanna know why? Because it takes no talent whatsoever. When you add the seltzer to the chocolate syrup and milk, the seltzer causes a chemical reaction that magically makes the drink all frothy and delicious. Even Tracy Morgan was amazed and delighted.

Squeeze some Fox's U-Bet chocolate syrup into a glass about a quarter of the way up, then fill another quarter of the glass with milk and stir until you have chocolate milk. Then keep stirring while slowly adding cold seltzer. Enjoy my heritage.

You won't regret doing something today.

You can't talk about New York without talking about everything this city has been through. We all remember 9-11, we all remember when the pandemic first hit New York. The rest of us were powerless, watching it all unfold on TV and listening to the reports on the news. I was worried about my dad, who was in his nineties and living in a retirement home. But the first person I knew who died of COVID was the great chef Floyd Cardoz, a master of modern Indian cuisine. It was terrible.

If you watch the show, you will remember that Floyd took me and my friend Rupa Balasubramanian to Ganesh Temple, the Hindu temple in Flushing, Queens. Rupa's family took her there as a little girl. Floyd said he first went there because of the food, not because of the temple. I had no idea what to expect. It was an amazing experience. I didn't know it at the time, but it turns out that Ganesh is the symbol of moving forward in life after facing an obstacle.

What are you doing right now? Reading this book. There might be better things to do. Put it down for a minute and call somebody up, go to lunch. Plan a vacation. Go out for an ice cream. Get a coffee. Go to the temple and break a coconut. Yes, right now. Go!

Helen: He's eating. Can you hear me?

Phil: Oh my God, that is so good.

Max: Hello?

(*Phil gets up from chair.*)

Helen: Where is he going?

Max: You have to move your chair back.

Helen: Max, leave me alone, please.

(*Phil suddenly appears in Helen and Max's room.*)

Phil: You have to try this, it's fantastic.

(*Phil holds up a plate of rugelach.*)

Helen: Which one?

Phil: Whichever you like.

(*Helen and Max take a rugelach.*)

Max: Are we supposed to eat it now?

Phil: Why not, it's so good.

Phil: I got the chocolate and this one is the cinnamon. You like it?

Helen: Mm, mmm.

Phil: All right, goodbye.

(*Phil leaves; Helen and Max stare at the computer.*)

Max: Now what?

And now, ladies and gentlemen, we take a break at Ice and Vice for the Academy Awards of Ice Cream Tasting...

...with your host, the incomparable Elaine May.

Basic B (Mexican vanilla with black lava sea salt)
Elaine: It tastes very white. Creamy, yet with a slight fruity taste that I can't define.

Yellow (buckwheat honey with turmeric and butterscotch sunflower seed chips)
Elaine: This is the next nominee. Really dramatic taste. I eat turmeric all the time, I'm yellow from it.

Opium Den (white sesame with toasted poppy seed and lemon bread croutons)
Elaine: It does have an opium-like flavor...from my experience.

9 a.m. (Vietnamese coffee with donut truffle)
Elaine: Hints, oddly enough, of Cuban tobacco.

Shade (smoked dark chocolate)
Elaine: Yum.

Red (hibiscus with rose and Swedish Fish fluff)
Elaine: As crazy as that flavor is, it's delicious.

Elaine: I want to say this now (talking to the ice cream tubs), no matter who gets the award, it's an honor just to be nominated. This is going to be so hard. For complexity, depth, originality, I have to go with...9 a.m. But I think you've all been wonderful, and I think 9 a.m. shares this honor with all of you.

There was an event at my hotel and I got to meet actual ballerinas:

Elina Miettinen, Georgina Pazcoguin, and Abigail Simon, superstars of the New York ballet scene. And I watched in amazement as they started pounding down the bar snacks. "Did you not eat dinner?" I asked. "No, we ate dinner," they said.

I told them that the stereotype I have of ballerinas is that they don't eat. They've got to fit into tights. "Oh, not all of us," they said. "We eat."

I knew right then in my head what my next scene was going to be. Who better to stuff your face with than ballerinas? I could invite the New York Giants, but that's not as fun or surprising for me. I decided I'm going to get takeout from New York's best places and show these ballerinas a good time in Central Park. We went all out and got fried chicken from Harlem; Charles's Pan-Fried Chicken, giant hero sandwiches from Faicco's; the classic pastrami sandwich from Katz's and a newer version from Harry and Ida's; Dan Dan noodles from Han Dynasty. And then to top it off, my dear friend Paulette Goto, who is a world-class pastry chef, came with the cake. It was a bacchanal. And then I danced away with the ballerinas. It's exactly how I always pictured my life in New York would be.

· · · ·

I loved showing Blue Hill at Stone Barns in the episode because it's literally half an hour from New York City in the Hudson Valley. That's nothing. It's still in the New

York metropolitan area, and you can easily go there and be in a whole other world.

Dan Barber is a genius. He's not just a chef but a visionary. One of the things I learned from him is that the same properties that make a fruit or vegetable nutritious is also what makes it delicious, like his Honeynut squash. So many chefs would have to dress it up with sauces and seasonings. He appreciates what it truly is, and you will, too.

Roasted Honeynut Squash

Serves 4

Seven years ago—almost by accident—I challenged vegetable breeder Michael Mazourek to build a better butternut squash. For Michael, it was the first time that someone had asked him to breed for flavor. For me, it was the discovery of a new kind of recipe—one that begins with the seed. Honeynut squash was the first brainchild of Row 7 Seed Company, packing three times the amount of beta-carotene in a palm-size gourd. You can buy Honeynuts at your local supermarket. Trust me, you'll never go back! —**Dan Barber**

2 10- to 12-ounce (280 to 340g) Honeynut squash	1 ounce (¼ stick/28g) unsalted butter, melted
Coarse sea salt	

Preheat the oven to 350°F (180°C). Slice the squash in half lengthwise and scoop out the seeds. Put the squash, cut side up, in a medium baking pan. Cover the pan tightly with foil and bake until a knife easily pierces the center, 40 to 45 minutes.

Remove the baking pan from the oven, let the squash rest for 5 minutes, and use a spoon to remove any juices that have pooled in the center cavity of each squash. (Save the juices for soup or discard.)

Flip the squash so the cut side faces down (do not recover the squash with foil), bake for 15 minutes, and let the squash rest for another 5 minutes. Use a spatula to flip the squash right side up, sprinkle the flesh lightly with salt, and bake for another 15 minutes. Brush the squash with the butter and let cool, uncovered, for about 5 minutes. Transfer each squash half to a plate and serve with a spoon.

Tip Honeynut squash are much smaller than many commercial squash varieties. Look for them at farmers markets and specialty markets like Whole Foods.

We couldn't leave New York without visiting the birthplace of the blues, my mother's kitchen.

I make fun of my mom's cooking. I do it for a living. I don't mean to disparage my mom. She was a great mom, a fantastic, funny person. She just never really cooked. She didn't have the time or the resources. She'd come home from work and have two rotten kids to deal with, plus Max; great food just wasn't the priority.

That scene at my parents' house is the only time we set something up on the show almost like a prank. It could have gone badly, but look how great my parents went with it. While we set up, Daniel Boulud (not only one of the greatest French chefs but one of the greatest chefs of any kind in the world) had to sit in the tiny hallway outside their door. We tried to give him a general time when we'd need him, but you don't know how long these things are going to take when you're filming. What a great sport.

The other thing was that my parents were so afraid the crew was going to break something. We've shot in many people's homes on the show. We've never broken anything. Then sure enough, one of the camera guys backed up in their small kitchen and hit the window. He didn't just hit the window, he cracked the window. My father exclaimed his immortal cry of "Oy!" I calmed him down.

"This is showbiz, Dad. We're going to replace the window."

Only in my parents' kitchen would that happen. The one place you need to be extra careful because they will never let you forget this.

My mom's soup will be the last thing I want to eat before I die. It's what will take me back to childhood.

Helen's 4-Star Matzoh Ball Soup

Serves 4 to 6

We'd never know what went into my mom's soup if Daniel hadn't asked all those questions at the table. She used chicken stock but also chicken bouillon, parsley and dill, boxed matzoh ball mix. Then she tells Daniel that no, she doesn't put the delicious chicken fat, the schmaltz, in the matzoh ball dough like everybody else does. She puts the schmaltz in the cooking water that she boils the matzoh balls in. That's the equivalent of throwing away the most Jewish part of the whole dish. We miss you, Mom.

1 3- to 4-pound (1.4 to 1.8kg) chicken or a mix of bone-in chicken breast and thighs

1 medium white or yellow onion, cut in half

1 large carrot, peeled and halved

1 medium celery stalk, halved

1 chicken bouillon cube

1 teaspoon plus 1 generous pinch dried parsley, divided

1 teaspoon plus 1 generous pinch dried dill, divided

1 teaspoon kosher salt

½ teaspoon finely ground black pepper

1 5-ounce (140g) package matzoh ball mix, such as Manischewitz

In a large stockpot, combine the chicken, onion, carrot, celery, chicken bouillon cube, 1 teaspoon each of the parsley and dill, salt, pepper, and about 2½ quarts (about 2.5L) of water. Bring to a boil, reduce to a simmer, and cook until the chicken is falling off the bone, 1 to 1½ hours. When

cool enough to handle, set a strainer over a large bowl and strain the stock.

Put about 1 cup (240ml) of the stock, half the cooked onion, the carrot, and celery in a blender. Blend until smooth, then stir vegetables into the stock. Pick the meat off the chicken and return it to the stock (discard the bones). Transfer the soup to a storage container, cover, and refrigerate overnight or up to 5 days.

Skim off the solidified fat (schmaltz) from the top of the chilled soup, put it in a medium pot, fill the pot about halfway with water, and bring the water to a boil.

Add the pinch of parsley and dill to the matzoh ball mix and shape the matzoh into ten to twelve balls. Gently drop the matzoh balls into the water, reduce to a simmer, cover the pot, and cook until the matzoh balls are no longer dark and doughy in the center (to check, slice one in half), about 20 minutes. Meanwhile, rewarm the soup over low heat and season the soup with salt and pepper, if needed. Use a slotted spoon to transfer 2 matzoh balls to each soup bowl, ladle the soup on top, and serve.

Matzoh Ball Soup with Dill Oil

Serves 8

This soup was inspired by Helen's rustic and delicious matzoh ball soup when Phil invited me to their home next to Bar Boulud on the West Side. It was a great homey and tasty broth. In my version, instead of sprinkling chopped dill on top, I make a dill oil to intensify the flavor. As I always have extra carcasses and bones, I also make a double-fortified chicken stock with both regular and roasted chicken bones for more flavor. —**Daniel Boulud**

About 3 quarts (about 3L) Double Chicken Stock (plus reserved chicken leg meat and diced vegetables), recipe follows, chilled

1½ cups (170g) matzoh meal, such as Streit's

3 large eggs, separated

1½ tablespoons grated white or yellow onion

¾ teaspoon grated garlic

1 tablespoon finely chopped fresh parsley leaves

½ teaspoon kosher salt

½ teaspoon finely ground black pepper

Vegetable oil, if needed

Dill Oil, recipe follows

Skim off the solidified fat (schmaltz) from the top of the chicken stock and reserve it for the matzoh balls. Put the strained chicken stock and reserved chicken leg meat and diced vegetables in a large Dutch oven or soup pot and rewarm the soup over low heat while you make the matzoh balls.

In a small saucepan, warm the schmaltz over low heat until melted. In a medium bowl, combine the matzoh meal, egg yolks (reserve the whites), onion, garlic, parsley, salt, pepper, and ⅓ cup (80ml) of water and use your fingers or a fork to mix until just combined. Add 6 tablespoons of the schmaltz (or, if you don't have enough schmaltz, a mix of schmaltz and vegetable oil) and mix well. The dough will be very crumbly.

In a stand mixer fitted with the whisk attachment, whip the egg whites on high speed to stiff peaks, 3 to 4 minutes, then use a spatula to fold the egg whites into the matzoh dough until just combined.

Shape the matzoh dough into roughly 1-inch (2.5cm) balls and roll the balls between your hands so the dough stays together; you should have about twenty-four matzoh balls. Bring a large pot of salted water to a boil. Add the matzoh balls, reduce to a simmer, and cook until the matzoh balls are no longer dark and doughy in the center (to check, slice one in half), about 45 minutes.

Use a slotted spoon or skimmer to transfer the matzoh balls to individual bowls (do not use tongs; the matzoh balls easily break) and ladle the hot soup on top. Serve the matzoh ball soup with the Dill Oil on the side.

Tips

- Use pure matzoh meal, not matzoh mix, which has added flavors. (You'll need about half of a 12-ounce/340g box.)
- Freeze any extra Double Chicken Stock for soups and stews, and save the extra Dill Oil as a base for salad dressings or to drizzle on baked fish or chicken.

Double Chicken Stock

Makes 4 to 4½ quarts (about 4L)

2 pounds (900g) chicken wings

1½ pounds (680g) chicken legs

6 quarts (5.6L) chicken stock, homemade or low-sodium store-bought

1 large white or yellow onion, cut in half

2 celery stalks

2 medium carrots, peeled

2 small parsnips, peeled

2 sprigs fresh thyme

1 bay leaf

2 whole cloves

2 teaspoons whole black peppercorns

2 teaspoons kosher salt

Preheat the oven to 400°F (200°C). Arrange the chicken wings in a single layer on a rimmed baking sheet and roast for 15 minutes. Use tongs to flip the wings and continue to bake until the opposite side is golden brown, about 15 minutes longer, and set aside.

In a large stockpot, combine the chicken legs and chicken stock. Bring to a boil and skim off and discard any foam that rises to the top. Add the roasted chicken wings, onion, celery, carrots, parsnips, thyme, bay leaf, cloves, peppercorns, and salt reduce to a simmer. Cook the stock, uncovered, for 45 minutes. Set a strainer over a large bowl, strain the stock, and use a spoon to press on the solids to release all of the liquid. (Do this in batches if needed.)

When the chicken legs are cool enough to handle, pick off the meat. Dice the celery, carrots, and parsnips into small (roughly ½-inch/12mm) cubes. Let the leg meat and vegetables cool completely, transfer a storage container, cover, and refrigerate until you are ready to make the soup or up to 5 days.

Return the chicken leg bones, wings, and strained stock to the stockpot. Bring to a simmer and cook the stock until richly flavored, about 1 hour. Strain the stock again and let cool. Transfer the stock to a storage container, cover, and refrigerate overnight or for up to 5 days.

Dill Oil

Makes about 1 cup (240ml)

2 cup fresh dill fronds (1 large or 2 small bunches), tough stems removed

1 cup (240ml) grapeseed or vegetable oil

Fill a small bowl with ice water. Bring a medium pot of water to a boil and add the dill fronds. Boil for 2 minutes, then strain and immediately submerge the dill in the ice water. Swirl the dill around in the cold water until cool and strain.

Roll up the dill in a kitchen towel and squeeze out any excess water, then transfer a blender. Add the grapeseed or vegetable oil, blend until smooth, and strain the oil through a fine mesh sieve (discard the solids). Transfer the oil to a storage container, cover, and refrigerate for up to 5 days.

New York is New York because this is where people from all over the world came for a new life.

I think the New York episode was one of our best shows. Not just because it's very personal to me, it's where my parents lived, where my brother and his family still live, it's where I grew up, and where I met the girl I was going to marry.

But without realizing it, when we get to the end and see the Statue of Liberty, you understand the entire episode is about immigration. The whole city is. Everyone you've met in the episode is an immigrant. My parents, too. It looms very large in our collective memory of what it means to be an American, to have come from somewhere else and to have settled here. That's what makes this country great.

New York!

FOR MY BEAUTIFUL BRIDE
MONICA HORAN ROSENTHAL
SIT NEXT TO ME AND I'M HAPPY
LOVE, THE HUSBAND

For PHILIP ROSENTHAL with love
from The Wife
MY WHOLE HEART
FOR MY WHOLE LIFE

›13‹

Marrakesh

Marrakesh is a beautiful, complicated, intense, wonderful city.

MARRAKESH WAS A PLACE I'D ALWAYS WANTED to go because of the way it's portrayed in the movies. It seemed so exotic, a world unto itself that you could just enter and be immersed in a whole other life and culture. You can go somewhere where the lifestyle is similar to how you live at home, and that's great, too. But for me, some of the best trips of my life have been when I went someplace totally foreign to me.

I've still never been anywhere like Marrakesh. I recommend it.

You know my favorite thing to do: hit the market first.

I never get tired of the marketplace no matter where I go. It's a microcosm of the society wherever you are. You're seeing everything and everyone; it's a feast of the senses. Marrakesh has some of the best markets I've ever been to, including the giant Jama El F'na Market. It's an ancient market, almost a thousand years old, that's now like the equivalent of Times Square in New York. You can be walking and suddenly there's a monkey on you, and the expectation is you're going to pause for a picture and pay the person who it belongs to. Then there are the snake charmers. You don't see

either of those in the show because I'd heard they don't treat these animals very well, so I want no part of that. I do want a part of everything else. The food, the shops, the people from all over the world.

Later, there's that scene when the shop owner offered me what I thought were eucalyptus crystals and asked me to smell it. He corrected me and said it was "metal crystal." I asked, "Crystal meth?" And he says, "Yes." It did look like crystal meth, or at least how I imagined it would look like from having watched *Breaking Bad*. (I passed.)

If you can laugh with others, you feel the world is one.

If any episode exemplified eating with families, it was this episode. That scene at the Amazigh family's house in the Atlas Mountains was one of the most memorable meals of my life.

When you eat there, they get paid for that, and of course they should. It's how they make a living. The magic happens when you sit down and get to spend real time with them. It's a fantastic way to get to know people you otherwise probably would never get to know.

When you're traveling, it also gives you perspective on what it's like to live wherever you're visiting. By any standards, this family's house is modest. And it seemed so precarious to me, built into the side of the cliff. It was like a house for mountain goats, but that's only because of how I live in my stupidly lucky life. But then I went up to their rooftop, and they have a priceless view. And they get how lucky they are.

My biggest takeaway was that this is the warmest, sweetest family. They were funny, too, and they were their own entertainment. They didn't need a TV show to watch. Such genuine hospitality. Ten minutes after I got there they invited me to come back anytime and stay with them.

And what we have in common? Dad can always embarrass his kids.

Everything we eat is a cross-pollination.

That lamb from Hadj Mustapha at Chez Lamine was amazing. It was just lowered into a hole, which is actually an underground oven, and cooked right there. You realize, "Wow this is where barbecue comes from. This is what a luau is." I love how people all over the world have figured these things out.

And there were no seasonings. What? None. When you eat it, you are tasting the animal, what the animal eats, and the clay of the oven. History is the seasoning here, the history of the place and the people. You also know it's special because it's the whole animal, and that means there is a respect for the animal. When you eat something like that, you're not just traveling, you're time traveling.

Mechoui

A lot of people asked me to get the recipe for that lamb. Here you go.

Get a whole lamb and don't add anything. Dig a hole. Get tiles from Morocco to line the pit. Light a fire, put the lamb in the pit, and cook the lamb for a very long time. Good luck.

Monica: Hello there!

Phil: You know I went to the bath, to the hammam. Dad, have you ever had a body scrub?

Max: My wife would do that.

Phil: It's like having your mommy give you a bath, it's insane. You put on these black disposable underwear, and they lie you on the marble floor, and then they take a bucket of water and throw it on you. And then the lady puts on a glove that is the kind of a sandpaper you would use if you were taking fifty-year-old paint off your house. And scrub, scrub, scrub. But then it becomes very nice, like, "I now shampoo you with almond. I now wash you with orange." Then juice of dates somewhere, I don't know where. And then they take you someplace else, this is the relaxation room. It's so beautiful, you can't believe it.

Max: They go every day?

Phil: They go once a week for this, to the hammam.

Max: Instead of taking a shower?

Phil: I don't think it's instead of taking a shower, but you go to the hammam as well.

Max: What does your body look like after?

Phil: A lobster. We should have been filming, except the audience doesn't need to see all that. Monica, I'd like you to do it to my father this evening.

Monica: I think he would like that; he likes the back scratcher.

Phil: Yeah, maybe just do the back. By the way, Monica, this one is for you. (*holds up a cookie*) This is filled with almond and flavored with rose.

Monica: That's me! My favorite thing.

Phil: Yeah, this is you. (*eats cookie*)

Monica: Oh, is it a little soft? Remember when I brought the rose sorbet to the *Raymond* set, and Brad Garrett said, "It tastes like my aunt Ethel's neck"?

How do you change a man's mind when a man is stupid?

Going to Project Soar, the nonprofit Maryam Montague founded that helps provide equal opportunities for teen girls in places where traditionally they haven't always had them, is something that has stayed with me. These girls are so smart, so articulate, and thrilled to be in school—all these things I'm describing are the opposite of me. When school is taken for granted, you don't appreciate it.

What these young women are doing is slowly chipping away at longstanding traditions and customs. It's like in the musical *Fiddler on the Roof*. The plot is about these three daughters, and each is gradually asking for a little more freedom. It's the story of the evolution of change, the struggle of hope and change and tradition, and how much you hold on to and how much you let go.

It's empowering. Girl power!

It's a given that you're gonna have a lot of tagines in Morocco, the dish that's named after the clay pot that it's cooked in. You can imagine getting a little tired of it. Trust me, you won't. That one we had on Amanda Mouttaki's food tour, the trid, was maybe my favorite. It was really, really delicious and had so many different flavors going on.

Amanda wins!

She also met her husband, Youssef, when she was on vacation in Marrakesh. So Youssef won, too.

Trid (Rfissa)

Serves 6

Trid, or rfissa, is one of the dishes rarely found in restaurants in Morocco but beloved in homes. How it is prepared and even served changes between regions and families. Rfissa is typically served for special gatherings; the most traditional time is right after a woman gives birth as it is believed the ingredients will give her strength to recover from labor. Some people add all the cooking broth to the serving dish while others serve the broth on the side so that people can choose how much extra they want to add.

Msemmen, the flaky, pan-fried flat bread served with rfissa, is also typically made at home. Indian parathas or even naan works if that's the only option. Whole chickens are traditional, but thighs also maintain the rich flavors true to the dish. Smen, a local fermented butter aged for up to two years that you find at Moroccan markets, adds even more richness. The hard-boiled

eggs and almond-stuffed dates are traditional and give different flavors and textures but can be left out.
—**Amanda Mouttaki**

2½ to 3 pounds (1.2 to 1.4kg) bone-in chicken thighs

2 medium white or yellow onions, thinly sliced

2 inch (5cm) piece ginger, peeled and finely chopped

1 tablespoon ras el hanout

2 teaspoons ground fenugreek

1 teaspoon ground turmeric

2 teaspoons kosher salt

1 teaspoon freshly ground black pepper

⅓ cup (80ml) extra-virgin olive oil

1 teaspoon saffron threads

⅔ cup (130g) dried brown or green lentils

1 medium bunch fresh parsley

1 medium bunch fresh cilantro

1 tablespoon smen or salted butter (optional)

6 whole msemmen, paratha, or other flatbread

3 hard-boiled eggs, peeled and halved (optional)

12 almond-stuffed dates (optional)

Put the chicken, onions, and ginger in a large bowl. In a small bowl, mix together the ras el hanout, fenugreek, turmeric, salt, and pepper. Whisk in the olive oil and pour the spice mixture over the chicken and onions. Use your hands to mix the chicken and onions in the spices until well coated. Cover and refrigerate at least 3 hours, preferably overnight.

Heat a large Dutch oven over medium heat. Add half the chicken (leave the onions in the bowl), skin side down, and cook until the skin is golden brown, 8 to 10 minutes. Transfer the chicken to a plate and brown the remaining chicken the same way.

Reduce the heat to low, pour off all but a few tablespoons of the fat from the pan, and add the onions to the pot. Cook the onions until soft and fragrant, stirring often, about 5 minutes. Add 1 cup (240ml) of water and scrape any caramelized bits off the bottom of the pot. Crumble the saffron between your fingers and add it to the pot, then add the strained lentils, chicken and any accumulated juices, and 3 cups (720ml) of water.

Remove the tough bottom stems of the parsley and cilantro and finely chop the remaining stems and leaves. Reserve a small handful of the parsley and cilantro leaves

for garnish. Add the remaining stems and leaves to the pot, bring to a boil, reduce to a simmer, and cook, stirring occasionally, until the chicken is falling off the bone and the lentils are soft, about 1 hour.

Add the smen or salted butter, if using, and season the rfissa with salt and pepper. Shred the msemmen or paratha into small pieces with your fingers and scatter the shredded bread on the bottom of a large, wide serving bowl or in individual serving bowls. Spoon the lentils and broth over the bread and arrange the chicken on top. Scatter the reserved parsley and cilantro over the rfissa, arrange the sliced eggs and dates, if using, on the side, and serve.

Tips

- Ras el hanout is a Moroccan spice mix that typically includes cumin, coriander, ginger, cinnamon, and cloves, though it varies by the spice shop.
- Use brown or green lentils, not hulled red (also called yellow) lentils, which fall apart in the stew.
- Paratha is available at Indian markets and often in the freezer section at Trader Joe's.

. . . .

We started the Marrakesh episode with the great chef Moha Fedal at the market. Ending the episode at Moha's house, with his beautiful wife, Hadisha; his sweet son, Malik; and their close friends was the perfect final scene for an episode that became about eating with families. (By the way, it turns out it was turmeric that Moha bought at the market. That has nothing to do with my cooking knowledge. I was right purely by luck.)

If you want to cook that dish with the Jerusalem artichokes that Moha tried to teach me how to make, you're gonna have to watch the show. If you were to ask me to re-create what I was making with any chef, I would have no idea. I was just trying to stay afloat. It's a good thing there were a lot of other delicious things on the table so I could give you this recipe that Moha wrote up instead. And it has three of my favorite things: chicken, garlic, and preserved lemon. I'll be missing my other favorite thing: Moha's family.

Schlemiel of Arabia.

Chicken with Preserved Lemons and Olives

Serves 4

As I told Phil, you must have concentration when you cook. We are serious, we have to respect the ingredients that we have. First we have to test them, taste them. How do you find it? We also need spices: my love, garlic, preserved lemon, and, of course, the king: saffron. And don't forget colors. —**Moha Fedal**

1 4- to 4½-pound (1.8 to 2kg) free-range chicken

2 medium (3 ounces/80g) preserved lemons

3 garlic cloves, minced

Generous pinch saffron threads

1 tablespoon peeled and finely chopped ginger or 1 teaspoon ground ginger

2 tablespoons freshly squeezed lemon juice

1 teaspoon coarse sea salt

1 teaspoon freshly ground black pepper

½ medium bunch fresh parsley, leaves and tender top stems, finely chopped

½ medium bunch fresh cilantro, leaves and tender top stems, finely chopped

1½ cups (220g) good-quality whole green olives, such as Castelvetrano, divided

⅓ cup (80ml) plus 2 tablespoons extra-virgin olive oil, divided

1 large white or yellow onion, finely chopped

1 medium lemon, cut into wedges

Rinse the chicken and pat it dry with paper towels. Rinse the preserved lemons, slice each in half, remove the seeds, and use your hands to tear the skins and flesh into small pieces (or roughly chop the lemons).

In a large bowl, combine the preserved lemons and garlic. Crumble the saffron between your fingers over the bowl. Add the ginger, lemon juice, salt, and pepper, and 2 tablespoons of water and mix well. Stir in the parsley and cilantro, add the chicken, and use your hands to cover the chicken in the seasonings. Cover and refrigerate the chicken for at least 3 hours or overnight.

Remove the pits from about ⅔ of the olives, roughly chop the flesh, and set aside.

Wipe most of the herbs and spices off the chicken (reserve the spices and marinade). Heat 2 tablespoons of the olive oil in a large Dutch oven over medium-high heat until hot. Add the chicken, breast side down, and sear until the skin is golden brown, 5 to 6 minutes. Use tongs to flip the chicken and brown the bottom, then brown both sides. Transfer the chicken to a plate.

Add the onions, remaining ⅓ cup (80ml) of olive oil, ¾ cup (180ml) of water, and reserved marinade and spices to the pot. Use a wooden spoon to scrape any caramelized bits off the bottom. Lay the chicken on top of the vegetables, cover the pot, and cook, flipping the chicken occasionally, until a digital thermometer reads 160°F (70°C) when inserted in the middle of the breast and thighs, about 45 minutes. Transfer the chicken to a plate.

Reduce the heat to medium and continue to cook the onions, stirring occasionally, until the liquid is reduced by about half about 10 minutes. Use a potato masher to roughly smash the onions to form a creamy sauce. Add the chopped olives and cook for 5 minutes. Season the sauce with salt and pepper.

Return the chicken to the pot, cover, and rewarm the chicken for a few minutes, then transfer to a serving platter. Spoon the sauce over the chicken, scatter the whole olives on top, and serve with the lemon wedges.

Marrakesh, or any foreign place, can be a little disorienting at first. But treat it like the first day of school. Don't expect to know everything on the first day.

Take the pressure off yourself a little bit, get a little acclimated. And then, before you know it, you start to enjoy things, and the next thing you know, you can be happier than you've ever been. Man, I loved being in Marrakesh. Can't wait to go back. And wherever you go, I want you to seek out families. Eat with the families! That's where magic happens.

·14·

Chicago

The people move you, the architecture moves you, the food moves you. Chicago moves you. In many ways, the promise of America is realized here.

I LOVE THE SPIRIT OF CHICAGO. IF YOU'VE NEVER been, I'd recommend going here to anybody. (Maybe not in January, if you can help it. It hurts, that winter. But I've been spoiled, maybe weakened, by Los Angeles weather.)

Chicago has what I think is the best architecture in America. We don't have a long history of grand buildings in this country like Paris or London. We don't have waterfalls in airports like you see in Singapore. But, we have Chicago. Not only is it filled with the greatest hits of American architecture, within the city you have the most amazing people and incredible food. There's nothing subtle about any of it—and that's exactly what makes Chicago so unforgettable. It's our handsomest city.

City of the Big Shoulders —**Carl Sandburg**

Going to Bang Bang Pies with Lily and meeting up with cousin Ben Shartar was the perfect thing to do on a sunny Chicago day. The food was incredible; Michael Ciapciak, the owner, kept bringing out more and more pies, and there was even candied bacon for poor Richard. Then those pigeons flew in and started hacking at our pie and tearing it apart with their beaks. They had no fear. It was like a Hitchcock movie.

All those pies were fantastic, but we thought the PB&J was the winner, so here's a recipe for Lily. Hold the pigeons.

PB&J Pie

Serves 8

We make our own homemade graham crackers for the crust. Here we've simplified the recipe to use store-bought graham crackers. We keep the jam flexible based on the season and our pie whims; you can use the jam recipe for any berry. Our favorite fruits for the PB&J Pie are raspberries and strawberries. —**Michael Ciapciak**

8 ounces (225g) cream cheese, room temperature

¼ cup (50g) granulated sugar

½ teaspoon molasses (not blackstrap)

½ teaspoon vanilla extract

¼ teaspoon kosher salt

1 large egg, room temperature

2 tablespoons heavy cream

1½ tablespoons sour cream

¼ cup plus 2 tablespoons (90g) creamy peanut butter spread, such as Jif

Graham Cracker Crust, recipe follows

Berry Jam, recipe follows

⅓ cup (50g) roasted salted peanuts, finely chopped

Preheat the oven to 275°F (135°C) degrees. In a stand mixer fitted with the paddle attachment, combine the cream cheese, sugar, molasses, vanilla, and salt. Mix on medium-low speed until very smooth, scraping down the sides of the bowl occasionally, about 5 minutes. Add the egg and mix until well incorporated. Add the heavy cream and sour cream and mix again. Add the peanut butter and mix until the filling is smooth and no lumps remain, 2 to 3 minutes.

Pour the filling into the Graham Cracker Crust and use an offset spatula to smooth the top. Bake the pie until the edges are set but the very center is still slightly jiggly, 40 to 45 minutes, and transfer the pie to a baking rack to cool for at least 1 hour. Spread the Berry Jam evenly over the surface of the pie and sprinkle the peanuts on top. Cover the pie with plastic wrap (do not let the plastic touch the custard) and refrigerate for at least 3 hours or up to 5 days before serving.

Graham Cracker Crust

12 whole graham crackers (170g; about 12 crackers)

3 ounces (¾ stick/85g) unsalted butter, melted

3 tablespoons granulated sugar

¼ teaspoon ground cinnamon

¼ teaspoon kosher salt

Preheat the oven to 350°F (180°C). Break up the graham crackers, put them in a food processor, and pulse until finely ground. (Or put the crackers in a large zip-top bag, seal the bag, and smash the pieces with a rolling pin.) Add

the melted butter, sugar, cinnamon, and salt and pulse until well combined; the mixture will be very crumbly. Firmly press the crumb base into the bottom and up the sides of a standard (not high-sided) 9-inch (22.5cm) pie pan.

Bake the crust until the edges begin to brown, 12 to 14 minutes. Use the crust immediately or let cool completely, cover tightly with plastic wrap, and store at room temperature for up to 2 days or freeze for up to 1 month.

Berry Jam
Makes about 1½ cups (360ml)

½ medium organic lemon	1½ cups (6 ounces/170g) raspberries
2 cups (8 ounces/225g) strawberries, quartered	¾ cup (150g) granulated sugar

Use a citrus peeler to remove the peel from the lemon in large strips, avoiding the white pith. Put the berries, peel and juice of the lemon, and sugar in a medium saucepan, and bring to a boil. Boil the fruit, stirring occasionally, until the berries have broken down and the jam is dark red and slightly thickened, about 15 minutes. Let the jam cool completely. Remove the lemon peel, transfer to a blender, and blend until smooth. Use the jam immediately or cover and refrigerate for up to 1 week.

Tips
- To avoid lumps in the filling, make sure the cream cheese is room temperature.
- When you cut the pie, wipe off your knife with a paper towel after making each slice to keep the jam from spreading into the peanut butter filling.

Deep dish pizza IS Chicago.

It's got too much sauce, too much cheese, too many toppings, most of them meat. It might be closer to a casserole than a pizza. Who cares? It's delicious, and it works.

Dinner and a show.

One of the best places to do that in Chicago is at one of the best Italian restaurants, not just in Chicago but in the country, Sarah Grueneberg's masterpiece: Monteverde. The whole concept of this place, down to the two nonnas making your pasta right in front of you, is incredible. Maria Perez, originally from Mexico City, speaks Spanish; Besa Xhemo, from Bologna, speaks Italian; but they have their own language of pasta.

That ragu, I couldn't stop eating it. It's an explosion of meat with pork shanks and homemade sausages, salami meatballs, and more salami. Sarah says it takes a coupla days to make, so she made you this much simpler version until you can get to her in Chicago. I'll be dreaming about this food in my pasta pajamas.

Salumi Sauce
Serves 4 to 6

I love this sauce! It is a quick, flavorful meat ragu inspired by our Ragu alla Napoletana, aka the bowl of love that Phil enjoyed at Monteverde. The bits of prosciutto and salami elevate the meaty flavor so it tastes like the sauce took hours to cook on the stove. (Our secret: it takes less than an hour.) I generally find that I do not need to add any salt or pepper at the end, as the salumi adds a delicious umami and seasoning to the sauce. Serve the sauce with your favorite pasta shape, Chicago-style: lots of sauce, lots of pasta! —**Sarah Grueneberg**

1 large carrot, peeled	1 28-ounce (790g) can whole peeled tomatoes
1 large yellow onion	
4 ounces (110g) sliced prosciutto or country ham	1 cup (240ml) dry red wine, such as Sangiovese, Chianti, or Pinot Noir
3 ounces (80g) mixed sliced salami (salami, soppressata, pepperoni, or similar)	1 4-inch (10cm) sprig fresh rosemary
16 ounces (450g) mild Italian-style sausage links	Kosher salt and freshly ground black pepper
2 tablespoons extra-virgin olive oil, divided	
4 tablespoons tomato paste	

Finely chop the carrot and onions. You should have about 1 cup of diced carrots and 2 cups of onions.

If using prosciutto, stack the slices on top of each other, roll the stack into a cylinder, slice into thin strips, and finely chop the strips. If using country ham, finely chop the meat. Chop the mixed salumi pieces the same way. Remove the Italian sausages from the casings and break up the meat with your fingers.

In a medium Dutch oven or large saucepan, heat 1 tablespoon of the oil over medium-high heat. Add the sausage and cook, stirring occasionally, until the fat has rendered and the sausages begin to brown, 8 to 10 minutes. Add the prosciutto or ham and salumi and cook, stirring often, until the cured meats begin to brown, 2 to 3 minutes, then strain (discard the fat).

In the same pot, heat the remaining 1 tablespoon of oil over medium heat. Add the carrots and onions and cook, stirring often, until the vegetables just begin to brown, 6 to 8 minutes. Stir in the tomato paste, then crush the tomatoes between your fingers as you add them to the pot with the tomato juices. Cook the sauce until slightly reduced, 3 to 4 minutes. Stir in the red wine, bring to a boil, and reduce to a simmer. Cover the pot and cook for 15 minutes. Stir again, cover, and cook until the sauce has darkened in color and smells fragrant, about 15 minutes.

Remove the pot from the heat, submerge the rosemary in the sauce, cover the pot, and set aside for 5 minutes. Discard the rosemary, season the sauce with salt and pepper, and use immediately, or keep warm over low heat, stirring occasionally, for up to 2 hours. Or, let the sauce cool completely, cover, and refrigerate for up to 1 week or freeze for up to 3 months.

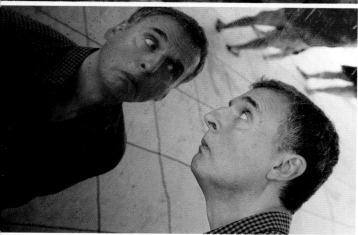

In Chicago, the food never stops, so one recipe from such a great chef is not gonna cut it. Sarah's tigelle, the flatbread with the burrata and melon she brought out for us before the pasta, was just as incredible. I could have eaten that all night. Turns out, you need a special press to make the bread, so this is the equally fantastic Prosciutto Butter that goes with it. For a normal person, this alone could be dinner. But who's normal?

Prosciutto Butter

Makes about 2 cups (380g)

Who doesn't love prosciutto and butter? At Monteverde, I love to schmear the Prosciutto Butter on our tigelle sandwiches. At home, I opt for the simpler version: on warm toasty bread and topped with radishes and dill. Leftover Prosciutto Butter has endless possibilities. At my house, it makes its way into a weeknight pasta, folded into scrambled eggs, spread on an egg sandwich, or simply served with a loaf of crusty bread. —**Sarah Grueneberg**

4 ounces (110g) sliced prosciutto or country ham

1 medium organic lemon

8 ounces (2 sticks/225g) unsalted European-style butter, such as Kerrygold, at room temperature

2 tablespoons minced chives

2 tablespoons minced fresh dill fronds

Freshly ground black pepper

If using prosciutto, stack the slices on top of each other, roll the stack into a cylinder, slice into thin strips, and finely chop the strips. If using country ham, finely chop the meat.

Zest and juice the lemon; you should have about 2 tablespoons of juice. Put the prosciutto, lemon zest and juice, butter, chives, and dill in a food processor and process, scraping down the sides of the bowl once or twice, until the butter is very fluffy, about 2 minutes. Season the Prosciutto Butter with pepper, and serve as desired, or cover and refrigerate for up to 1 week. (Let the butter come to room temperature before serving.)

Phil: Yes! Success. How are we?

Monica: You look like you're in a pub.

Phil: I'm in a beautiful building from 1890. It was a men's club until after World War II, when they let women in because they needed the business.

Max: So now there are women there?

Phil: Yeah, I see some, even. Dad, what do you remember about Chicago when you lived here? Did you like it?

Max: The wind blows you away.

Phil: I'm telling you, it hurts. I've been here in the winter. I can't take it.

Max: They had good restaurants to eat in.

Phil: They still do.

Max: And we had really good pizza in our neighborhood.

Phil: Very good! I'm eating pizza. I've had like two or three pizzas already.

Max: Did you accomplish everything you wanted?

Phil: I've accomplished everything I've wanted. I have done massive amounts of eating. The food here is very heavy, but it is delicious. Do you have a joke for me today, Dad?

Max: You know my jokes are all old jokes.

Phil: Yes, but you have a young, new audience.

Max: I don't change jokes. I change friends.

Phil: That's it!

Max: I'll tell you one, my famous old joke.

Phil: Yes, please.

(*Max holds one hand up to his ear, and right at that moment, his real phone happens to ring.*)

Phil: Wow, that was a very good imitation of a phone, Dad.

(*Max mimes dialing a phone.*)

Max: You can tell it's an old joke, right?

Phil: Yes, the dial phone.

Max: Hello? Dr. Schwartz? This is Mrs. Shapiro. Remember I was there this morning for my checkup? Could you look around and see if you maybe saw my panties hiding someplace? I left my panties, I think, at your place. Take a look, please. Okay. Hello? You didn't find it? No? I must've left them at the dentist.

Phil: That's wonderful. And with that we say goodbye!

I'll concede that my good buddy Jon Harris, who you also saw in the New York episode on the boat with Al Roker, *may* have beaten me at both bocce and shuffle-board when we were in the Game Room of the Chicago Athletic Association, and that may be because he's a hustler. We celebrated his victory with a great Chicago dog; in fact, at the Athletic Association, you get a *foot-long* Chicago dog. Even better.

Footlong Chicago Dog

Serves 4

In Chicago, there are two basic ways you can get a hot dog: Chicago-style or Maxwell Street–style. I grew up on Maxwell Street–style dogs (mustard, grilled onions, and sport peppers) but Chicago-style is more common. The origins go back to the 1920s; they contain a lot of ingre-dients you really don't see in many other foods: celery salt, sport peppers, Chicago's uniquely neon green relish. But for some reason, when they all get together, it just works. This is a case where even a chef has to take a step back and say, "Don't mess with a good thing." Less inno-vation and more preservation. I know a lot of people say it's an unforgivable sin in Chicago to put ketchup on a hot dog. But honestly, drag the dog through the garden two, three times, and you'll never even think of ketchup again. Trust me, it's a better way to live! Growing up we didn't even have ketchup in the fridge. This is the clas-sic Chicago recipe, only with footlong franks and buns that we use in the Game Room at the Chicago Athletic Association. (They can be hard to find; regular dogs and franks also work.) —**Max Robbins**

1 small white onion, finely chopped	Ballpark (classic yellow) mustard
3 Roma tomatoes, cored and finely chopped	1 teaspoon kosher salt
8 dill pickle spears	4 all-beef hot dog franks, such as Nathan's or Vienna Beef, preferably footlong
16 pickled sport peppers, such as Vienna	
Chicago-style sweet pickle relish, such as Vienna	4 hot dog buns, preferably footlong
	Celery salt

Line a baking sheet or large plate with paper towels. Put the onions in a strainer, rinse well under cold running

Sometimes you have a feeling you're going to experience something special. You just don't know how special.

water, and transfer to the paper towels to drain. Set the diced tomatoes, pickle spears, and pickled sport peppers in separate piles on the paper towels to drain.

Fill a large, wide saucepan halfway with water. Bring the water to a simmer, reduce the heat to low, then add the salt and franks. Gently cook the franks until warmed throughout (do not boil), 8 to 10 minutes, and turn off the heat. Lay a baking rack over the saucepan, place the hot dog buns on top, and put a large bowl upside down over the buns. Steam the buns until warm, 2 to 3 minutes, and transfer to serving plates.

Use tongs to remove the franks from the hot water, lightly pat each dry on the paper towels, and place them on the buns.

Nestle 1 pickle spear on each side of each frank (for a total of 2 spears per hot dog) and dollop a little relish on top. Scatter the diced tomato and onion over each and drizzle the mustard across the top of each hot dog in a zigzag pattern. Tuck the sport peppers inside the buns, sprinkle 2 to 3 pinches of celery salt on top of the franks, and serve.

Tip Chicago's signature neon green sweet pickle relish and pickled sport peppers are available online from Vienna Beef (viennabeef.com) and other specialty retailers.

We'd done a lot of final dinners by this point in the show, but this was the first time we'd filmed one at a church. I'm usually not in a church, so I didn't know what to expect.

I can tell you that the Ebenezer Missionary Baptist Church is a national treasure. This place is *the* birthplace of gospel music in America, going back to the first choir here in 1931. Mahalia Jackson, Bo Diddley, Dinah Washington . . . they all started out in the choir here. Martin Luther King Jr. preached here. That whole place, that whole experience, was incredible. When the pastor asked everyone to greet the newcomers, and I was embraced so warmly by everyone, I thought about converting. And then when the congregation began to sing, I actually recognized a song from my childhood: *Amen*, and an already beautiful day became transcendent.

You want to be uplifted? Come here. You want community? Come here. Come to Chicago.

15

London

London is the gateway drug to Europe. It feels a little like New York but also a lot like European cities. But what it really feels like is the comfort of childhood; it's the setting of our collective stories.

To me, London really does feel like it's out of a children's storybook, so I thought that would be a fun way to start the episode, reminding us of *Peter Pan*; my favorite, *Mary Poppins*; and even *Harry Potter*—they all take place in a kind of fantasized London. That's a great way to get your kids excited to hop on a plane and come here.

Another reason this city is so great? The architecture is incredible; it's modern and historic at the same time. And if you're like me, the best part is that the food, which had not always been this city's finest attribute, has caught up with everything else here.

London, it turns out, may actually be better than any fairy tale.

. . . .

One chef who's had a lot to do with why there's so much fantastic food in London today is Yotam Ottolenghi. He's a real genius, the way he combines flavors. At Rovi, where I met my immensely talented friend Dan Patterson, the creator of *Whose Line Is It, Anyway?* for lunch, the whole restaurant concept centers around vegetables. If I'm going to take on a sandwich, it's usually not going to be one filled with just vegetables. But that shawarma sandwich with celery root wasn't just a vegetable sandwich, it wasn't just a vegetable pretending to be meat like the veggie burgers you see everywhere, it was *better* than meat—I'm not kidding. And better than most burgers I've ever had in my life.

Consider this your lucky day: you're gonna have to go to London to try the best vegetable sandwich in all of England because it's a recipe Yotam wisely doesn't give out. We also talked about shakshuka, which, if you follow Yotam's cooking, you know he makes a lot of different ways. He wanted you to have this one that's packed with enough spinach to count as all your vegetables for the week.

Green Shakshuka

Serves 6

This dish often appears on our brunch table at home on weekends. It's the perfect dish for entertaining: delicious and stunning to look at. Created by my husband, Karl, based on a Turkish recipe, it has a similar impact as shakshuka, with the eggs nestling in a sea of greens and finished off with chilli butter. Urfa pepper (page 47) is worth seeking out. If you don't have any on hand, use another chile pepper and cut the quantity in half.
—**Yotam Ottolenghi**

2 medium bunches Swiss or rainbow chard

1¼ cups (300ml) chicken or vegetable stock, preferably homemade

2 pounds (four 8-ounce/225g bags) baby spinach

3 tablespoons extra-virgin olive oil, plus more for the baking dish

1 large white or yellow onion, finely chopped

2 garlic cloves, minced

1¼ teaspoon sea salt, divided

3½ teaspoon ground cumin

6 large eggs

2 ounces (½ stick/55g) unsalted butter

¾ teaspoon urfa pepper

1 cup (240ml) plain Greek-style yogurt, room temperature

Wash and dry the chard well and remove the stalks. Trim off the coarse ends of the stalks and chop into ½-inch (12mm) pieces. Roughly chop the leaves and set the stalks and leaves aside in separate piles.

In a large stockpot, heat the chicken or vegetable stock ot over medium-high heat. Add about half the spinach (or however much fits in the pot) and stir until the spinach wilts. Add the remaining spinach, stir again, and turn off the heat.

In a large Dutch oven or stockpot, heat the olive oil over medium-high heat. Add the onions, garlic, and ¼ teaspoon of sea salt and cook, stirring occasionally, until fragrant, 3 to 4 minutes. Add the chopped chard stalks and cumin and cook until the onions are translucent, about

5 minutes. Stir in the chard leaves and cook until wilted, 3 to 4 minutes. Add the spinach and stock to the pot and cook, stirring occasionally, until the chard stalks are tender, about 10 minutes. Stir in the remaining 1 teaspoon of salt.

Set a strainer over a large bowl, strain the greens, and press down on the vegetables with the back of a spoon to release any excess liquid.

Return the strained stock to the pot and cook over high heat until reduced to about ⅓ cup (80ml), about 10 minutes. Then stir in the strained greens and season with salt, if needed. Use the greens immediately, or let cool, cover, and refrigerate overnight.

Preheat the oven to 425°F (220°C) and lightly oil a 9x13-inch (23cmx33cm) casserole dish. Gently rewarm the greens, if needed, in a sauté pan over low heat.

Scatter the greens evenly throughout the baking dish and use your fingers to make six evenly spaced, shallow indentations for the eggs. Carefully break an egg into each indentation, cover the tray tightly with foil, and bake for 5 minutes. Remove the foil and bake the shakshuka until the whites are almost set but the yolks are still very runny, 6 to 8 minutes longer. (The eggs will continue to cook when taken out of the oven.)

Meanwhile, melt the butter in a small saucepan over medium heat, swirling the pan occasionally, until the butter begins to foam and turn golden brown, 1 to 2 minutes. Then stir in the urfa pepper. Dollop large spoonfuls of yogurt in between the baked eggs, drizzle the butter over the shakshuka, and serve.

Borough Market was my first love.

Some people bring magic just by being in the room.

Mary Poppins, of course, but a handful of real people, too.

I'm sure you remember Steven and David Flynn, the Happy Pear twins in our Dublin episode. The moment I met them, I knew I wanted to have them back on another episode. In the words of my wife, "Why aren't they the poster for the show?"

Here's why: Steven and David always have an agenda. Like their healthy crap agenda they put me through.

. . . .

It was the very first market I fell in love with in the world, and it's still one of my favorite places in all of London. There's been a food market in this spot for a thousand years, and then in the 1700s it was converted to this permanent space. Just walking around to the different restaurants and stands, like we did in that scene with our longtime friends Tom and Cathy McGowan, is an adventure. You can't go wrong with anything you get here, from classics like bubble and squeak from Maria's Market Cafe that Monica demolished, to that duck confit wrap that's like an insanely decadent burrito. (You need to try that wrap. The place is called Le Marché du Quartier.) But you must save room for the world's best grilled cheese at Kappacasein.

The Best Toastie

Bill Oglethorpe worked for years at Neal's Yard, one of the world's best cheese stores, which happens to be right around the corner from the market. This guy sampled every combination of cheese to find the best for his grilled

The perfect breakfast spot, the perfect dining companion, the perfect toast that comes in the perfect little slotted thing.

cheese sandwich. *He puts more cheese than seems possible on the best sourdough bread (which he also spent years searching for) from the Paris bakery, Poilâne, and then toasts up the sandwich so the cheese gets perfectly melted and the fat oozes out. The best. Here's my take:*

Spread some good salted butter on 2 slices of day-old sourdough sandwich bread. Chop up the thinnest slice of red onion, a little green onion (or baby leek), and some garlic and mix those together. Put a thin layer of that on one slice of bread. Mound a giant handful of shredded aged cheddar (Neal's Yard) on top. Heat up a panini press and cook the sandwich for a couple minutes until the cheese has just melted. (Don't press down on the top of the panini press too hard or the cheese will come out.) Eat that while you look at flights to London.

After I got to have breakfast with a Lady, the sweet and lovely Sophie Winkleman, I got to have a drink with My Lady at Dukes . . .

. . . where Monica and I had the pleasure of corrupting our nice, new young friend, *Great British Bake-Off* star Liam Charles. Dukes is where Sir Ian Fleming came to drink martinis and, legend has it, wrote the first James Bond novel. The martinis here aren't like the "shaken, not stirred" martini James Bond orders because the right way to do it is "stirred, not shaken." But at Dukes, they don't even do that.

Here's why: the gin comes straight out of the freezer so there's no ice. No need to shake or stir. Genius Alessandro Palazzi, who has been the bartender at Dukes for years, swirls a bit of vermouth in your glass and then dumps it on the carpet. He then pours about five shots of gin or vodka into the glass and then adds a lemon peel. Not just any lemon peel; these giant lemons are from the Amalfi coast.

Monica's Martini (The Vesper)

Put a giant martini glass, a bottle of gin, and a bottle of vodka in the freezer to chill. When everything is icy cold, fill the glass with two shots of gin, two shots of vodka, ½ shot of Lillet Blanc, and 2 to 3 dashes of bitters. Drop an orange peel in the glass and hand it over. Take cover.

· · · ·

If it were up to me, I'd have kept eating the puffballs at Brat with Nigella. Then Tomos brought out that whole turbot fish that looks like it's in this butter sauce, but it's not. It's just the amazing way this fish is cooked. I'd never had anything like it.

What happens when these delicate fish are very slowly roasted is the fat, bones, and cartilage start to melt and become what looks like sauce over the fish. It sounds simple, but things like that never are. Tomos kindly wrote an essay for you here explaining what you need to do to make the dish. Get the wrong fish, cook it wrong, it's not going to work. My way: book a reservation at Brat instead.

Basque-Style Grilled Fish

Serves 4

Before opening Brat, I traveled extensively throughout the Basque country, visiting restaurants, farmers, and fishermen. I always had the idea of a restaurant driven by open-fire cooking focusing on whole fish and vegetables. When I spoke to fishermen and local restaurant owners in the port towns, such as Getaria, I started to understand the importance of "terroir." Not only to the fish, but how it influenced their cooking methods. I was familiar with the term terroir with wine but hadn't thought about it so much in relation to fish. This was an important moment for me. It was the first time that I realized that where the fish comes from can directly link to how the fish tasted and how it could be cooked.

I have tried to apply this approach to sourcing fish in the UK, becoming very connected with exactly where the fish is caught and preparing it appropriately. You can do the same with similar varieties of fish in your area. We believe it's one of the best ways to eat the fish and allows you to taste and appreciate the terroir of the fish. I hope you will consider this more a technique, as it is meant to be, than a true recipe. It takes some time to master this style, from maintaining the right temperature of the fish to creating the gelatinous pil pil sauce. —**Tomos Parry**

Sourcing

- Turbot is readily available in the UK and is farmed in much of Europe. Finding turbot here may be easy, but finding out where the fish was caught and what kind of diet the particular fish would have been eating is essential. This translates directly to the gelatin and fat content of a turbot and is key to the enjoyment of eating this simple dish. Cooking a whole turbot—one that comes from the best sources—symbolizes much of what we do at Brat. Other flat fish that have similar qualities include Dover sole, lemon sole, halibut, brill, or flounder. Ask your fishmonger or fishermen which of these are in season and is particularly fatty that day—a good fishmonger will know what you mean. The fattier the fish, the better it cooks over fire.

Cooking Method

- When I first started cooking, chefs would always tell me to cook fish quickly, then let it rest. As I studied how Basque (and Japanese) chefs cook, I noticed they were aiming to almost roast the fish over the fire, not so much grill it in the traditional form. At Brat we also cook the fish slowly over the fire. After you burn your fire down and let it develop into glowing embers, the temperature should be a lovely glowing heat but not raging hot. This allows the skin to roast, the collagen to develop, and the deep flavors to exude from the bones. I would compare it to roasting a piece of meat. The longer you can leave the fish cooking on the bone, the more complex and delicious the flavor.
- The second key is to spray the fish with a vinaigrette, known as the Lourdes water in the Basque country, as it cooks. Every restaurant in the Basque country has their own recipe. (Our version includes chardonnay vinegar, olive oil, fish stock, and lemon juice.) The purpose of basting helps protect the skin and crisp up the fins as the fish cooks. The acidity also helps break down the natural collagen in the fish, which is essential for the pil pil sauce that is made out of the gelatin that oozes out of the fish combined with the vinaigrette, which emulsifies as you gently move the fish from side to side after cooking.

1 whole 3-pound (1.4kg) turbot or two 1½-pound (680g) Dover sole or similar flatfish

1 cup (240ml) fish stock, preferably homemade

½ cup (120ml) good-quality extra-virgin olive oil

⅓ cup (80ml) white wine vinegar

3 tablespoons freshlysqueezed lemon juice

Sea salt (optional)

Let the fish rest at room temperature while you prepare the vinaigrette and grill (up to 30 minutes). Put the fish stock, olive oil, vinegar, and lemon juice in a measuring cup, stir to combine, and pour about half the mixture (the "Lourdes water") into a clean spray bottle. Set aside the remaining Lourdes water for the sauce.

Prepare a grill over medium indirect heat.

Lightly sprinkle the fish on both sides with sea salt, only if needed, to taste. (If the fish stock is very salty, don't salt the fish.) Gently place the fish in a large stainless steel fish (or net) clamp, put the fish clamp on the grill, and spray the fish on both sides with about ¼ of the Lourdes water.

Phil: Hi, Dad. How are you? You were in London with us once. And then we went on from London to Italy. Do you remember that?

Max: Yes. The luggage didn't get onto the plane.

Phil: That's what he remembers from his trips. "So, I understand you've been all around the world?" "Yes, I know it by the complaints I had at each stop." Didn't it get there around the same time?

Max: A couple days later.

Phil: So, I understand you have a special guest star today, Dad? Is that right?

(*Max shakes his head no.*)

Phil: There's no one there to visit you today?

Max: Oh yes, Judy Gold.

Phil: But she's not so special?

(*Judy sits next to Max.*) **Judy:** I'm not special?

Phil: Hi, Judy. You schlepped all the way from Uptown.

Judy: I rode my bike, as you can see from my sweat.

Max: Should I put on the air-conditioning?

Phil: Wow, he doesn't put on the AC until people are fainting.

Judy: I'm putting it on, Max.

Max: The air-conditioning?

Judy: Can I? Or will you be mad?

Max: I'll do it.

Judy: Oh my god, just like my father, "I'll do it!"

Phil: "I'll do it! Because I know you, and you're going to put it on high, and it only needs to be on low."

Judy (*to Max*): Do not touch that thermostat!

Phil: "I can save fifteen cents!" I understand there's some breakfast there for you. Because you're not getting paid, so we had to give you something.

Judy: What? I'm not getting paid? (*Judy is delivered plates with breakfast.*) My god, look at that, Maximillian.

Phil: That is a Full English. You've got the eggs, you've got a tomato, you've got some bangers. You know what, when it's breakfast time for you, you know what time it is for me? High tea! (*Phil is delivered a plate of scones.*) Thank you.

Judy: Oh, that's good, Phil.

Phil: And you know what else I have? I have a date!

(*Monica sits next to Phil in London. Judy and Monica scream in excitement.*)

Phil: Judy, why don't you tell everybody what's new with you.

Judy: I wrote a book, *Yes, I Can Say That*, and it's about freedom of speech from the perspective of a comedian.

(*Continued on next page*)

Phil: It's so important, especially today, am I right, ladies and gentlemen?

Judy: Yes you are, folks.

(*Phil is delivered a tray of desserts.*)

Phil: Whoa! Dessert just arrived!

Judy: Is that cotton candy? I'm a little jealous.

Phil: Yeah, dessert. This is like a mini Yoo-hoo.

Max: Is that chocolate milk?

Phil: It's chocolate peppermint. (*Phil holds up a cake pop.*)

Judy: Ohhh, is that red velvet?

Phil: There's chocolate cake inside. (*To Monica*) What do you think this is? A little chocolate pudding?

Judy: Chocolate pudding is my favorite! Oh my god, what is that?

Monica: It looks like there's passion fruit inside.

Judy: Is it good? This is torture. I'm not doing this again.

Phil: That's why people watch the show.

Judy: Yeah. Is there a gym at the hotel?

Phil: Yeah, I use it every day. I have to.

Judy: Really?

Phil: This doesn't happen by itself. (*sits back in chair to show off body*)

(*Judy and Monica cackling.*)

Phil: Why are you laughing so hard?

Judy: Because it was funny.

Phil: Cut!

Grill the fish (do not close the grill) for 10 minutes. Spray the fish again on both sides with about ¼ of the Lourdes water and grill for another 10 minutes. A digital thermometer should read about 130°F (55°C) when inserted into the center of the fish. Spray the fish again with ¼ of the Lourdes water, grill for 10 minutes, then spray the fish with the Lourdes water one final time. Grill until the fish skin is golden brown and the flesh is opaque, about 10 minutes (for a total cooking time of about 40 minutes).

Remove the fish clamp from the grill and use one or more large spatulas to carefully transfer the fish to a rimmed baking sheet and let the fish rest for 10 minutes. Use sharp scissors to cut out the spine of the fish and pour the reserved Lourdes water on top. Grip the sides of the sheet pan with your hands and gently move the pan in a circular motion until the pan juices emulsify (you should see small globules of gelatin oozing out of the fish) to create a sauce. Carefully transfer the fish to a serving platter, pour the pil pil sauce on top, and serve.

Tip The cooking temperature is key to slowly cooking such a delicate fish and making the pil pil sauce after the fish grills. (If the meat is too hot the collagen will melt away, too cold and it will remain solidified.)

· · · ·

At the final reunion dinner in London, I wanted to invite some friends of mine you hadn't met who weren't in this episode or any other, the incredibly talented British director Gurinder Chadha (*Bend It Like Beckham*) and chef, food host, and member of the Most Excellent Order of the British Empire, Ching-he Huang. I knew they'd get along with all of our other friends—Tom and Cathy, Dan, Sophie, and Brett Graham, who cooked that amazing dinner for us out at Aynhoe Park. It remains one of the most fun lunches of my life.

Shamil Thakrar, the owner of Dishoom, kept bringing out more and more food. Okra fries; lamb chops; that bacon, egg, and cheese on their homemade naan; and this fantastic spicy fried chicken. You can't go wrong. I will hit Dishoom on every trip to London.

Chilli Fried Chicken

Serves 6 as an appetizer or 4 as a main course

Our chilli (how we spell chile) fried chicken was one of the dishes enjoyed by Phil and his friends when we had the pleasure of warmly welcoming them to Dishoom King's Cross. One of our best loved dishes, it is inspired by an Indo-Chinese favorite from Leopold Café. A Bombay institution, Leopold's is one of the cherished Irani cafés to which Dishoom pays loving homage. If you find yourself in Bombay, Leopold's is well worth a visit for plentiful plates of chilli chicken and chilli cheese toast (another of our favorite Bombay comfort foods). In the meantime, we hope this home version satisfies. A glass of sweet chai is the perfect accompaniment and complements the chilli heat nicely.

We use Indian green chillies, but you can replace them with Thai bird's eye (we'd recommend using a little less, as they are a touch hotter) or another chilli with some heat. Strong (bread) flour is our preference, but regular (all-purpose) flour will work just as nicely.
—**Naved Nasir**

1½ pounds (680g) boneless, skinless chicken thighs	Generous pinch salt
½ small bunch fresh cilantro (leaves and tender top stems), finely chopped	Pinch ajinomoto (MSG) (optional)
	1 cup (120g) cornstarch
3 tablespoons malt vinegar	½ cup (60g) bread or all-purpose flour
3 tablespoons dark soy sauce, or regular soy sauce plus ½ teaspoon honey	Vegetable oil, for frying
	Chilli Sauce, recipe follows
1 large egg, lightly beaten	2 green onions, finely chopped
2 teaspoons white pepper or finely ground black pepper	2 limes, cut into wedges

Cut the chicken into 1-inch (2.5cm) pieces if serving as an appetizer, 2-inch (5cm) pieces if serving as a main course.

In a large bowl, mix together the cilantro, malt vinegar, dark soy sauce or regular soy sauce and honey, egg, salt,

pepper, and ajinomoto, if using. Add the chicken and mix until the chicken is well coated in the sauce.

Mix together the cornstarch and flour in a small bowl. Scatter the dry ingredients over the chicken and use your hands to coat the chicken in the batter (the batter will be very sticky). Cover and refrigerate the chicken for at least 6 hours, preferably overnight.

Preheat the oven to 250°F (120°C) and lay a baking rack on top of a sheet pan. In a large iron skillet or Dutch oven, heat about 1 inch (2.5cm) of vegetable oil over medium-high heat. When the oil is very hot (about 325°F/165°C), add about half the chicken (do not crowd the pan) and fry until golden brown on the bottom, 2 to 3 minutes. Use tongs to flip the chicken and fry the other side until golden brown and the internal temperature reads 160°F (70°C) on a digital thermometer, about 2 minutes. Transfer the chicken to the baking rack–lined sheet pan to keep warm in the oven while you fry the remaining chicken the same way.

Put the Chilli Sauce in a large bowl, add the hot fried chicken, and toss the chicken in the sauce until well coated. Arrange the chicken on a serving platter, scatter the green onions on top, and serve with the lime wedges.

Chilli Sauce

Makes about ¾ cup (180ml)

2 tablespoons vegetable oil

10 garlic cloves, minced

1 large red onion, finely chopped

1 4-inch (10cm) piece fresh ginger, peeled and finely chopped

⅓ cup (80ml) dark soy sauce, or regular soy sauce plus 1 teaspoon honey

3 tablespoons rice vinegar

2 to 3 tablespoons seeded and finely chopped hot chillis, such as Indian or Thai bird's eye

1½ teaspoons granulated sugar

Pinch ajinomoto (MSG) (optional)

In a medium saucepan, heat the vegetable oil over medium heat. Add the garlic and fry, stirring often, until golden brown, about 2 minutes. Strain the oil into a small bowl and return the oil to the pan (reserve the garlic).

Add the onions and ginger to the saucepan and continue to cook over medium heat, stirring occasionally, until the onions are translucent and fragrant, about 5 minutes. Add the dark soy sauce or soy sauce and honey, simmer for

2 minutes, then stir in the rice vinegar, chilli peppers, sugar, ajinomoto, if using, and fried garlic. Reduce the heat to low and cook the sauce, stirring occasionally, until thickened and a thin layer of oil has risen to the top of the saucepan, 8 to 10 minutes. Turn off the heat and use paper towels to dab the top of the sauce to remove as much of the excess oil as possible. Use the Chilli Sace immediately, or cover and refrigerate for up to 1 week. (Let the sauce come to room temperature before using.)

Tips
- The batter for this fried chicken is mixed together several hours ahead of frying (or overnight), making it an easy recipe for a party or quick dinner.
- Malt vinegar, made from malted barley, is available at well-stocked grocery stores.
- Chinese-style dark soy sauce, available at most Asian markets, is slightly thicker and sweeter than most widely available soy sauces.

London is so spectacular in every way.

It's so civilized, it's so pretty, it's just so polite and sweet. It was heaven to be back in this town with these people.

I can't sing and I can't dance like Dick van Dyke, but there is one scene in *Mary Poppins* that I think I can nail ...

16

Seoul

Seoul may feel a little daunting at first, it's so huge. But when I'm faced with a place like this, I find it's best to just jump in.

SEOUL IS ONE OF THE MOST MODERN SOCIETIES on Earth, at the cutting edge of technology, music, movies, and, yes, food. Korean food is truly one of the most unique cuisines, a mix of so many flavors in each bite.

And for somebody like me, whose foreign language skills are compromised at best, Korean was one of the toughest nuts for me to crack. I stayed up at night trying to get "thank you" right. *Gamsahabnida.*

In fact, here's what I've learned traveling to so many foreign countries: if you don't speak the local language at all, the most important phrase to learn is "thank you." I've found that it's good for almost any situation. It works for:

"Very nice to meet you."
"Cheers!"
"Excuse me."
"I'm sorry, I was just a stupid tourist and you're nice."

When in doubt, say, "Thank you."

A lot of the world's most unique and most delicious dishes come out of hard times.

Budae jjigae, the Korean "army stew" I had with Tom Caltabiano, a writer on *Raymond*, and Khee Lee, our mutual friend, is a good example of that. Khee was explaining how the soup was created in the early 1950s, right after the armistice was signed that ended the Korean War. Koreans were struggling to find enough to eat, so they would get surplus food from American army bases like hot dogs, veggies, tofu, and Spam, and then combine it with their specialties: kimchi, tofu, noodles, dumplings, rice cakes, or whatever was available. The stew that came out of those difficult times is now loved in Korea, the United States, and beyond.

If you want a great version, write this down: *Samcheongdong Jukkumi Kalguksu*, then pull the paper out when you get to Seoul and show it to your cab driver. Or, if you're taking the subway (a great way to get around the city, by the way), show it to anybody you meet. (Actually, why not invite them to come to the restaurant with you?) When you get to the restaurant, order the budae jjigae!

Korean Army Stew

The ingredients in this soup might not sound very enticing, but together, trust me. Like so many Korean dishes, you want good, fresh kimchi. It gives the stew a good punch.

Heat up a lot of broth (vegetable, chicken, or beef) or ask your local Korean take-out place if they ever sell the extra broth from any of their soups. Add a handful of good kimchi (with the juices), chopped cabbage, and whatever else you have in the pantry and fridge: sliced Spam, hot dogs, cooked ground beef, ramen noodles, Korean dumplings, soft rice cakes, even baked beans. Let everything cook together for a while and season the soup with whatever you like (fish sauce, soy sauce … ?). Put some of the soup broth in a kettle so people can add as much broth as they want to their soup, and put everything else in a giant bowl on the table. Let everybody pick out the choice bits with chopsticks.

I got the idea to taste all of the chips in this episode after tasting the different whiskies in the Dublin episode.

Like whiskey in Ireland, chips are a thing in Korea. Chips that taste like fried chicken, black pepper crab, spicy ramen chips, "late-night roasted chicken," even sweet chips that taste like churros and butter caramel popcorn.

I wanted to taste them all for the first time with you, that's why we did it back at the hotel and not in the middle of the convenience store. (By the way, those shrimp chips really do smell like a bad day at the docks when you first open a bag, then you taste one, and you can't stop eating them.)

Chips, people! Another good reason to travel.

. . . .

That lunch with Jessie Kim and Sokeel Park, the South Korea regional director of Liberty in North Korea, was one of the most emotional moments for me in the

series. Jessie had escaped from North Korea as a teenager and hadn't had many of the foods she grew up with while now here in Seoul. It was so touching, so beautiful, that the simplest thing—the potato dumplings that her grandmother used to make (turn the page)—could have such an effect on a person. These are not just foods, they're memories.

North Korean Potato Dumplings

Makes about 12 dumplings

When I was growing up, rice and flour were rare commodities. After the Soviet Union collapsed, North Korea was no longer able to provide for its own people, and the devastating famine hit. My grandma always made potato dumplings for me whenever I was hungry, even when food was not easy to get. I did not fully understand the situation in North Korea and nagged my grandma for dumplings made of rice or flour. It's the one thing I regret the most in my life. This version represents my grandma's unconditional love and instantly brings me home. I long for the day when I can welcome friends from all around the world to my hometown in North Korea, share steaming hot dumplings, and dance the night away.

This recipe makes enough dumplings to share with friends. They are traditionally served without sauce, but sometimes I will put out one of my favorite North Korean–inspired sauces for dipping. (I use it in my cooking classes, where I hope to meet you sometime.) Traditionally, the potatoes are finely grated by hand, but I use a blender to make it easier (a professional-style high-speed blender works best). The one trick is you need to make sure to remove all the water content from the potatoes to extract the starch or the dough will not bind properly. —**Jessie Kim**

About 3 pounds (1.4kg) russet potatoes	¾ cup (180ml) kimchi, strained and finely chopped
1 teaspoon fine sea salt	2 teaspoons granulated sugar
2 tablespoons vegetable oil	1 teaspoon soy sauce
2 garlic cloves, minced	1 teaspoon toasted sesame oil
4 ounces (110g) ground pork	

Line a large colander with a large nut milk bag and set the colander in a large bowl.

Fill a large bowl about halfway with cold water. Peel and roughly chop the potatoes, adding the potatoes to the bowl of water as you chop them to keep them from discoloring. (Discard the peels.)

Scoop out about half the potatoes from the water, put them in a blender with 1 cup (240ml) of fresh water, and blend until the mixture is the consistency of a milkshake. Transfer the potato mixture to the nut milk bag, process the remaining potatoes the same way, and add them to the bag. Tie up the nut milk bag securely so no liquid can seep out. Place a heavy saucepan or a bowl filled with water on top of the bag and set aside to drain for 10 minutes.

Lift the nut milk bag out of the colander and use your hands to firmly squeeze the bag over the colander, like you are wringing out a wet towel, until the water has been released. Transfer the colander to the sink and add the potatoes. (Do not discard the potato water in the bowl.)

Prepare a steamer according to the manufacturer's instructions. Or, fill a large Dutch oven with about 1 inch (2.5cm) of water and set a large colander (with legs or on a stand) inside the pot; the bottom of the colander bowl should sit above the level of the water. Add the potatoes to the steamer or colander, cover, and steam until tender, about 20 minutes. Transfer the potatoes to a large bowl to cool for about 10 minutes.

Meanwhile, in a large sauté pan, heat the vegetable oil over medium heat. Add the garlic and stir until fragrant, about 30 seconds. Add the pork and stir the meat until it just begins to brown, about 2 minutes. Add the kimchi, sugar, and soy sauce and cook, stirring occasionally, until the liquid has mostly evaporated, about 5 minutes. Turn off the heat and stir in the sesame oil. Season the dumpling filling with salt and set aside until cool enough to handle.

Carefully strain off the water in the bowl used to strain the potatoes and use a rubber spatula to scrape up the white starch at the bottom of the bowl. Add the starch to the steamed potatoes and use a fork or your hands to

If you want to feel old and insignificant, walk with a K-pop star like Eric Nam down the streets of Seoul.

gently mix the dough until just combined (do not overmix). You should have about 3 cups (680g) of potato dough.

To make the dumplings, turn out the potato dough onto a work surface and fill a small dish with water. Wet your hands and put about ¼ cup (55g) of dough into the palm of one hand. Flatten the dough with your fingers and shape it into a disc about 3.5 inches (9cm) in diameter; it should be slightly thicker at the edges than in the center. Set the dough round on the work surface and put about 1 scant tablespoon of the pork-kimchi dumpling filling in the center. Dip a finger in the water and run it around the bottom edge of the dough round, then fold the top of the dough over the filling to create a half moon shape. Pick up the dumpling again and use your fingers to gently press the edges of the dough together to seal them. Shape and fill the remaining dough the same way; you should have about 12 dumplings.

Stand the dumplings, seam side up, in the steamer or in the colander in the Dutch oven. Cover and steam until the dumplings are firm and a fork or chopstick inserted into the dumplings comes out clean, 16 to 18 minutes. Serve the dumplings immediately.

Tip   Once the dough has been made, these dumplings are easy to shape and assemble. But work quickly, as the uncooked potato dough will discolor if left to rest for too long before steaming the dumplings.

. . . .

I've had all kinds of food experiences around the world, but I'd never been to an airline's catering kitchen before we went to the Korean Airlines headquarters for the episode. Who would want to? The expectation is that airline food is going to be bad. It's almost a requirement: eat before you get on the plane. The problem

with feeding people on a plane is the chefs are working with all these strict limitations, so the real artistry is in overcoming that.

Still the single best dish I've ever gotten on an airline I had on my way to Korea: samgyetang. The stewardess brings out this little crock, opens the lid for you like you're at a fancy restaurant, and there's a whole baby chicken inside. When you slice open the chicken, it's stuffed with rice. If you ever have a cold, I might suggest this chicken soup even *over* the Jewish version. You won't believe how delicious it is. By the way, I got the nicest rejection letter I've ever gotten for anything when we asked for this recipe from the airline. This huge corporation was so nice in saying no. That says a lot about these people, this culture.

But we had a lot of other great samgyetang all over Seoul. One was a crew dinner at Tosokchon Samgyetang.

If you go there, you're going to have to wait in line. Do that. Another was from our hotel, the one you saw on the call with Dad. And here it is.

Samgyetang

Serves 2

Samgyetang is a boiling-hot ginseng chicken soup. ("Sam" refers to ginseng, "gye" means chicken, and "tang" soup.) The dish is extremely popular on boknals, the hottest days of summer. You'll see people lining the streets at the most popular samgyetang restaurants as it is considered a nourishing food. As the Korean saying goes, eating this hot soup on a hot day is "fighting the heat with heat." Food is medicine in Korea, and samgyetang

is meant to help you rebalance your hot and cold energy. It's also delicious—a fact that holds true any time of year.

The chickens we use at the Grand Hyatt Seoul are very young and tender, about the size of Cornish hens (a good substitute). The soup is not salted during cooking; instead, sea salt is served at the table so everyone can season the dish to their taste. —**Ik Sun Son**

½ cup (100g) sticky rice, such as sushi rice

2 Cornish hens or very young chickens, about 1½ pounds (680g) each

2 3-inch (7.5cm) pieces fresh ginseng, preferably tender young roots, peeled, divided

2 green onions, thinly sliced, plus 2 whole green onions, divided

10 garlic cloves, divided

6 fresh or dried jujubes, rinsed

4 fresh chestnuts, peeled (optional)

1 2-inch (5cm) piece ginger, peeled

Sea salt and freshly ground black pepper, for serving

Put the rice in a strainer and rinse well under cold running water until the water is no longer cloudy. Transfer the rice to a medium bowl, cover with cold water, set aside to soak for 20 minutes, then strain.

Meanwhile, rinse the Cornish hens, pat dry with paper towels, and put the birds upright in a large Dutch oven or stockpot, cavity facing up. Thinly slice 1 piece of ginseng and stuff half the slices inside each cavity (if the roots are older and too tough to slice, leave the ginseng whole and reserve it for the broth). Divide the sliced green onions, 4 garlic cloves, jujubes, and chestnuts, if using, among the two chicken cavities, then stuff the birds with the rice. (It's fine if some rice falls into the pot.)

Tie the legs of the birds together with kitchen twine. Use kitchen scissors or a small knife to pierce two to three holes in the excess skin on either side of the breast, then use the twine to sew the skin together to close the cavity. Lay the birds side-by-side, breast side up, in the pot and add the remaining ginseng (or both if 1 wasn't sliced), whole green onions, garlic, ginger, and 2 quarts (about 2L) of water. The water should almost cover the birds; if not, add a little more to the pot.

Bring the water to a low boil, reduce to a simmer, cover the pot, and cook until the meat is almost falling off the bone and the rice is tender, about 45 minutes. Slide a spatula underneath each bird and use tongs to carefully transfer them to large soup bowls (try not to break the flesh). Remove the ginseng and ginger from the broth (discard both). Spoon several cups of the hot broth over each bird, scatter the remaining green onions on top, and serve the soup with the sea salt and pepper on the side.

Tips

- For another meal, pick off any leftover meat from the birds and add it to the leftover broth for later.
- Fresh ginseng (also called galangal), an earthy root vegetable, is available at some Asian markets but can be difficult to find (it is not the same as ginger). The flavor of dried ginseng is typically very mild and won't impart the same flavor as fresh but could be used in the broth.
- Jujubes are also available at most Asian markets.

I've found that people everywhere want to share their culture with you.

In a place like this that's so huge, so chaotic, with signs you can't read, the locals are your way around the uncertainty. Share their stories. Help you navigate the new things. Because they're proud of where they live. All you've got to do is make a little effort. You just have to ask.

To everyone in Seoul, I don't want to forget to say the most important thing: gamsahabnida. 감사합니다

Phil: Dad, I got something special for you today. (*holds up a bowl of soup*) This is Korean chicken soup. It's so much like what you know as chicken soup, and it's so delicious. It's called samgyetang. If I told you this came from Fine and Schapiro in New York, you would say, "Yes, this is excellent chicken soup."

Max: So what's going on over there?

Phil: I love it here. It's sprawling. Twenty-five million people live in the metropolitan area of Seoul. What year were you in Seoul?

Max: 1944. I found this, can you see? (*holds up a picture of a Navy ship*)

Phil: A ship, a big ship.

Max: The ship that took us from the Philippines to Korea.

Phil: Wow, what was that like?

Max: I was there five days on the ship. I was sick four days.

Phil: You were young. What were you? Like, nineteen years old?

Max: Yes.

Phil: Could you have imagined that your son would . . .

Max: . . . someday be in Korea?

Monica: And celebrating it.

Phil: And loving it. And having delicious food, and meeting wonderful people.

Monica: Where are you going today?

Phil: You know, it's the last day, and I like to have a reunion of everyone we've met throughout the week. And we'll go for Korean barbecue.

Monica: Oh, how great.

Max: Something like you have in LA? Where you sit at the table, and they put on the fire, and a pot, and you throw everything on there?

Phil: Yes. I love it. What's your joke today?

Max: Mr. Cohen goes to the doctor, and he feels very weak and helpless and low energy, and has no sex life. And the doctor says, "Do you do any exercises?" And he says, "No." "Do you walk a little?" "No." "I'll tell you what you do. You start walking every day, one block, two blocks. Before you know it, you'll be walking a quarter mile, half a mile. Call me back in about four months, five months, and let me know how things go." So he calls him back. "Mr. Cohen, how are you? Are you walking?" "Oh boy, am I walking, really great." "And has your sex life improved?" He says, "I don't know. I'm thirty miles from home."

Phil: Monica, you're laughing like you've never heard that joke. I'm toasting you and everyone with a spoonful of chicken soup!

17

Montreal

I can't say enough nice things about Montreal.
It's sweet, charming, and it's Canada, so
everybody's nice! There's a spirit of love here.

MONTREAL FEELS A LOT LIKE EUROPE TO ME. You get that feeling just walking down the street, you see it in the architecture and at the parks, and you certainly taste it in the food. And French is spoken by half the population—only don't say French or French Canadian, this is *Quebeçois*, because we're in the province of Quebec. It's easy to forget it's only a one-hour flight from New York.

I thought I knew what makes a great bagel.

The New York water, right? At least that's what I'd always heard.

At St-Viateur Bagel Shop, they put honey in the water they use to boil the bagels. In New York, that would be like cheating. But the first time I went to St-Viateur, I was blown away. When we found out we were going to Montreal for the show, I had to go back and share with you the best bagels I've ever had in my life. Does that make me a cheater?

And this time, I got to meet the great Italian Joe Morena, who started working at the shop in 1962 when he was fourteen years old and is now the owner. You gotta love a guy who chooses the Bagel Life. We instantly connected. I always say, Italians and Jews, we're the same. All problems are solved with food, and your mother never leaves you alone. Of course, Joe is so sweet, he thinks that's a beautiful trait in a mother. He's not wrong.

Joe's Bagel

You can't have Joe's Bagel without one of Joe's bagels. Another reason to go to Montreal. (By the way, you can now also order St-Viateur's bagels online, which I do.)

Split open a St-Viateur sesame seed bagel and toast it if you want. Spread ricotta cheese on the inside, top the cheese with fresh figs, and eat it.

How do we choose a city for the series?

Paul Toussaint asked me that question when we were at Agrikol, his Haitian restaurant.

It's changed somewhat since the early episodes. But it really comes down to where I want to eat. Then is the place hospitable? Is it fun? Will people like this? Does it offer more than just food? As I said, in the first version of the series back on PBS, we started with some of Earth's Greatest Hits: Paris, Tokyo, Barcelona, Los Angeles, Hong Kong, and Florence. I thought that's what people would want most, accessible, popular places. Places they could see themselves going that weren't such a stretch. And of course, they're all fantastic.

We got a tiny bit more adventurous as we went on. And we realized people were a lot more adventurous than we thought. More adventurous than I'd ever been. Bangkok, Saigon, and Tel Aviv were all in the first season of the new show. We had more American cities starting in the third season, too. I wanted to get people to travel in their own towns. Not just feel like they had to get on a plane, not everyone can afford that. We also went to places that I know well like Chicago and of course, New York.

Later, as the show went on, we had fans telling us places we should go. Your hometowns, your favorite cities. Those have been some of the best tips. And

people featured in the show shared their opinions, too. The Mississippi Delta episode was entirely because of Julia Reed. She wouldn't stop talking about it when we were in New Orleans. It's not a place I would have thought to go, but I'm so glad we went. You should, too.

When Paul was talking about Haiti, I said right then and there we should go. When we got renewed for the fifth season, we actually did look into it, but it didn't work out that time. Sometimes it comes down to where else we are filming so we can make our budget work. Other times it's something beyond our control, what's happening in that part of the world. When we were picking places for the fifth and sixth seasons, places you might see in the next book, things were opening back up after the pandemic—or at least that's what we thought. We also thought we were going to Japan right after the Olympics, but no one could go yet. In

a way, that's also serendipity. We'd never have gone to another place if that didn't happen, and hopefully, there will be another opportunity to go back to all the places we missed.

In the end, Richard and our team do a lot of research. As much as I hate to admit it, if Richard tells me I should go, we go.

. . . .

That scene with Paul at Agrikol was my first time trying Haitian food with all of its African, French, and Caribbean influences. (Since the show, that restaurant closed, but he opened a new place, Kamúy, in the city.) Everything was fantastic.

It was also my first real "rhum" sour. Richard especially loved the cocktail, so I got him the next recipe. I sometimes do nice things for him.

Rhum Sour

Makes 1 cocktail

Nothing is better than sipping a great rhum sour and enjoying good food surrounded by Caribbean artwork and music. An appreciation of all art—food, drink, paintings and sculpture, music—is a part of me and the experience at Kamúy.

My version comes from a moment I passed with Win Butler and Régine Chassagne of the band Arcade Fire at Hotel Florita in Haiti. It was the first time I enjoyed a spicy rhum sour like that; the experience was epic. I had to create an extraordinary rhum sour with a special scotch bonnet syrup to share that moment with others around the world. **—Paul Toussaint**

2 ounces (60ml) Agricole or Clairin rhum, or unaged white rum

1 ounce (30ml) Scotch Bonnet Syrup, well stirred, recipe follows

1 ounce (30ml) freshly squeezed lime juice

1 lime wedge

Fill a rocks glass with ice. Add the rhum or rum, Scotch Bonnet Syrup, and lime juice, gently stir, and serve with the lime wedge.

Scotch Bonnet Syrup

Makes about 1 cup (240ml)

1 Scotch bonnet chile pepper, sliced in half

1 1-inch (2.5cm) piece ginger, peeled

1 3-inch (7.5cm) piece lemon peel

1 3-inch (7.5cm) piece orange peel

1 whole star anise

2 cardamom pods, smashed

1 cinnamon stick

1 cup (200g) granulated sugar

1 teaspoon Angostura bitters

In a medium saucepan, combine the Scotch bonnet pepper, ginger, lemon and orange peel, star anise, cardamom, cinnamon stick, sugar, and ⅔ cup (150ml) of water. Bring to a boil, then turn off the heat and let the syrup cool completely. Strain the syrup and add the bitters. Transfer the syrup to a jar, cover, and refrigerate for at least 3 hours or up to 2 weeks. (Stir the cocktail base before using.)

Tips

- Rhum refers to a spirit made from fresh sugarcane juice, rather than molasses, the base of most widely available rums. Any unaged white rum can be substituted.
- If you can't find Scotch Bonnet peppers (small, round, bright orange hot chile peppers), habañeros can be used.

. . . .

This pikliz recipe, the classic Haitian condiment, is also for Richard to enjoy . . . don't tell him it's incredibly spicy.

Pikliz

Makes about 3 cups (720ml)

I love Haiti; it's my culture. Merging those Caribbean traditions with modern styles of cooking is how I share that with others. Pikliz is a popular traditional Haitian condiment that we like to use everywhere and with everything. It can spice up an entire meal or a single dish like baked fish, grilled meat, sandwiches, even fries. Like any pickle, if you store pikliz in the vinegar, refrigerated, it will keep for weeks. Any leftover vinegar can be used on its own to add balance and acidity to whatever you are making. **—Paul Toussaint**

½ small green cabbage

1 medium carrot, peeled

1 medium white onion

1 to 2 Scotch bonnet or habañero chile peppers, halved

½ small bunch fresh parsley, leaves and tender stems, finely chopped

¾ to 1 cup (180 to 240ml) distilled white vinegar, as needed

¼ cup (60ml) freshly squeezed lime juice

¼ cup (60ml) vegetable oil

1 tablespoon plus 1 teaspoon kosher salt

Shred the cabbage, carrot, and onions on the large holes of a box grater. Put the cabbage, carrot, onions, chile peppers, parsley, ¾ cup (180ml) of the vinegar, lime juice, vegetable

oil, and salt in a medium bowl. Mix well and transfer the vegetables and brine to one or two large jars. If needed, add up to another ¼ cup (60ml) of vinegar so the vegetables are fully submerged in the brine. Refrigerate the pikliz for at least 3 hours before serving or for up to 1 month.

Tip Freshly made pikliz has a bright flavor and crunchy texture that becomes spicier as the condiment ages.

. . . .

Self-service restaurants like Olive et Gourmando, Dyan Solomon's bakery and café, can be wonderful places to meet people. You go to the counter, order your food, and while you wait at one of the tables, you can start up a conversation with someone at the next table. Like I did with that adorable little girl, Isha, who was in town with her family from New Jersey—which happens to be not far from where I grew up.

The other great things about Olive et Gourmando? Every bite is delicious, and you can get breakfast *and* lunch at the same time. We all need vitamin P, so here's Dyan's famous Cubano sandwich.

The Cubano

Serves 6

I dragged the Cuban sandwich back with me from my time working in Boston with chef Corinna Mozo at Chez Henri. Corinna made a more authentic version of a Cuban sandwich (the kind you might actually find in Cuba) that was on a crusty, airy baguette with ham, cheese, mayo, and cornichon pickles, flattened and heated through over a charcoal grill. It was insanely delicious and marked me for life!

When we finally bought a panini machine a few years into owning Olive, the first thing I thought about was how I could re-create Corinna's Cuban sandwich with our own little twist. We decided on using two types of pork (pancetta to add a smoky element, as well as thin slices of house-roasted, tender pork loin), Gruyère cheese, and then instead of adding sliced pickles, we created a

spicy pickle mayo (also a good addition to sandwiches, hamburgers, and hot dogs) and make our own panini. Crispy, juicy, spicy, salty, and with the perfect touch of acidity, this sandwich is perhaps the most craveable item on the menu at Olive.

As for the smoked pancetta, it is an artisanal product made here in Quebec that has been hot smoked, so it is fully cooked, then we thinly slice it. Smoked pancetta is very smoky and fatty, so it balances the roast pork. If you can't find it, I would suggest a smoky ham.
—Dyan Solomon

Roast Pork Loin, chilled, as needed, recipe follows	Cuban Mayonnaise, recipe follows
6 panini or ciabatta sandwich loaves (or 2 large ciabatta loaves)	Kosher salt and freshly ground black pepper
18 slices thinly shaved Quebec-style smoked pancetta or smoked ham (8 ounces/220g)	12 slices deli-style Gruyère cheese (12 ounces/340g)

Remove the Roast Pork Loin from the refrigerator about 30 minutes before serving. Brush off any braising liquid (do not rinse the pork) and thinly slice the pork about ¼ inch (6mm) thick.

Preheat a panini press according to the manufacturer's instructions. If using a large panini or ciabatta loaf, slice each into 6-inch (15cm) sandwich-size pieces and cut each in half lengthwise. Lay 3 to 4 slices of pork loin on each bottom half of bread, lay 3 slices of pancetta or ham over the pork, and spread about 2 tablespoons of Cuban Mayonnaise evenly over the surface of the meats. Lightly sprinkle the salt and pepper over the mayonnaise, lay 2 slices of Gruyère over the mayonnaise, and close the sandwiches.

When the panini press is hot, grill the panini in batches until the cheese is melted and the bread is golden brown, 3 to 5 minutes, and serve hot.

Cuban Mayonnaise

Makes about 1 cup (240ml)

½ small bunch fresh cilantro, both leaves and tender top stems, roughly chopped

¼ medium red onion, roughly chopped

2 tablespoons roughly chopped dill pickles, preferably gherkin

½ cup (120ml) mayonnaise

1 tablespoon canned chipotle peppers in adobo sauce

2 teaspoons freshly squeezed lime juice

Pinch kosher salt and freshly ground black pepper

Put the cilantro leaves and stems, red onion, and pickles in a food processor and pulse until finely chopped. Scrape down the processor bowl, add the mayonnaise, chipotles, lime juice, salt, and pepper, and process until smooth. Use the mayonnaise immediately or cover and refrigerate for up to 1 week.

Roast Pork Loin

1 tablespoon kosher salt

2 teaspoons freshly ground black pepper

1 tablespoon extra-virgin olive oil

1 3- to 3½-pound (1.4 to 1.6kg) boneless, center-cut pork loin with a fat cap

Preheat the oven to 425°F (220°C).

In a small bowl, mix together the salt and pepper. Rub the olive oil all over the pork, then season with the salt and pepper. Put the pork on a sheet pan, fat side up.

Roast the pork for 15 minutes, reduce the oven temperature to 325°F (165°C), and continue to roast until a digital thermometer reads 145°F (63°C) when inserted in the middle (the pork will continue to cook as it cools), 40 to 50 minutes longer. Remove the pork from the oven, tent the meat lightly with foil, and let cool completely. Transfer the pork and any pan juices to a loaf pan, cover, and refrigerate overnight or up to 5 days.

Tips

- You can make the sandwich with your own roast pork loin leftovers, or make Olive et Gourmando's simple pork roast. (You'll have plenty of leftovers to make more sandwiches.)
- Don't substitute the more widely available European-style pancetta, which is raw and must be cooked, for the Quebec-style smoked pancetta.

Alone you are nothing in life.

That was one of my favorite things anybody said on the show. We think of the most famous chefs as these solitary geniuses, mad scientists in a food laboratory. But most of those I've met are like Martin Picard, who give as much or more credit to the talented sous chefs and team around them who make everything happen. And if you're crazy enough to open a place like Cabane à Sucre (the Sugar Shack), his place outside the city, you're going to need a lot of help to make so much fantastic food. We've had some incredible dinners on the show, but nothing like this one.

There was caviar, duck, foie gras, a pig's head, oysters with duck hearts, giant salads . . . it was death by what you love. For me it bordered on insanity, but I have to say, everything I had was delicious. A meal like this anywhere else would cost hundreds of dollars, but the whole thing there costs $56.

By the way, my friend Jeff Gordinier retired a couple of years after we shot that scene. He started his final article as the food critic for *Esquire* magazine by saying that our dinner together at the Sugar Shack was a real turning point for him. (Look it up, it's a great read.) "They're trying to kill us," is what he said on the show.

I always say, you can't eat this way every single day. But you should enjoy it when you do. It's also why we have these things called gyms. And yes, I work out every day.

This is like a slab of caramel that comes out after you've eaten more than you ever have in your life. Tell me this doesn't become your new favorite Thanksgiving pie.

Martin's Maple Pie

Serves 8 to 10

The maple pie is our Au Pied de Cochon baby that merges tradition (maple syrup), innovation (condensed milk), and gluttony (dulce de leche). In other words, the maple pie is a sin already forgiven.

A pastry crust works well with the sweet maple filling, but you could use a graham cracker crust depending on your vibe. —**Martin Picard**

Unsalted butter, room temperature, for the pan

All-purpose flour, for dusting

1 unbaked 9-inch pie dough, preferably homemade, chilled

½ cup (120ml) canned sweetened condensed milk (about half a 14-ounce/400g can)

½ cup (120ml) Dulce de Leche, recipe follows

½ cup (120ml) good-quality maple syrup

5 large egg yolks, lightly beaten

Pinch fine sea salt

Preheat the oven to 425°F (220°C) and set a rack in the top third of the oven. Lightly butter the bottom and sides of a 9-inch (22.5cm) nonstick springform (cheesecake) pan with a removable bottom and line the bottom with parchment paper.

Roll out the pie dough on a lightly floured work surface into a round about 1 inch (2.5cm) larger than the springform pan. Lay the crust in the bottom and up the sides of the pan and flatten the edges like a tart. The crust should go about ¾ inch (18mm) up the sides of the pan. Freeze the crust for 15 to 20 minutes.

Line the bottom and sides of the crust with aluminum foil and top the foil with enough pie weights or dried beans so they come up the sides of the pie pan. Put the pie crust on a sheet pan and bake until the crust has set and no longer looks doughy in the center, 10 to 12 minutes. Remove the foil and weights and bake until the edges just begin to brown, about 10 minutes longer.

Reduce the oven temperature to 350°F (180°C). In a medium bowl, whisk together the condensed milk, dulce de leche, maple syrup, egg yolks, and salt until well combined. Pour the filling into the crust (it should come to or almost to the top of the crust), then use an offset spatula to spread a little of the filling over the edges in a few places so it caramelizes in spots while baking. Bake the pie for 15 minutes, reduce the oven temperature to 300°F (150°C), and continue baking until the edges are set and slightly darker in color but the very center is still slightly jiggly, 18 to 20 minutes longer. Immediately run a knife along the edges of the pan to loosen the sides, transfer the pie to a baking rack, and let cool completely.

Serve the pie at room temperature or cover and store at room temperature for up to 5 days.

Dulce de Leche

Makes about 1 cup (240ml)

1 14-ounce (400g) can sweetened condensed milk

Remove the label from the can (do not open the can). Put the can in a large Dutch oven or other high-sided pot. Cover the can with several inches of water, bring to a simmer, and cook, adding more water as needed, for 2½ hours. (Be sure the can is always completely covered in water by several inches or it can pressurize and explode.) Let the Dulce de Leche cool completely and use immediately, or refrigerate the can (unopened), for up to 3 months.

Tips

- You'll have enough homemade Dulce de Leche to make two pies (which are more like a tart than a classic American-style pie). Or use the leftovers to sweetened drinks (iced coffee, milkshakes), or as a caramel sauce on ice cream.
- If using a graham cracker or store-bought pastry pie crust, blind bake the crust (without pie weights) until just beginning to brown at the edges, about 10 minutes, or according to the recipe or manufacturer's instructions.

Max's Bagel

Joe likes his sesame bagel with fresh ricotta cheese and figs, things you'd find in the Italian countryside. My people like their bagels covered with fresh cheese that's been turned into a dense paste, then we top it off with the freshest fish that's been covered in salt and smoked until it's a dream. The best.

By the way, we did manage to get some bagels from St-Viateur sent back to Dad after we shot that scene. His review? "I only like challah now."

Get a sesame bagel. Split it in half and toast it, then spread cream cheese all over the inside, cover the cream cheese with smoked salmon, sliced tomato, some onions, and capers and make a pot of coffee. (Max: Use the Keurig; it's easier.)

So that's Montreal. A little French, a little English, kind of like Europe, and kind of not.

What brings it together are the people, local or immigrant, whatever language they speak, sharing themselves with their neighbors. Speaking of the spirit of love, you know whose bed I stayed in in Montreal? The one John and Yoko stayed in during their famous Bed-in for Peace. I knew Monica had to be part of this experience, and since Montreal's only an hour away from New York . . .

Phil: Hi, Ma!

Helen: Hi, Philip, how are you?

Phil: Your hair looks beautiful!

Helen: Thank you.

Phil: I was talking to Dad.

Max: What?

Monica: We're all having a good hair day.

Phil: You are. Mom, you look very nice. How you doing?

Helen: Fine.

Phil: Yeah? Have you been to Montreal?

Helen: Yes.

Phil: You like it?

Helen: Yes.

Phil: Can I show you my favorite thing about Montreal? This is one of the best things about this city . . . which is very much like going to France, half the population speaks French, all the signs are in French and English, some no English.

Max: The ones that speak English, they don't want their children to know what they're saying.

Phil: The way you spoke German when I was growing up? That was your bit. I remember: *"Das Kind ist nicht normal."* [*The kid is not normal.*] (*holding up bagel*) Look at this. Okay, so these are truly great.

Monica: That's sesame, right? That's my favorite.

Max: Is it soft?

(*Richard laughs*)

Phil: Dad's number one requirement for food? Soft. "It could taste like crap, but if it's soft, I'm eating it." I have to say, they're the best bagels I've ever had.

Max: Cream cheese and lox, they don't have that? (*Phil holds up the cream cheese.*) Oh, okay.

Phil: You know the great thing about cream cheese, Dad? It's very soft.

18

Rio de Janeiro

They call Rio the Marvelous City for a very good reason. And it's absolutely spectacular in so many ways: the scenery, the spirit, the music, the food, and the caipirinhas.

MY ONLY FRAME OF REFERENCE FOR RIO DE Janeiro was from *The Producers*. "Rio by the Sea-o." I also knew they had great music, a Carnival that tops all others . . . and that it was going to be hot.

But that's only a fraction of what I found in this incredible—and huge—city. Brazil is the biggest country in Latin America with more than 200 million people, and Rio is its second biggest city. I've never seen anything like the sheer beauty of this place. There's the water, and the beaches, and then you have these valleys and then mountains jutting up, one with a statue of the very famous gentleman on top. And the food is as incredible, with its European, African, and Indigenous influences.

But if anything captures the essence of Rio, it's that scene at Confeitaria Colombo. I wanted to use the photograph you see here for the cover of this book because for me, it embodies what the whole series is about: I'm the luckiest guy in the world, and the world can be a beautiful place. And I want you to have what I'm having. It's only good if you can share it. Everyone at Colombo was stopping to taste pastries as I was handing them out. Most other places, people might say, "No, thank you." Not in Brazil. Not only that, I got kisses.

When I'm in a tropical climate, the first thing I want to try is the fruit.

There are a couple places I've been around the world where the fruit is like nowhere else. I'm no agricultural expert, but I've learned that a climate that's fantastic for fruit means you'd better pack some extra antiperspirant.

I encourage you to taste the locally grown fruit when you're traveling. I had some of the best fruit of my life in Rio, like that mango I had with Tom Le Mesurier, a British expat who leads food tours in town, at Praça Nossa Senhora da Paz, the square in Ipanema where they have a local market. It wasn't a mango like we get at most grocery stores in the US. This was a tiny little mango, a manga carlotinha, the mango

Phil: Hello there! I'm in Rio, which is honestly one of the more spectacular places on the Earth.

Max: I've seen the pictures. They're beautiful. With the mountains, the sea. I mean, what else can you have there?

Phil: "What else can you have?" That should be their motto. Rio de Janeiro. What else could you have? Here's something I could have. Oh look, they brought me this specialty, brigadeiros. (*holds up a chocolate candy*) This is Portuguese for "super fudge ball."

Max: Is it chocolate?

Phil: It's so crazy soft with little chocolate sprinkles on the top. Oh my god, is that good. And this . . . (*holds up cheese bread*) Cheese bread.

Max: Cheese bread?

Phil: Yep.

Phil: Oh, Monica, I'm bringing you something. Have you ever had cachaça?

Monica: Is it liquor?

Phil: I know the way to my wife's heart. It goes through a bottle. But this, holy cow! This place we went is called the Academie de Cachaça. Your heaven.

Monica: Favorite university.

Phil: Yes, your favorite university.

Monica: What do they make it from?

Phil: Sugarcane, so it's like rum, but it's lighter than rum. I'm telling you, you could drink three of them like it's Hawaiian Punch. And then you're dead . . . because it comes at you later, like a thief in the night, and mugs you. You really feel it. Dad, do we have a joke today?

Max: I have a story with the beach joke.

Monica: The beach joke.

Phil: The beach joke. He has a file. "Rio . . . is there a beach there? Then we do the beach joke."

Max: This mother with a child, they're playing on the beach. And all of a sudden this big wave came and swept the child off the beach. The mother got hysterical and prayed to God, "God, please, it's my only son, I'll pray every day, please get him back to me." And then another wave comes and the kid comes back, and the mother was so happy. "Thank you, God, thank you so much. Whatever I promised, I'll keep." "By the way, one more thing: He had a hat."

Phil: C'mon, that's a good joke.

Monica: We're very happy you've had such a good time, and my favorite part was definitely you dancing.

Phil: I'm a hell of a dancer. Don't you think, Dad?

Max: So-so.

of mangoes, that's only available for about a month. I smuggled some home.

By the way, fruit makes a very good breakfast when you're traveling, another reason to start out at a local market. Sometimes it's also very good at the hotels. And it's light, so you can still do all the food scenes you've got coming up.

Cassava Flour Pancakes

Tom and I had these pancakes at the market. They're made from what we call yucca in the US, which goes by the name cassava, or manioc, in Brazil. If you extract the starch from the root vegetable, you magically end up with tapioca flour. Here's what else I learned from Tom and watching that nice local woman make this pancake, but don't take it from me. If you really want to know how to make them, rewatch the episode or, even better, go to Praça Nossa Senhora da Paz on a day the market's open, and let them show you how.

Finely grate a cassava until it turns into powdery tapioca flour. (Or maybe you could buy tapioca flour and add a little water, but this wasn't wet like a pancake batter; it was very dry.) Now scatter the tapioca flour into a hot skillet, and it should melt together and make a pancake. Sprinkle a little dried oregano and the local queso coalho (a fresh cheese; "squeaky like cheese curds" is what Tom called it) on top. Let the cheese melt, then flip the pancake in the air like you know what you're doing, and let the other side brown. If the pancake ends up on the floor, pick it up, wipe it off, and pretend nothing happened.

. . . .

Those caipirinhas, my first, at the Academia da Cachaça, where I went with our lovely local fixers, Jazmin Castillo and Nanda Varanda, were so good. I brought Monica home a bottle of cachaça, but that was the one time a bottle of booze I picked up while traveling was really for me. I can't believe I'd never had either the liquor or the cocktail before that trip.

You're gonna need something to eat after all those drinks, and this feijoada, the local specialty, will do it. It's a black bean stew with pork loin and ribs, different sausages, beef jerky, there's even bacon to help sop up all the alcohol.

Feijoada

Serves 6 to 8

The very Brazilian feijoada, part of our cultural heritage, could not be left off the menu when Academia da Cachaça opened in 1985. To accompany the dish, a good dose of a cachaça or a caipirinha, and friends, lots of friends around, are required. —**Eveline Sidi**

1 pound (450g) carne seca, biltong, or other lightly seasoned beef jerky

1 pound (450g) boneless pork loin or thick-cut pork chops

1 pound (450g) pork baby back ribs

1 cup (220g) dried black beans

6 ounces (170g) smoked sausage links, preferably paio or andouille

6 ounces (170g) spicy smoked sausage links, preferably linguiça or kielbasa

4 ounces (110g) bacon, roughly chopped

½ medium white or yellow onion, finely chopped

4 garlic cloves, minced

Kosher salt and freshly ground black pepper

1 ounce (¼ stick/28g) unsalted butter, more if needed

1 cup (100g) manioc (cassava) flour (optional)

Collard Greens, recipe follows

3 oranges, cut into sections

Cooked white rice, such as Seasoned Rice (page 73), for serving

Put the jerky in a small bowl, cover generously with water, soak for 30 minutes, strain, and roughly chop the jerky.

In a large Dutch oven or soup pot, combine the jerky, pork loin or chops, ribs, dried beans, and 6 cups (1½L) of water and bring to a boil. (If the meats are not completely covered, add a little more water.) Skim off and discard any foam that rises to the top of the liquid. Reduce to a simmer, partially cover the pot, and cook, stirring occasionally, until the beans are tender and the pork rib meat easily separates from the bone, about 1½ hours. If the cooking liquid ever falls below the level of the beans, add just enough water to fully cover the beans. Add the sausage links to the stew, partially cover the pot, and simmer for 30 minutes.

Meanwhile, heat a sauté pan over medium-high heat. Add the bacon and cook until the fat has rendered, about 5 minutes. Reduce the heat to low. Add the onion and garlic and cook, stirring often, until the bacon is golden brown and the onions are soft, 3 to 4 minutes. Strain the bacon and onions (discard the bacon fat), add the bacon-onion mixture into the stew, and season with salt and pepper.

Wipe out the sauté pan with a paper towel, return the heat to medium-high, and add the butter. When the butter has melted, stir in the manioc flour and cook, stirring constantly, until lightly toasted, about 5 minutes. (If the flour is ever too dry to stir, add a little more butter.) Transfer the toasted manioc flour to a small serving bowl.

Remove the pork loin or chops from the stew and cut the meat into several large chunks; leave the ribs whole or pull off the meat and discard the bones. Slice the sausages into several large pieces and return all the meat to the stew. Season the stew with salt and pepper and serve immediately or keep warm over low heat for up to 2 hours.

Serve the feijoada family-style with the rice, collards, orange slices, and manioc flour, if using (to sprinkle on top of the stew) on the side.

Collard Greens

Makes about 1½ cups (225g)

2 large bunches (about 1¼ pounds/560g) collard greens

1 tablespoon vegetable oil

4 ounces (110g) bacon, roughly chopped

Submerge the collard greens in cold water to remove any grit and shake off the excess water. Holding the stem end of each, run your hand down the length of the stems to remove the leaves (discard the stems) and roughly chop the leaves. You should have 6 to 8 cups of greens, packed.

Bring a large pot of water to a boil, add the vegetable oil and collards, and blanch the collards until wilted, about 2 minutes, then strain. When cool enough to handle, squeeze the extra water out of the collards.

Heat a large sauté pan over medium heat. Add the bacon and cook, stirring occasionally, until golden brown and crispy, 5 to 6 minutes. Pour off and discard most of the bacon fat. Add the collards and stir until well combined. Use the collard greens immediately or cover and refrigerate for up to 3 days. (Rewarm the collard greens before serving.)

Tips

- Linguiça (a garlic and paprika–spiced smoked sausage) and paio (a spicier smoked sausage) are available at well-stocked Latin markets and specialty grocers (andouille and kielbasa can be substituted).
- Many American-style beef jerkies are heavily seasoned and contain ingredients like soy sauce; look for milder carne seco or South African biltong without additives (or, soak a more heavily spiced jerky in several changes of water).
- Manioc flour, made from finely ground cassava root, is available at many Latin markets.

Here's something I'd recommend to anybody: take the cable car up Sugarloaf Mountain. All of us, even the jaded camera guys who've been to even more spectacular places around the world than I have, were blown away. Being there, at the top of Rio at sunset, having that drink, a caipirinha, it one of *the* drinks of my life. Absolutely spectacular.

The Best Caipirinha

They use a lot more limes than what we usually find here in the States. I recommend it.

Cut 2 limes in half and juice 3 of the halves. Cut the other lime half into quarters, save 1 of the quarters, and put the rest of the limes in a sturdy glass. Add 1½ tablespoons of granulated sugar and use a muddler or the back of a spoon to smash the limes and sugar until the sugar dissolves (keep smashing, it takes a while). Take out the limes, add 1½ ounces cachaça, and fill the glass

with ice. Pour in about ¾ of the lime juice, stir that, and taste, and add a little more lime juice if you want. Throw the other lime quarter into the glass and enjoy.

There are diamonds everywhere. You just have to look.

You can't come to Rio without noticing the favelas all up in the hillsides. These neighborhoods started out as shanty towns more than one hundred years ago. Today, they're permanent neighborhoods housing a quarter of the city's population. We don't always think to go these places when we travel, but the favelas are full of the life and culture that define this city.

It also happens to be a great place to get a bite to eat. Chef Flavia Quaresma took me to meet another great chef, João Diamante, who was born in the neighborhood and saw what happened when his friends got into drugs and gangs. Today he runs a program called Diamantes na Cozinha (Diamonds in the Kitchen) through his restaurant, Na Minha Casa, that teaches kids in the neighborhood how to work and have a career in the food and restaurant industries. It's a win-win for the neighborhood, and it's a win for all of us, too.

By the way, you can get that Brazilian cream cheese, the one that's like the runny, good part of the brie, at markets back in the US (and I'm guessing a lot of other places around the world, too). Say it with me: *requeijão* (rey-kay-*sh*aow). You need to try this stuff.

It boils down to one thing: people. People thinking about people. This makes for a better world. —**João Diamante**

Go somewhere with the guy who knows what's around and let him drive the car. Just be a passenger with your mouth open.

We're in chapter eighteen, and I've probably told you a dozen times to go where the locals go; even better, go with a local. Sorry for the repetition, but I want it to stick.

In that scene where Guga Rocha, a great chef and all-around good person who happens to be well versed in Brazilian food history, took me to Aconchego Carioca where they serve traditional food, and we got the local dessert. Basically, it's their cheese, which is one of those springy, fresh cheeses, and guava jam. But at this restaurant, they go one step further and fry the cheese. Yes! Good idea.

Guga also took me to Cervantes, the place next to Bar Do David (also great, by the way). I wouldn't think to put pineapple on a sandwich with steak, *and* this sandwich also has chicken liver pâté. It was one of the best steak sandwiches I'd ever had. Go easy on the hot sauce.

Pineapple Steak Sandwich

Make this and then tell me pineapple isn't your new favorite thing in a steak sandwich.

Get a Portuguese roll (or a soft hoagie roll) and cut it in half. Cook some steak, filet mignon if you have it, then throw a couple slices of pineapple into the pan to heat up. Slice up the steak, dip the roll in the pan juices, now put the pineapple, steak, and a thick slice of chicken liver pâté inside and sprinkle some hot sauce on top. Eat that. Go to bed.

No one
enjoys
me falling
more than
Richard.

I love these little candies. They're sweet and creamy and chocolatey, which is perfect when you want just a little something to tide you over to the next meal or caipirinha. (By the way, if you're ever in LA, Maya's Brigadeiro makes delicious little gourmet ones.)

Brigadeiros

Makes 18 candies

The brigadeiro is a traditional Brazilian dessert, a true family favorite. No party in Brazil, especially children's parties, is complete without them. At the Copacabana Palace, we offer them to guests as a welcome amenity, but it's not unusual for guests to request the candies to take home. —**Nello Cassese**

1 ounce (¼ stick/28g) unsalted butter, plus more for the bowl and shaping the candies

1 14-ounce (400g) can sweetened condensed milk

1 tablespoon cocoa powder

1 tablespoon instant chocolate powder, such as Nesquik

About ½ cup (100g) chocolate sprinkles

18 small paper or foil candy cups

Lightly butter a small stainless steel bowl or baking dish. In a medium saucepan, combine the condensed milk, cocoa powder, chocolate powder, and butter. Bring to a simmer and cook, stirring constantly with a rubber spatula, until the candy filling thickens and no longer sticks to the bottom of the saucepan, 8 to 10 minutes. (When you run the spatula across the bottom of the saucepan, it should leave a clean trail.) Remove the saucepan from the heat, scrape the filling into the buttered bowl, and let cool completely.

Put the chocolate sprinkles in a small bowl. Lightly coat your hands in butter and shape the cooled candy into eighteen balls (about 1 tablespoon each). Roll the balls in the chocolate sprinkles and put each in a candy cup. Transfer the brigadeiros to a storage container, cover, and store at room temperature for up to 5 days.

My time here in Rio has shown me so much, but one thing stands out.

As much as I love the landscape, the setting, the feeling of this magical place, it's the people, the people, the people! It's always the people.

Not just because yes, they're physically beautiful, but because of their spirit, their smiles. I made friends real quick here. And it turns out, that's the secret to life.

Make friends.

19

San Francisco

San Francisco is one of the most beautiful cities on the face of the Earth, the Paris of the Pacific. But what's most beautiful about this majestic city? It has embodied the very best that America can be: the United States of America.

I WANTED TO START THIS EPISODE BY TELLING THAT story about San Francisco having the worst guy possible running the city just as it was expanding at the turn of the twentieth century. The mayor who was elected in 1902 was a huckster, a showman with no political experience at all. He was the most corrupt mayor in the United States at the time. He and his cronies cheaped out on everything. They were supposed to be building an infrastructure but took most of the money for themselves. They let the city be built with cheap wood in an area that already had major earthquakes. Then in 1906, there was the Big One that destroyed half the city. But even more of the city was lost because of the fire that erupted after the earthquake. It was absolutely devastating.

But here's my favorite part of the story: An Italian immigrant named A. P. Giannini had started a bank a couple years before the earthquake. And *he* was the one out on the street, not the politicians, after the earthquake, after the fire, giving loans to the locals so they could rebuild. This beautiful city was saved by an immigrant. And now, that bank is the Bank of America. Of course I think about that when I watch the episode now. Good story.

Two words: chocolate croissant.

I feel it's my civic duty to show you the very best things you may eat in your entire life. My favorite, favorite thing and something I never miss when I'm in San

Francisco is Liz Pruitt's chocolate croissant. Things this good don't stick around long, so you need to get to Tartine, the world-famous bakery she started with her partner Chad Robertson, early. The glaze is so beautiful it breaks like fine glass, then there's the luscious croissant pastry, and then the chocolate, which is so dark and delicious, *and* there is A LOT of chocolate inside. I don't want to disparage the French, but they could put a little more chocolate in their croissants.

. . . .

One of my favorite things about traveling is you never know where your next great meal is going to come from. When my friend and culinary genius Kenji López-Alt took me to La Torta Gordo, I didn't expect anything. I'd already polished off a chocolate croissant and that strawberry bread pudding at Tartine, and a maple bacon donut at Dynamo Donuts. I was good. But I was completely unprepared for that Mega Cubana that Armando Macuil, the mastermind behind this architectural wonder of the sandwich world, laid down in front of us.

This is the ultimate sandwich. It's a party, a sandwich Dagwood would make. One of the key things has to be the bread. It's the foundation of any sandwich, but with this sandwich, it's structurally essential. What is going to carry this thing? If Armando used two Wonder bread slices, this sandwich wouldn't have a chance. It's also clear there is great thought behind this sandwich. It could have been arbitrary and just a mess, but there is consideration behind the flavors. How much fun would it be to make this sandwich as your family activity one night? Everyone gets a different job. "You're in charge of the pork, you're in charge of the chicken, you're in charge of the eggs." I'm in charge of eating.

The Mega Cubana

Serves 4

There is a sandwich popular in Mexico City, the torta Cubana, that inspired this one. I do have the regular Cubana on the menu, but one day I was looking at all my ingredients in the kitchen, what I had to use. So I said, "Let's make a monster Cubana!" I put refried beans, grilled red onions, pickled jalapeño, sliced avocado, and queso fresco on the bread, then the first meat layer, which is our famous spicy pulled pork. Then chicken Milanesa, sliced turkey, ham, and hot dogs, and on top of that, chorizo eggs and American cheese. When I finished building the sandwich, I put it on the scale. It was a little over three pounds. I thought most people might be scared of it, but maybe somebody would be brave enough to try this "mega" Cuban, so that's what we called it. Instead of being scared of it, people started asking for it.

One thing: Before we add the meats, we put the sandwich in a grill (panini) press so the bread gets all crispy first, but also because you don't want to flip the sandwich on the griddle or in a pan. It's too heavy.
—Armando Macuil

4 large telera or San Francisco–style French sandwich rolls

4 tablespoons mayonnaise

1 medium avocado, peeled and thinly sliced

5 ounces (140g) queso fresco or panela, crumbled or thinly sliced

½ cup (120g) canned refried beans

12 to 16 pickled jalapeño slices, such as Mezzetta

2 tablespoons vegetable oil, divided

½ medium red onion, thinly sliced

2 hot dog franks

16 thin slices deli-style ham (8 ounces/220g)

16 thin slices deli-style turkey (8 ounces/220g)

4 ounces (110g) fresh Mexican-style chorizo or spicy breakfast sausage

1 cup (125g) leftover pulled pork, finely chopped, preferably without barbecue sauce (see Tips)

Chicken Milanesa Cutlets, recipe follows

4 large eggs, lightly beaten

4 slices American cheese

Slice the telera or San Francisco–style rolls in half lengthwise and spread 1 tablespoon of mayonnaise on the inside of each top roll. Divide the avocado slices and queso fresco or panela among each roll half.

Spread about 2 tablespoons of refried beans on each of the bottom halves of the rolls and lay 3 to 4 jalapeño slices on top.

In a large sauté pan with a lid, heat 1 tablespoon of the oil over medium-high heat. Add the onions and cook, stirring occasionally, until softened, 3 to 4 minutes. Divide the onions among the bottom rolls and close the sandwiches.

Slice the hot dogs in half crosswise, then slice each half lengthwise into three strips. Arrange 4 slices of ham in four separate piles and lay 4 turkey slices on top of each so the deli meats lay fairly flat (this makes the sandwiches easier to close) but are roughly the size of the bread.

Crumble the chorizo or sausage into the sauté pan and cook over medium-high heat, stirring occasionally, until no longer pink, 3 to 4 minutes. Transfer the sausage to a plate and pour off and discard the fat.

Add the hot dog slices to the pan and cook until lightly seared on both sides, 2 to 3 minutes. Add the pulled pork (keep the meats in separate piles), stir a few times to rewarm the pork, cover the pan, and turn off the heat.

Preheat a panini press. When the panini press is hot, add the sandwich rolls, gently close the lid, and grill until the bread is lightly golden brown, 3 to 4 minutes. (Do this in batches if needed.) Transfer the sandwiches to plates.

Meanwhile, on a griddle or in a large skillet, heat the remaining 1 tablespoon of vegetable oil over medium-high heat. Add the chicken cutlets and cook, flipping occasionally, until warm, 1 to 2 minutes. Arrange the chicken cutlets in a single layer on a sheet pan or large dish and cover to keep warm.

Add the sausage to the griddle or skillet, pour the eggs on top of the sausage, and cook, stirring occasionally, until the eggs just beginning to set, 2 to 3 minutes. Lay the American cheese slices on top of the eggs.

Open each sandwich; some of the toppings on the rolls will have shifted sides; you can leave them as is or rearrange them. Divide the pulled pork among each bottom roll.

Top each chicken cutlet with a few hot dog slices and 1 ham and turkey stack. Use a spatula to cut the chorizo-fried eggs into quarters and lay 1 quarter on top of each ham and turkey stack. Slice a spatula to underneath each chicken cutlet and transfer each meat stack to a bottom roll. Gently close the sandwiches, use a serrated knife to gently cut each sandwich in half, and serve.

Chicken Milanesa Cutlets

1 large (6 ounces/170g) boneless, skinless chicken breast	1 large egg, lightly beaten
¼ teaspoon kosher salt	⅓ cup (40g) fine bread crumbs
½ cup (60g) all-purpose flour	1 tablespoon vegetable oil

Slice the chicken in half crosswise, then lengthwise through the middle to make 4 cutlets. Use the smooth side of a meat mallet to pound the chicken to between ⅛ and ¼ inch (3 to 6mm) thick. Sprinkle the salt over the chicken, then the flour, and toss the chicken in the flour until well coated.

Put the egg in a medium bowl and the bread crumbs in a separate bowl. Dip the chicken in the eggs, then the bread crumbs.

Heat the oil in a large skillet over medium-high heat. Add the chicken and cook until golden brown, 2 to 3 minutes. Flip the chicken and cook until no longer pink in the center, about 2 minutes. Use the chicken cutlets immediately or cover and refrigerate for up to 3 days. (Rewarm the chicken before serving.)

Tips
- A local bakery makes extra-large telera rolls, the wide flat loaves with a sturdy exterior and soft interior used for Mexican sandwiches, especially for La Torta Gordo bakery; this recipe uses smaller telera rolls, available at Latin markets, or San Francisco–style rolls available at most grocery stores.
- You can use any leftover pulled pork, like the Oven-Barbecued Pulled Pork (page 294); Armando uses a similar spicy (not sweet) barbecued pork.
- The trick to this recipe is timing. Warm up the fillings when you put the bean-filled rolls on the panini press.

Going on a boat is not the antidote for "boozsh-goozsh." Thank you, Richard.

I need to clear the air.

I did not get sick from any place you saw in this episode. I've heard some theories floating around out there. We don't film any episode in the order you see it, so it was not from anyplace you saw right before that moment.

And if I was going to get sick, I'm glad the only time it happened while we were filming was in the United States, where we have the strictest food laws anywhere. I know if I'd gotten sick in any other country and I'd shown that, people would say they'd never go there.

By the way, I'm pretty sure I know what I ate. I'm not going to tell you what it was because it doesn't matter. There are occupational hazards in any job. "Boozsh-goozsh" is one of them. The show must go on. By the way, "boozsh" represents food coming back up; "goozsh" means the other way.

. . . .

I met the great Alice Waters almost twenty years ago, and I've been in love with her ever since. She is royalty in the food world, and for good reason: she happened to create the way we eat in America. She's responsible for the farm-to-table movement, the farmers markets everywhere (those peaches from Frog Hollow were so

delicious), the Edible Schoolyard. She doesn't stop. And she's just the most charming, lovely lady. Here's another thing I love about Alice: she likes eating fruits and fresh salads with her hands. When you see me do it, I'm not a slob. I'm eating like Alice Waters.

She's kindly written this recipe for us to show off the flavors of the best fruit from the farmers market, which, by the way, is one of my favorite places to go in any city, even though I don't cook. It's like going on a mini trip around your local community with all the produce varieties from different nearby farmers. And there are usually plenty of samples to taste. The one at the Ferry Building in San Francisco is one of the best in the world.

Alice Waters's Fresh Peach Crisp or Cobbler

Serves 8

I am forever falling in love with the fantastic range of peach varieties available. Learning to discern these subtleties of texture and flavor—learning to distinguish an Elberta peach from a Sun Crest—is a thrill for me. Using hand-selected produce that is still full of life and vitality, just picked from the vine or pulled from the ground, is what makes cooking not just good, but irresistible.

We only eat peaches at the peak of their season, so when they come, we have to think about every possible way to use them. A perfectly ripe peach is utterly divine on its own. Cut them in half and grill or bake them with a

touch of honey or sprinkle of sugar. Turn them into delicious pies and crisps, alone (you can use one variety of peaches or mix several varieties together) or with mixed berries. Use them for the base of a summer fruit compote or a garnish in a berry soup. —**Alice Waters**

4 pounds (1.8kg) ripe peaches (10 to 12 large)

1½ tablespoons all-purpose flour

1 tablespoon granulated sugar (optional)

Crisp Topping or Cream Biscuits, recipes follow

Lightly sweetened whipped cream or premium vanilla ice cream, for serving (optional)

Preheat the oven to 375°F (190°C). Bring a large pot of water to a boil. Add the peaches, blanch them for 15 seconds, then strain. Rinse the peaches under cold water and use your fingers to slip off the skins (discard the skins). Cut the peaches in half, remove the pits, and slice the flesh into roughly ⅓-inch (8mm) sections.

Put the peaches in a large bowl, sprinkle the flour and sugar, if using, on top, and use your hands to gently toss the peaches in the dry ingredients. Pile the peaches into a deep, 9-inch square (22.5cm) casserole dish or a 10-inch (25cm) baking dish.

To make a crisp, scatter the Crisp Topping over the peaches and bake for 25 minutes, rotate the baking dish from front to back, and reduce the oven temperature to 350°F (180°C). Bake until the topping is golden brown and the fruit is bubbling around the edges, 20 to 25 minutes (for a total cooking time of 45 to 55 minutes).

To make a cobbler, evenly space the Cream Biscuits on top of the peaches and bake until the biscuits are golden brown and the fruit is bubbling, 40 to 45 minutes.

Let the crisp or cobbler cool for 20 to 30 minutes before serving with the whipped cream or ice cream, if using.

Crisp Topping

⅔ cup whole unsalted pecans (65g), almonds (90g), or walnuts (80g)

1¼ cups (150g) all-purpose flour

6 tablespoons dark brown sugar, packed

¼ teaspoon ground cinnamon (optional)

¼ teaspoon fine sea salt

6 ounces (1½ sticks/170g) unsalted butter, chilled

Preheat the oven to 375°F (190°C). Spread out the nuts on a sheet pan and bake until lightly toasted, 5 to 6 minutes. Transfer the nuts to a cutting board to cool and coarsely chop.

In a medium bowl, combine the nuts, flour, brown sugar, cinnamon, if using, and salt and stir until well combined. Cut the chilled butter into roughly ½-inch (12mm) pieces and use your fingers to rub the butter into the dry ingredients just until the mixture has a crumbly texture. Use the crisp topping immediately, cover, and refrigerate for up to 3 days, or freeze for up to 1 month.

Cream Biscuits

Makes 8 biscuits

1½ cups (180g) all-purpose flour, plus more for rolling out the dough

1 tablespoon plus 1 teaspoon granulated sugar (optional)

2 teaspoons baking powder

¼ teaspoon fine sea salt

3 ounces (¾ stick/85g) unsalted butter, chilled

¾ cup (180ml) heavy cream, divided

In a large bowl, combine the flour, sugar, if using, baking powder, and salt. Cut the chilled butter into roughly ½-inch (12mm) pieces and use your fingers to crumble the butter into the flour until the butter is roughly the size of peas. Pour all but about 1 tablespoon of the cream into the flour mixture and use a fork to roughly incorporate the cream into the flour, then use your hands to knead the dough 3 to 4 times until the dough just begins to come together. (Do not overwork the dough.)

Turn out the dough onto a lightly floured work surface and use a rolling pin to roll the dough into roughly a 6-inch (15cm) circle. Use a biscuit cutter to cut the dough into roughly 3-inch (7.5cm) rounds, then reroll any scraps to cut the final biscuit; you should have about eight biscuits. Use the dough immediately, or cover with plastic wrap and refrigerate for up to 6 hours. Just before baking, lightly brush the top of each biscuit with the reserved cream.

Tip   You can make both the peach base and toppings ahead and bake the dessert about an hour or so before you plan to serve it.

One of my favorite moments ever was in this episode, when we met those wonderful guys in their truck.

The crew wanted an exterior shot of me walking up one of San Francisco's famous hills, so I started schlepping. All of a sudden, one fellow on this truck recognized me and said, "Hi." So I went over there. And every single one of those guys was terrific.

I asked what they were eating, and they invited me to crash their lunch.

By the way, we tried to track down "The Lady" for a recipe, but couldn't find her. If you know her, or see my friends from the truck, tell them I said thank you, and that she's my second favorite Lady.

I met Thomas Keller when the great James L. Brooks had the crazy idea to cast me as a chef in the movie *Spanglish*. Thomas was the culinary consultant on the film and we became friends. And since he happens to be in the nearby Napa Valley and helped put it on the map, I wanted to take you out to America's Tuscany to meet him.

Alice Waters and Thomas Keller are like the mother and father of how modern America eats. Not just the artistry. You've got all of this great produce largely because of what Alice started. Then you've got Thomas, arguably America's greatest chef, within an hour. Thomas can take a peanut butter and jelly sandwich and turn it into an incredible macaron. He's a wizard, a meticulous wizard, and having him watch me try to cook is like having Michael Jordan watch me try to dunk.

What's great about that scene at Ad Hoc is we're standing in the kitchen with one of the best chefs in the world, and we're eating Thomas Keller's fried chicken right out of the fryer. Anything right out of the fryer is going to be good, but anything from Thomas Keller anytime, anywhere, is going to be better than good. I've never had better fried chicken.

Thomas Keller's Fried Chicken

Serves 6

Fried chicken is a great American tradition. It had fallen out of favor when we opened Ad Hoc more than fifteen years ago, but it's really made a comeback. If there is a better fried chicken than this, I haven't tasted it.

If you have two large pots and a lot of oil, you can cook the dark and white meat at the same time; if not, cook the dark meat first, then turn up the heat and cook the white meat. (You can rewarm the chicken for a minute or two in a hot oven and to ensure the crust is crisp.) It's worth seeking out smaller free-range chickens. They're a little easier to cook properly, and pieces this size result in

the optimal meat-to-crust proportion, which is such an important part of the pleasure of chicken.

Phil ate the chicken right out of the fryer, but it's ideal to let the chicken rest for a few minutes after it comes out so it has a minute to cool down. Forget Colonel Sanders, baby. —**Thomas Keller**

2 3- to 3½-pound (1.4 to 1.6kg) organic, free-range chickens	1 tablespoon plus 1 teaspoon cayenne pepper
Chicken Brine, room temperature or chilled, recipe follows	1 tablespoon plus 1 teaspoon kosher salt
Peanut or canola oil, for frying	1 quart (950ml) buttermilk
6 cups (720g) all-purpose flour	Kosher salt and freshly ground black pepper
4 tablespoons garlic powder	Fleur de sel or fine sea salt (optional)
4 tablespoons onion powder	Small handful fresh rosemary and thyme sprigs, for garnish
1 tablespoon plus 1 teaspoon sweet paprika	

Trim off any excess skin from the chicken. Put the chickens, breast side down, on a work surface and use a cleaver or other sturdy, sharp knife to cut along each side of the backbone and remove it from each chicken (save the backbones for stock).

Turn each chicken over and locate the joints that connect each thigh to the chicken. Cut through the joint to separate the legs, then cut through the joint connecting each thigh and drumstick to separate them.

Turn each chicken over again and remove the pointed breastplates (heel bone) by making a shallow cut on each side of the tip of the bone, then use your fingers to remove it. Cut each breast in half lengthwise, then cut each piece in half crosswise so you have 4 pieces per breast.

Cut off the wings at the joint that attaches them to the breast. You should have 2 legs, 2 thighs, 4 breast quarters, and 2 wings per chicken.

Pour the Chicken Brine into a large container or several zip-top bags (if using multiple containers or bags, divide the herbs and garlic among them). Add the chicken and refrigerate for 10 to 12 hours. (Do not brine the chicken any longer or the chicken will become too salty.)

Remove the chicken from the brine (discard the brine) and rinse the chicken under cold water. Pat the chicken dry with paper towels and let rest at room temperature for about 1 hour.

Line one sheet pan with parchment paper and lay a baking rack on top of a second sheet pan.

In a large bowl, combine the flour, garlic powder, onion powder, paprika, and cayenne pepper and mix well. Pour about half of the dry ingredients into another large bowl. Put the buttermilk and kosher salt and black pepper, to taste, in a third large bowl. (When adding salt, keep in mind there is a lot of salt in the chicken from the brine.) Set up a dipping station: the chicken, one bowl of dry ingredients, the buttermilk, the second bowl of dry ingredients, and the parchment-lined sheet pan.

Put the baking rack–lined sheet pan near the stove and preheat the oven to 400ºF (200ºC). In a Dutch oven or other large pot, heat 2 to 3 inches (5 to 7.5cm) of oil over medium-high heat.

Just before frying, dip the chicken thighs into the first bowl of dry ingredients, turning to coat (pat off any excess flour), then dip them into the buttermilk (let the excess buttermilk run back into the bowl). Then dip them in the second bowl of dry ingredients. Lay the thighs on the parchment-lined pan.

When the oil is very hot (about 325°F/165°C), use tongs to carefully lower the thighs into the oil. (Fry the thighs in batches if needed to avoid overcrowding the pot.) Fry the thighs for 2 minutes, then carefully move the chicken pieces around in the oil (redistributing the pieces helps them cook evenly), and continue to fry, flipping the pieces occasionally, until the skin is a deep golden brown and crispy and a digital thermometer reads 160°F (70°C) when inserted in the middle of the thighs, 10 to 12 minutes. Transfer the thighs to the baking rack, skin side up.

Meanwhile, coat the chicken drumsticks in the dry and wet ingredients. Retest the oil temperature, then fry the drumsticks the same way you fried the thighs. (They should take roughly the same amount of time.) Transfer the drumsticks to the baking rack, lay them meat end up (rest the drumsticks against the thighs) to drain, and sprinkle the thighs and legs with the sea salt, if needed.

Add more oil to the pot, if needed, and reheat the oil.

Meanwhile, coat the chicken breasts and wings in the dry and wet ingredients. Fry the breast pieces until the skin is deep golden brown and crispy and the internal temperature is 160°F (70°C), 7 to 9 minutes. Transfer to the baking rack, skin side up. Fry the wings until golden brown, about 6 minutes. Transfer to the rack and sprinkle both the breast and wings with the sea salt if needed.

Arrange the chicken breasts and wings on a serving platter. Put the sheet pan with the thighs and legs in the oven and bake just until the chicken is hot, 1 to 2 minutes.

Meanwhile, put the rosemary and thyme sprigs in the cooking oil (it should still be hot). Fry until crispy, a few seconds, and transfer to paper towels to drain. Add the chicken thighs and legs to the serving platter, tuck the herbs in between the chicken pieces, and serve.

Chicken Brine

Zest and juice of 2 medium organic lemons

10 garlic cloves

½ small bunch fresh thyme

½ small bunch fresh parsley

6 bay leaves

¼ cup (85g) clover or similar honey

1 cup Diamond Crystal or ⅔ cup Morton kosher salt (140g)

2 tablespoons black peppercorns

In a large stockpot, combine the lemon zest and juice from both lemons, the garlic, thyme, parsley, bay leaves, honey, salt, peppercorns, and 2 quarts (about 2L) of water. Bring to a boil and stir to dissolve the salt. Remove the brine from the heat, let cool completely, and add another 2 quarts (about 2L) of cold water. Use the cooled brine immediately or cover and refrigerate for up to 3 days.

Tip

• The difference in quantity between Diamond Crystal (Keller's preference) and Morton's kosher salt is due to crystal size and weight, so different amounts for each are given in the brine, which calls for a large quantity of salt. If using another brand, it is best to weigh the salt.

Sometimes all you can do is make things a little bit better.

There's always going to be somewhere you go where people are going through tough times. Food can be a very good way of showing people that you care about them. I wanted to do the final San Francisco dinner at the Family House.

This is such a special place. Families can stay together here, eat together instead of having to find someplace else near the hospital, while their child is going through cancer treatments. They get to remain a family. It was probably the most special reunion we had on the show.

And every kid likes pizza, so we brought along a real pizza champ, Tony Gemignani. (By the way, one of the best pizzas I've ever had in my life was a Chicago deep-dish pizza from Tony's place in San Francisco, Capo's.) I'll never forget watching the way those kids' faces lit up when Tony started twirling the dough in the air. Food, the great connector, one of my favorite ways to say "I love you."

Phil: Look how beautiful you look! (*Monica smiles*) I'm talking to my dad. You too, Monica, you look beautiful.

Monica: Thanks. You like my pink top?

Phil: I do.

Max: I like how you shaved. Shaven, you look much better.

Phil: Monica actually suggested the beard because I think she was tired of the face.

Monica: Mix it up.

Phil: How's it going over there? I know Monica is staying with you a bit.

Max: Yes.

Phil: Is she doing a good job? Or is it, "enough already"?

Max: We have help so she's adding on to the help.

Phil: So you're saying you don't need her, really.

Max: No.

(*Monica laughs*)

Phil: I'm having fun in San Francisco. Monica, you've been to Tartine.

Monica: I have.

Phil: Hee-hee-hee . . . (*holds up a croissant*) My favorite thing.

Max: What's that?

Phil: This is the chocolate croissant. I mean . . . like Paris.

Max: This is for one person?

Phil: That should be the name of it. But listen to this when you bite it. (*bites croissant, loud crunch, crumbs fall*) I am ruining the computer. You have a joke for us today?

Max: I don't know if you heard that an old man was in a cab and there was a big accident. And he was thrown out of the cab and he landed on the sidewalk. And some good Samaritan took off his jacket and put it under his head and said to him, "Are you comfortable?" And he said, "Eh, I make a living."

Phil: It's like an old song you like hearing over and over. All right, Burns and Allen, I gotta go.

(*Monica hugs Max and Max pats her head.*)

Phil: Awww, you like your daughter-in-law?

Max: She's okay.

Phil: All right, I love you! We'll see you later.

Monica: We love you, Richard!

Phil: What do you mean? I just said, "I love you," and I get back, "We love you, Richard!"?

Monica: We love you, too, Philip.

Phil: Aww, thanks. At least I have croissants to keep me company.

The Capri

Don't let Capri's size fool you. This is a world-class chef.

Cut up a pineapple into little pieces and slice up some black and green olives. Get some pizza dough, stretch it out, pound it with your fists to flatten it, and spread tomato sauce over the dough. Scatter shredded mozzarella cheese on top (if you're funny, you get extra cheese), then very carefully arrange the pineapple and black olives on top. Pop out the pimentos ("only the finest") from the green olives and add those, and bake the pizza. The best.

"The pursuit of happiness" has always been my favorite phrase in the Declaration of Independence.

What other country allows for that? To be able to pursue what you love, that's everything. There's no place that embodies that more than San Francisco.

I love this city. I love that everything, no matter how dark it seems, how terrible, everything can have a rebirth.

What I am saying is: There is hope, people!

20

Singapore

It's an embarrassment of riches here in Singapore, the convergence of so many influences. The world is great when we mash it up.

SINGAPORE WAS A REAL DISCOVERY FOR ME IN this episode. In the introduction, I told you that I knew very little about Singapore before I went there. I'd heard it was strict with a lot of rules, and there certainly were some interesting rules:

No walking nude around your house, no bothering people with your musical instruments, no chewing gum is allowed in the country. And my favorite, no peeing in the elevator.

Is Singapore a city, an island, a country? Turns out, it's all three. There's a lot of history here, too, as a port city, a British colony, and an autonomous republic. It's got awe-inspiring architecture with quaint little villages mixed in between, and the whole city seems to have been built in and around beautiful Mother Nature with these very modern skyscrapers that seemingly erupt from the jungle. Something that simply serves a purpose becomes something spectacular instead. Even the airport is incredible with the world's tallest indoor waterfall. And I've never been to a place where the food is so much a part of the culture, actually *is* the culture.

. . . .

One word I heard over and over in Singapore was "preservation," especially when it came to the hawker stalls, which are these local institutions where people go to eat incredible meals for a price that would be unheard of most places. Damian D'Silva is one of those people on a mission to preserve the culinary culture in Singapore. The Hainanese Chicken Rice we had at the Maxwell Hawker Center was basically chicken, rice, and chile peppers with some condiments. You eat it at room temperature, so you can really taste all the subtle flavors. Damian re-created the one we enjoyed together for you here. Make it, and you'll understand why people go out to hawker stalls to eat.

Hainanese Chicken Rice

Serves 6

My whole culinary life is dedicated to Singapore's heritage cuisine. I strive to bring "lost" dishes from all the different ethnicities in this great city to the Singaporean and the world's palate.

The chicken rice that you will see in most hawker centers around Singapore evolved from a dish called Wenchang chicken (also a reference to the breed of chicken). It's traceable to Hainan Island off the coast of southern China where people made the dish at home; it was later popularized in Singapore by a hawker who peddled his offerings along a Hainanese enclave in the city in the late 1940s. As the story is told, he put the chicken rice in two baskets that were attached to a wooden pole and slung it over his shoulder. That hawker eventually started a stall in a coffee shop along Purvis Street, but it was his apprentice, Swee Kee, who eventually left to start Singapore's most iconic chicken rice restaurant. In its early years, his namesake Swee Kee restaurant was known for breeding its own chickens, so there was always a fresh supply of birds kept at the back of the restaurant.

Swee Kee is the main reason chicken rice is so popular today. They did everything right, from the texture and taste of the bird to the fragrant and grainy texture of the rice and the tart chili sauce and ginger paste (flavored by the oil from the chicken stock) served as accompaniments. Unfortunately, Swee Kee closed its doors in 1997. But they left such a great impact that today, no matter where you are in Singapore, there will always be a chicken rice stall or two somewhere close.

When making the dish at home, an organic, free-range chicken makes the best soup; it is worth seeking out. The backbone and surrounding bones make the most flavorful broth, but you can use bones from a whole chicken or even chicken wings or feet. For the rice, it's best to go to an Asian market and get very fresh dried rice. If the rice is "old" (many places, it unfortunately often is), you will need more cooking liquid. Finally, salt is gently massaged into the skin of the chicken, which removes any "impurities" to ensure a glistening skin. It needs to be done thoroughly but gently as you do not want to bruise the skin. Think of it as a facial. —**Damian D'Silva**

1 4- to 4½-pound (1.8 to 2kg) free-range chicken, preferably with head and feet attached

3 tablespoons plus 1½ teaspoons kosher salt, divided

Chicken Broth, recipe follows

4 green onions, divided

2 medium bunches fresh cilantro, preferably with roots attached

10 fresh or frozen pandan leaves, divided

1 6-inch (15cm) piece ginger, peeled, plus 2 tablespoons finely chopped ginger, divided

3 tablespoons soy sauce

2 cups (400g) long-grain rice, preferably basmati or jasmine

2 medium shallots, finely chopped

3 garlic cloves, minced

2 large cucumbers or 8 small Persian cucumbers, sliced

2 tomatoes, quartered

Hainanese Chile Sauce (page 292)

Ginger Paste (recipe follows)

Trim any excess fat from the chicken and cover and refrigerate the fat (it will be used for the rice). Gently rub the chicken skin and flesh with 2 tablespoons of the salt until the salt partially dissolves into the skin. Let the chicken rest for 10 minutes, then rinse well under cold running water.

Put the Chicken Broth in a medium Dutch oven or soup pot with a lid; the pot should be just large enough to snugly fit the chicken and broth so the bird is submerged while it cooks. Stuff the chicken cavity with 2 green onions and 1 bunch of cilantro. Tie 4 pandan leaves into a knot and add the leaves, the peeled ginger, and 1 teaspoon of salt to the pot.

Bring the chicken broth to a low boil over medium heat. Carefully slide the chicken into the hot broth, reduce the heat to low, and simmer for 20 minutes. Use tongs to carefully flip the chicken (try not to break the skin) and continue to cook the chicken until the meat is tender and a digital thermometer inserted into the thigh and breast reads 160°F (70°C). Turn off the heat and let the chicken cool in the cooking broth for about 30 minutes.

Transfer the chicken to a bowl and discard the cilantro and green onions in the cavity. Remove the pandan leaves and ginger from the broth (discard all the vegetables).

Use a spoon to skim off about 1 tablespoon of the oil on the surface of the broth and transfer it to a small bowl. Add the soy sauce and about ¼ cup (60ml) of the chicken broth to the oil and set the seasoned soy sauce aside until ready to serve.

Put the rice in a strainer and rinse well under cold running water until the water is no longer cloudy. Transfer the rice to a medium bowl, cover with cold water, and set aside to soak for 20 minutes. Then strain.

Put the reserved raw chicken fat in a small iron skillet or other heavy-bottomed pan and cook the fat over low heat until you have 3 to 4 tablespoons of melted fat. Discard any bits of skin or gristle and increase the heat to medium. Add the shallots and cook, stirring occasionally, until softened, about 3 minutes. Reduce the heat to low, add the garlic and chopped ginger, and cook until fragrant, about 2 minutes. Add the rice and stir until the grains are glossy and well coated in the fat, 2 to 3 minutes. Add 3 cups (720ml) of the chicken broth and the remaining ½ teaspoon of salt. Tie the remaining 6 pandan leaves into a knot and add them to the pot. Bring the broth to a low boil, reduce the heat to low, cover the pot, and cook the rice until tender, 12 to 15 minutes. (Or, cook the rice in a rice cooker, if preferred.) Remove the pandan leaves, fluff the rice with chopsticks or a fork, and cover the pot to keep the rice warm.

When ready to serve, arrange the sliced cucumbers in a single layer on the bottom of a large serving platter.

Put the chicken on a wood cutting board, breast side up, and use a cleaver or other sturdy, sharp knife to cut off the head and feet, if using. (Put one palm on top of the cleaver and press firmly down to work through the bones.)

To divide the chicken in half, cut through the breastbone, all the way through the chicken, just to the left or right of the backbone. Remove the whole backbone, cut it into three to four pieces crosswise, and reassemble the backbone down the middle of the serving platter. Put the head and feet at opposite ends of the platter, if using, like you are rebuilding the whole chicken.

Cut off the breasts, cut each breast in half crosswise, then cut the breast meat (with the bones attached) into roughly 2-inch (5cm) pieces.

Separate the thighs, legs, and wings at the joints. Cut the thighs into two to three pieces and separate the wings into two pieces (the drumette and wingette). Arrange the breast meat on top of the backbone, the thighs and legs near the feet, and the wings near the head of the bird to re-create the chicken's original shape on the plate. (As you cut and reassemble the chicken, some of the meat may fall off the bones.) Spoon about half of the seasoned soy sauce over the chicken and arrange the tomatoes alongside.

Thinly slice the remaining 2 green onions, roughly chop the remaining 1 bunch of cilantro, and scatter both on top of the chicken. Serve the chicken at room temperature with the warm rice, the seasoned soy sauce, ginger paste, and Hainanese Chile Sauce.

Chicken Broth and Ginger Paste

3 pounds (1.4kg) assorted chicken bones, preferably including backbones, or 2 pounds (900g) chicken feet and/or wings

1 5-inch (12.5cm) piece of ginger, peeled, plus two 6-inch (15cm) pieces "young" ginger, divided (see Tips)

6 pandan leaves, tied into a knot

In a large stockpot, combine the chicken bones or feet and wings and 4 quarts (about 3.75L) of water. Bring to a boil and skim off and discard any foam that rises to the top. Add the ginger and pandan leaves, reduce to a low boil, and cook the broth, uncovered, until reduced by about 1 inch (2.5cm), 45 minutes to 1 hour. Use a spoon to skim off and reserve about 1 tablespoon of the oil on the surface of the broth. Let the broth cool for 45 minutes to 1 hour. Set a strainer over a large bowl, strain the broth (discard the bones), and let cool completely.

Meanwhile, peel and roughly chop the young ginger. Put the ginger and reserved oil from the broth in a blender and blend until smooth. Add 1 to 2 tablespoons of the Chicken Broth, if needed, to create a smooth paste.

Use the Chicken Broth and Ginger Paste immediately or cover and refrigerate both for up to 3 days.

Tips
- The whole chicken is used—and enjoyed—in this dish, down to the last bits of meat on the bones.
- Fresh or frozen pandan leaves (from a tropical plant that imparts a subtly grassy flavor) and cilantro (also called Chinese parsley) with the roots attached are available at most Asian markets.
- Look for "young" ginger, the smaller, juicier, and sweeter roots of a younger plant (available at Asian markets and many farmers markets) rather than the tough, knobby mature roots often found at grocery stores for the ginger paste (the latter results in a very fibrous ginger paste).

Hainanese Chile Sauce

Makes about ½ cup (120ml)

This is the traditional sauce served with Hainanese Chicken Rice, but you can enjoy it with other dishes. Use fresh Thai bird's eye chiles if you like your sauce hot, or substitute a milder chile pepper. —**Damian D'Silva**

4 ounces (110g) Thai bird's eye chiles (about 35), or similar small, hot chile peppers	2 teaspoons chicken broth oil (see Tips) or vegetable oil
4 garlic cloves	1 teaspoon granulated sugar
Juice of ¼ lime, or to taste	¼ teaspoon fine sea salt
1½ tablespoons rice vinegar	

Remove the stems from the chile peppers and scrape out most of the seeds (if desired for a less spicy sauce). Put the chile peppers and garlic in a blender and blend until finely chopped. Scrape down the sides of the blender. Add the lime juice, vinegar, vegetable oil, sugar, and salt and blend to a smooth paste. Season the sauce with more lime juice and salt, if needed. Use the chile sauce immediately or cover and refrigerate for up to 3 days (if chicken broth oil was used) or up to 2 weeks (if vegetable oil was used).

Tips
- This sauce is typically made with the reserved oil on top of the chicken broth that is used to make Hainanese Chicken Rice (use that if you'd like).
- Using vegetable oil allows the spicy sauce to be stored for a longer period of time.

I'm always going to begin and end a trip with something to eat. But I will veer off the food path occasionally to go sightseeing. And gather a few souvenirs for when I get back home.

Taking that bumboat water taxi was my kind of sightseeing. You don't need a tour guide. You go at night on the Singapore River, and you see this city of the future gliding by. It's so peaceful and romantic. Have a Scotch while on board, and you'll see what I mean. Before tourists, the bumboats would carry supplies in from the big ships offshore.

And speaking of souvenirs, I am totally the guy who takes the shampoo or conditioner from the hotel if I like it. Or a couple of their tea bags, which I did take from Raffles in Singapore. I always try to take a little bit of whatever is takeable as a souvenir wherever I'm staying. Just the smell of the shampoo or the flavor of that tea takes you back to that magical place. Here's something else I got from the Raffles Hotel and brought back just for you:

The Silent Killer (Singapore Sling)

The height of colonial elegance in Singapore is the fabled Raffles Hotel, named after the British officer who founded this country. It's also home of the Long Bar, birthplace of the legendary Singapore Sling. Go there and maybe you'll meet my friend Rodolfo, the nice bartender who mixed up my drink in that fancy shaker wheel. Slug some peanuts on the floor for me.

Start with the booze: Put 1 ounce (30ml) gin, ½ ounce (15ml) cherry brandy, ¼ ounce (7.5ml) Bénédictine, ¼ ounce (7.5ml) Cointreau, and a dash of Angostura bitters in a cocktail shaker with a lot of ice. Now add 4 ounces (120ml) pineapple juice (Raffles uses Malaysian Sarawak pineapples), ½ ounce (15ml) lime juice, and slightly less than ½ ounce (10ml) grenadine, shake that up well, and strain it into a tall glass. Put a maraschino cherry and pineapple wedge on top, and enjoy.

Speaking of legends, here's my favorite kind: a sandwich. I said in that scene at Burnt Ends that if I ever have a cookbook, Dave Pynt was gonna have to give us this recipe. You're already dead from the giant steak, from all the courses, because everything Dave does is incredible. But then . . . you gotta have dessert, right? And then dessert comes, and it's the best pulled pork sandwich in the world.

A sandwich this good can't be just one recipe. First you've got to make the meat. You rub the pork with these spices and the next day roast it until it's so charred you'd think somebody put it on the grill. Eat some of that for dinner. The next day, call up a bunch of friends and have them make all the other stuff for the sandwiches. And when that's all done, call me.

The Pork Sanger

Serves 12

We make our own brioche buns and ferment jalapeños with horseradish for forty days to make the pickles for this sandwich. At home you can use good-quality brioche buns and jarred pickled jalapeños. —**Dave Pynt**

Oven-Barbecued Pulled Pork, as needed (recipe follows)

12 good-quality brioche buns

2 pounds (900g) sharp Cheddar cheese, coarsely grated

1 cup (240ml) Chipotle Aioli, recipe follows

Red Cabbage–Apple Slaw, recipe follows

1 16-ounce (480ml) jar pickled jalapeños, such as Mezzetta, drained

Preheat the oven to 350°F (180°C).

Spread out the pork and any pan juices in a large roasting pan, cover the pan tightly with foil, and bake until warm, about 15 minutes. Transfer the pan to a serving table (keep the pan covered) while you assemble the sandwich components.

Arrange the buns, cut sides facing up, on two sheet pans and scatter the cheese evenly on top. Put the buns in the oven and bake until the cheese is melted and the edges of the buns are lightly toasted, 6 to 8 minutes.

Meanwhile, put the Chipotle Aioli, Red Cabbage–Apple Slaw, and pickled jalapeños in separate serving dishes and arrange them on the table, after the pork, in that order.

To assemble the sandwiches, have everyone put a handful of the pulled pork on the bottom buns and drizzle about 1 tablespoon of aioli over the pork. Pile a generous spoonful of the coleslaw and 2 to 3 pickled jalapeños on top, close the sandwiches, and serve any remaining coleslaw on the side.

Oven-Barbecued Pulled Pork

The pork shoulder needs to be cooked low and slow until it almost blackens, which we do in the oven to give it the same effect as barbecue. The tray of champagne vinegar, lemons, and water beneath the meat keeps it moist and adds flavor. —**Dave Pynt**

1 7- to 8-pound (3.2 to 3.6kg) bone-in Boston butt or picnic shoulder roast, with a nice fat cap

2 tablespoons smoked paprika

1½ tablespoons granulated sugar

1½ tablespoons packed light or dark brown sugar

1½ tablespoons fine sea salt

1½ tablespoons freshly ground black pepper

2 teaspoons chili powder

2 teaspoons ground cumin

2 teaspoons celery salt

1 teaspoon garlic powder

1 teaspoon hot paprika

2 teaspoons cayenne pepper, divided

1 medium organic lemon, thinly sliced

½ cup (120ml) champagne or white wine vinegar

Trim the thick skin off the top of the pork roast, if needed (leave the fat cap).

In a small bowl, mix together the smoked paprika, granulated sugar, brown sugar, salt, black pepper, chili powder, cumin, celery salt, garlic powder, hot paprika, and 1 teaspoon of the cayenne pepper. Rub the pork evenly with the spice mixture. Wrap the pork back up in the butcher paper or plastic wrap with any remaining spice mixture (the excess spices will soak into the pork as the pork rests) and refrigerate overnight.

Preheat the oven to 450°F (230°C). Put a rack in the lower half of the oven and remove any top racks. Scatter the lemon slices, champagne or white wine vinegar, and remaining 1 teaspoon of cayenne pepper in the bottom of a large roasting pan and set a baking rack on top of the pan.

Put the pork, fat side up, on the baking rack, transfer the roasting pan to the oven, and pour 4 cups (950ml) of water into the pan.

Roast the pork for 30 minutes, reduce the heat to 300°F (150°C), and continue to roast for 2 more hours. Tent the pork loosely with foil, add another 4 cups (950ml) of water to the pan, and roast until the pork falls apart when pierced with a fork, 5 to 5½ hours (for a total roasting time of 7½ to 8 hours). Check the water level in the pan occasionally and add another 2 cups (480ml) of water if the pan ever appears dry.

Let the pork cool for at least 1 to 1½ hours and shred or finely chop the meat. Return the pork to the roasting pan and toss the meat in the pan juices. Use the pork immediately, or cover and refrigerate for up to 5 days. (Rewarm the pork in a low oven before serving.)

Chipotle Aioli

Makes about 2½ cups (600ml)

2 large eggs plus 1 egg yolk, room temperature	2 garlic cloves, roughly chopped
1 teaspoon Dijon mustard	2 to 3 canned chipotle chiles plus 3 tablespoons adobo sauce
2 teaspoons freshly squeezed lemon juice	½ teaspoon fine sea salt
2 cups (480ml) extra-virgin olive or grapeseed oil	

Put the eggs and egg yolk, mustard, lemon juice, and 3 to 4 drops of water in a blender and blend on low speed until the yolks are pale yellow, about 5 seconds. With the blender running, drizzle in the oil a few drops at a time until the mixture emulsifies, then slowly pour in the remaining oil in a steady stream. Transfer the aioli to a medium bowl (do not rinse out the blender).

Put the garlic, chipotle peppers and adobo sauce, and salt in the blender and blend until smooth. Scrape the mixture into the bowl with the aioli, mix well, and add more adobo sauce, if needed. (The aioli should be spicy.) Use the aioli immediately, or cover and refrigerate for up to 3 days.

Red Cabbage–Apple Slaw

Makes 7 to 8 cups (about 1.8kg)

1 medium red cabbage, cored	1½ tablespoons fine sea salt
1 large carrot, peeled	1 to 1½ cups (240 to 360ml) Chipotle Aioli
1 medium green apple, cored	

Grate the cabbage, carrot, and apple on the large holes of a box grater or in a food processor fitted with the grater attachment. Transfer the vegetables to a large bowl, add the salt, and use your hands to toss the vegetables in the salt until well combined. Set the slaw aside at room temperature for 2 hours. Transfer to a strainer and squeeze the slaw firmly with your hands to release as much of the water as possible. Use the slaw immediately or cover and refrigerate overnight (strain again, if needed, before using). When ready to serve, add the Chipotle Aioli and mix until well combined.

The more I travel, the more I realize how important architecture is to a city itself and to the world as a whole.

The skyline of Singapore really is one of the architectural Wonders of the World. The government even regulates it to maximize the space but also to provide benefits to its citizens. It's just gorgeous. That was Moshe Safdie's waterfall at the airport, which is incredible. But I've never seen anything like his infinity pool on top of the Marina Bay Sands hotel, which I got to tour with the incredibly talented Charu Kokate, the lead architect for Moshe Safdie's Singapore projects (including the hotel and airport). It seems impossible. My knees get a little weak thinking about it.

KF Seetoh, who I affectionately dubbed KFC, is the local champion of Singaporean food culture. He's on a mission to save the local hawker stalls from disappearing. He and other traditional food advocates pushed to have it declared a UNESCO Intangible Cultural Heritage, which aims to preserve cultural traditions, performing arts, and similar crafts.

KFC took me to Changi Village, where the hawker specialty is the Malay dish nasi lemak, or "rich rice." The rice is cooked with coconut milk and topped with anything fried: chicken, fish fillets, whole anchovies,

eggs. The key is the sauce, which every hawker stall makes in their own unique way. KFC pulled the next recipe together for you, based on the very best hawker secret recipes.

The hawkers are protecting our culinary legacy. The public hawker centers alone serve up 1 million meals. People don't cook because we have been spoiled by cheap deliciousness. I fear we are going to lose a lot of them unless way more is done. —**KF Seetoh**

Phil: Look what I have. (*pulls out a coconut with a straw in it*)

Max: What is it?

Phil: What does it look like?

Monica: Looks like a coconut.

Phil: Very good. There's a dish here for you, Dad. Chicken rice. You can put the spicy chili sauce in it if you want, you mix up the rice, and you put the chicken over it. It's the national dish.

Max: Is that for breakfast, lunch, or dinner?

Phil: I think they eat it all the time.

Monica: Is it very international there? Like architects from all over the world are building in Singapore?

Phil: There's a famous Israeli Canadian architect named Moshe Safdie. He and his firm built the largest infinity pool, and it's on top of this massive hotel.

Max: You can't swim over the edge, right? Is there a protection someplace?

Phil: They don't let you swim over the edge of the building, no. Would you like to swim in a pool like that?

Max: No. I don't like to swim in a pool, period.

Monica: But he likes looking at it.

Max: Looking at it is okay.

Phil: Do you have a joke?

Max (*whispering to Monica*): What's his favorite singer? The, the . . . one with the guitar. What's his name?

Monica: Bruce Springsteen.

Max: Bruce Springsteen. I think Bruce Springsteen went there, and they named the city after him. Sing-a-poor.

Richard (*talking in background*): That's his joke for the day?

Phil: Wow. That's the joke of the day?

Max: Sing-a-POOR.

Phil: I got it the first time.

Max: A poor singer.

Phil: Believe me, it gets funnier the more you explain it. That can't be the joke, though.

Max: I can tell you another joke, but I don't know if you can use it.

Phil: We already have one of those, but go ahead.

Max: Mr. and Mrs. Goldberg went to the doctor. Mrs. Goldberg said, "Would you examine my husband?" So, he checks him out, and the doctor comes back and says, "Your husband has a problem with sex. He says to me, 'The first time it's good, but the second time I start perspiring, and I sweat, and I'm completely soaked after the ordeal.'" The doctor says to the wife, "Could you explain that to me?" And she says, "Yes, the first time is in November and the second time is July."

Phil: Very good! Max, everybody!

Max: Do you know a guy named Fred Sumner?

Phil: No, why?

Max: He introduced me to your mother.

Phil: And?

Max: And he died.

Phil: Sorry.

Max: That's showbiz.

Richard: Thanks for the good ending!

Nasi Lemak Sambal

Makes about 2 cups (480ml)

There are plenty of incantations of a nasi lemak sambal recipe. It's quite different in Singapore (sweeter and drier) than Malaysia (a little wetter and spicier). This is my recipe nailed from forcing hawkers to reveal (or else!) the secrets, and marrying all up.

The amount of chiles and palm sugar is up to you. The frying process is slow, over a low to medium fire, until the paste absorbs all the oil and then releases it again to create a sheen of spicy oils (the oil is also used to preserve the sambal). Serve the sambal with coconut rice and anything else you like: fried chicken, fish or egg, some crispy anchovies. Remember . . . all else are mere actors. —KF Seetoh

6 to 8 dried Thai bird's eye chiles

4 to 6 fresh Thai bird's eye or similar small, hot chile peppers

1 cup (240ml) vegetable oil

½ cup (110g) peeled and finely chopped shallots (about 2 medium)

½ cup (110g) minced garlic (12 to 15 cloves)

2 teaspoons minced galangal or 1 teaspoon minced ginger plus ¼ teaspoon lemon zest

2 teaspoons minced lemongrass (white root end only)

1 tablespoon (15g) Malay-style dried shrimp paste ("belecan"), finely chopped

¼ to ½ cup (50 to 100g) ground palm sugar or lightly packed light or dark brown sugar

Soak the dried Thai bird's eye chiles in warm water for 15 minutes, strain, and dry on paper towels. Remove the stems from the dried and fresh chile peppers, scrape out most of the seeds (if desired for a less spicy sauce), and finely chop both.

Put the oil and 1 cup (240ml) of water into a wok or large skillet. Add the dried and fresh chiles, shallots, garlic, galangal, lemongrass, shrimp paste, and palm or brown sugar and bring to a low boil over medium heat. Reduce the heat to low and cook, stirring occasionally, until the oil rises to the top of the aromatics and forms a separate layer, about 20 minutes. Let the sambal cool completely and use immediately, or transfer to a large jar (including the oil), cover, and refrigerate for up to 1 month.

Tips

- Use the leftover sambal oil to fry rice and vegetables, seafood, or chicken.
- Both Malay-style dried shrimp paste (also called belacan, a firm, sun-dried block that is very different from less pungent sauce-like shrimp pastes) and palm sugar (whole or already ground) are available at most Asian markets.

Singapore: incredible food, awe-inspiring architecture, and the sweetest and most genuine people.

It's not a big place, but something tells me I only scratched the surface. I'll be back.

21

Mississippi Delta

Edith Wharton had a quote: "One of the great things about travel is you find out how many good, kind people there are." That was never truer than about the Mississippi Delta.

I SAID IN THE SHOW THAT I HAD BEEN HEARING that I should check out the Mississippi Delta. If it wasn't for my wonderful friend Julia Reed, who I met when we were filming the New Orleans episode, I'd never have thought it was a place I should check out. (Julia grew up in Greenville, Mississippi.) When I researched the area, it had so many of the things I love: amazing food, yes, but also a rich history and, of course, that incredible music.

My preconceived notion of this area was that I would be going into the movie *Deliverance*. And I couldn't have been more wrong. We were welcomed so warmly, everywhere we went. I know you will be, too.

By the time we did the Mississippi Delta episode, I'd met so many wonderful kids from all over the world.

Then I had the pleasure of meeting, quite accidentally, Alexander.

Desiree Robinson and her husband started the Cozy Corner, a fantastic barbecue restaurant in Memphis,

Tennessee, in the 1970s. Alexander was at his great-grandmother's restaurant almost every day, and yet he had never wanted to try any of the stuff I was eating. I called him over and convinced him to at least try the Cornish hen. Everyone gets it here, and it's fantastic. He pulls off a leg, takes a giant bite, and says, "I like it!" before he's even chewed it. He tried the ribs, he liked those, too. I'm in! He's even going to try the potato salad, until I ruin everything by telling him it's cold. Alexander says, "I hate cold." So I tell him, "No, you don't, and you know how I know? Because you like ice cream."

He comes back with, "You get to lick that, and I have to chew this with my teeth." I get him to put a teeny bit on his fork, and he takes the tiniest lick, and I swear, before it even hits his tongue, he says, "I don't like it. I taste the coldness." That would have been the perfect ending. But then he drops the Cornish hen leg in his lap and has sauce all over his face, and comes back with, "I bet my mama will know what I did today . . . because there's a mess on my face."

Same with my mom.

Fried Bologna Sandwich

Alexander's favorite thing at his great-grandmother's restaurant is the fried bologna sandwich. Go to Memphis and try it, and you'll thank Alexander. It was so delicious, as opposed to my bologna sandwiches growing up, which were Oscar Meyer with mayo and those thin, packaged slices of processed bologna on white bread. But here, it's a thick slab of bologna that's been skilleted, sauced, coleslawed, and put on a delicious roll. You want to go home and slap your parents.

Go to your deli and tell them you want one of those huge rolls of bologna and a tub of coleslaw (extra mayo; this is the South). Get some good barbecue sauce and good soft buns. Cut the bologna into thick slices, fry that up in a pan, and cover the bologna in barbecue sauce. Put the bologna on the buns and pour some more sauce over the whole thing, add your coleslaw, and eat it with a towel.

Every day is Judgment Day.

In Memphis, I had the honor of being a judge at the Mississippi Boulevard Christian Church's Men's Cook-off. The last time I judged food was on an episode of *Iron Chef*, and this was far more exciting.

I was so fortunate to be paired with the lovely Marian Douglas Starks, who grew up in Alabama but has lived in Memphis most of her life. She was the chef, I wasn't. But maybe we could come together over the food.

My one frustration in that scene was that I couldn't really talk to the other judges. Those other people across the table from us doing the entrées were serious about their judging. I asked about the chicken, and they didn't want to talk. They had a job to do.

Marian was the reason that scene worked. I like a scene like that where I can talk and bond with who I'm with. I love when she tried the chicken salad, then put it down after a tiny bite and said, "Eww, it's got apples in it, yuck." I don't know what's supposed to be in chicken salad in the South. I guess not apples. Then we compared notes, and I told Marian I thought the

tortilla soup seemed a little salty, and she agreed. We both loved the broccoli cheese cornbread, so we had the winner. By the way, that indoor food festival after the competition was so much fun, I converted.

Maybe the best part about traveling is sitting with people you just met and sharing a meal with them.

There's no place that shows that more in our series than that scene at Jim & Samella's House in Memphis. The restaurant is in an actual house, and not just any house, but the house across the street from where owner and chef, Talbert Fleming, grew up eating his grandma's cooking, helping her cook. Now he's turned the house into a full-blown restaurant that serves some of the best Southern food in the country.

I was blown away by how decadent the food was there. How about that gravy that comes in a mug? It was so delicious, and just what you wanted to wash down all of the Southern specialties on the table: fried chicken, fried potatoes that looked like kugel, shrimp and grits, Crown Royal–buttered apple waffles. (I almost just fainted again.) And then when you've eaten more than four humans should, out comes the grand finale: chicken-fried lobster tails. What?

The first thing I thought was, "Why would you do that to a lobster tail?" It's battered like it's chicken. Okay, that doesn't sound terrible, but must we chicken-fry everything, people? And then I tasted it, and the answer is: Yes, we must!

But as great as that meal was, what I remember most about being at Jim & Samella's was not only my dining companions, but the feeling you get from this wonderful community: warm.

Chicken-Fried Lobster Tails

Talbert's fried lobster tail turned out to be one of the best lobster tails of my life. I'm no chef, but it's like the frying process seals the meat so the flesh steams inside that batter, so you get the seasoning of the crunchy coating and the lobster meat is tender and juicy. If you watch Talbert make this in the episode, you'll see the recipe seems simple: just batter and fry the lobster. I'm going to guess it's a little trickier than that, like if you use too much coating and there's too much crust it won't taste right, like if you made a cake and added too much sugar.

Get a couple lobster tails and take off the top of the shells so you can see the meat, but leave the bottom (where the legs would be) of the shells on. Heat up a lot of oil in a pot for frying and make a batter, the kind that you'd use to fry up chicken, and season the batter how you like. Dip the lobster tails in the batter, then fry them up until they're crispy on the outside but the meat is still tender. Watch your friends' heads explode.

It doesn't matter how you open a mind. Sometimes you've gotta open a mouth first and the mind will follow.

Places like Delta Meat Market are an example of the Brooklynization of the world. Young people move in or move back to a place they grew up after they lived elsewhere because they discover they love their hometowns (and maybe the cheap rent is an incentive). It's how growth happens in every community. Young folks come up with something that the town didn't have before, like a hip restaurant with a cool chef behind the stove serving things like French fries with hanger steak like you'd get in France, only with the regional specialty, Hoover Sauce, and piles of American blue cheese on top.

And the locals go nuts for it. A new style of cooking becomes the norm, what locals now expect, and pretty soon, that evolution of tastes will bring other food businesses to town: a new butcher or seafood shop, an artisan gelato place, a great brewery. It's how the world was made, and keeps being remade.

Honey-Roasted Turkey Sandwich

Serves 6

My paternal grandmother lived next door to me when I was growing up. That's how I learned how to cook (my mom went back to school to become a nurse and help support the family). Me and my grandma cooked all sorts of things together, but we loved to make cornbread together. We decided the trick was stirring the mix in the bowl one hundred times with a wooden spoon.

It's kind of like the best of both worlds in this roasted turkey sandwich. The Duke's mayo I grew up on is still there, even if the rest is a little fancier than my grandma would have done. —**Cole Ellis**

Honey-Roasted Turkey Breast, as needed, recipe follows	12 slices whole grain sandwich bread, lightly toasted
12 slices thick-cut bacon (16 ounces/450g)	2 large beefsteak or heirloom tomatoes, sliced
Parmesan-Basil Mayonnaise, recipe follows	4 cups (about half a 5-ounce/140g package) arugula, loosely packed

Remove the Honey-Roasted Turkey Breast from the refrigerator about 30 minutes before serving and use your hand or a paper towel to brush off the congealed braise (do not rinse the turkey).

Thinly slice enough turkey about ¼ inch (6mm) thick so you have several slices for each sandwich.

Meanwhile, in a cast iron skillet or sauté pan, fry the bacon over medium heat, stirring occasionally, until golden brown, 6 to 8 minutes. Transfer the cooked bacon to a paper towel.

Spread about 1 tablespoon of Parmesan-Basil Mayonnaise over each slice of bread. Lay 3 to 4 slices of turkey on each bottom slice of bread, lay 2 slices of bacon over the turkey, then place a few tomato slices and a small handful of arugula on top. Close the sandwiches, cut each in half, and serve.

Honey-Roasted Turkey Breast

1 cup (340g) honey	2 garlic cloves
½ cup Diamond Crystal or ⅓ cup (70g) Morton kosher salt (see Tip page 282)	1 6- to 7-pound (2.7 to 3.2kg) bone-in turkey breast
2 sprigs fresh thyme	

In a medium saucepan, combine the honey, salt, and 1 quart (950ml) of water. Bring to a low boil, stir to dissolve the salt, and remove the pot from the heat. Add the thyme and garlic and let the brine cool completely.

Fill a turkey brining bag with 2 quarts (about 2L) of water. Add the cooled brine and submerge the turkey in the brine. Remove the air so the turkey is fully submerged in the brine (add a little more water if needed). Seal the bag and refrigerate overnight.

Remove the turkey from the brine and pat dry (discard the brine). Transfer the turkey to a large roasting pan and let sit at room temperature for 1 to 1½ hours.

Preheat the oven to 275°F (135°C).

Roast the turkey, basting the flesh with the pan juices about every 30 minutes, until golden brown and a digital thermometer inserted into the thickest part of the breast reads 160°F (70°C), 2½ to 3 hours, depending on the size of the turkey. Remove the turkey from the oven, loosely tent with foil, and let cool completely. Transfer the turkey and the pan juices to a storage container, cover, and refrigerate overnight or up to 5 days.

Parmesan-Basil Mayonnaise

Makes about 1 cup (240ml)

⅔ cup (150ml) mayonnaise, preferably Duke's

⅓ cup (70g) grated parmesan cheese

1½ tablespoons finely chopped basil leaves

1 garlic clove, minced

1 tablespoon freshly squeezed lemon juice

Kosher salt and freshly ground black pepper

In a medium bowl, whisk together the mayonnaise, parmesan cheese, basil, garlic, and lemon juice until well combined. Season the mayonnaise with salt and pepper. Use immediately or cover and refrigerate the mayonnaise for up to 5 days.

Tips

- You'll have leftover turkey to make more sandwiches, or serve half the turkey breast hot out of the oven one night, and save the rest for sandwiches.
- The brine can also be used for a smaller whole turkey (about 12 pounds/5.5kg or less); for a larger bird, increase the amount of brine by 50 percent. Refrigerate the turkey in the brine for up to 2 days before roasting (the roasting time will vary by weight).

There are differences at most tables.

Jim's Cafe has been around since 1909. Julia and my new friend Hank Burdine, a "gentleman farmer" as they say in the South who serves as the local historian, said I had to go to Jim's Cafe and find the Table of Knowledge.

These six men have met for lunch at Jim's almost every day for decades. Even though they have their differences, they never let them get in the way of their friendship or their sandwiches.

That scene was a real lesson for how things could be. What we see on TV is often the worst of the worst: conflict, prejudice, hate. But in reality, we saw the opposite everywhere we went on the series, not just the Mississippi Delta. We go to these places expecting something that's not the reality. Most of the time people are nice,

Max: Did you get a haircut?

Phil: I did, right before I left.

Max: There's not much hair left.

Phil: Look who's talking.

Max: This is Memphis?

Phil: Yes, where the Mississippi Delta begins, and then Highway 61 takes you along the Mighty Mississippi.

Max: The people look like they're very friendly.

Phil: You know what? Absolutely right. That's the best part. There's such diversity, and everybody gets along with everybody. What's happening in New York?

Monica: We did have kind of an interesting morning in that we had our eggs, this is four eggs now, and all of them were double yolks.

Phil: What? You hit the jackpot! Dad, that's like Christmas, Hanukkah, and New Year's all rolled into one. (*Monica hugs Max*) We hit the jackpot!

Monica: Okay, can I tell you one more thing? Yesterday, we saw a ladybug outside the window, and we opened the window...and another ladybug flew in, and then we got that one.

Phil: So not just double yolks...two ladybugs.

Monica: Double ladybug.

Phil: This must mean something.

Monica: What's this mean? It's very spiritual.

Max: Okay. What else is new?

Phil: Dad, welcome to my world.

Max: Very interesting.

Monica: "You're a fascinating woman," is that what you're thinking?

Phil: I get to hear stories like that all the time. I heard you played Password the other night?

Monica: Max made up the word.

Phil: He didn't want to play, but he wanted to give you the words.

Max: Cultivate.

Phil: That's a very hard Password.

Monica: I think it was too hard, and we couldn't get it. And then Max said, "I'll use it in a sentence."

Max: Yesterday I was waiting for a bus, but it was too cult-ti-vate so I took the subway.

Phil: So, no one can get the word. And it turns out he only wrote the word so he could do that joke. What else?

Max: Escort.

Phil: And you used it in a sentence?

Max: I had to jump over the fence but I didn't make it. I got my es-cort.

Phil: It's a very good show I've got here. I must say. When you're on, it's a very good show. I think I've got a nominee for the Table of Knowledge.

When they lose the skillets, it's all over. —Julia Reed

they want to be nice. Most people don't want to fight, but that's not exciting to talk about. It's not good for ratings.

"You know what happened today, when these two factions met, and they're on opposite sides of a thing? They all had lunch and got along."

. . . .

There may be no place more special in all of the South than Doe's Eat Place. It's legendary. Liza Minnelli, Judy Garland, Willie Nelson, and Johnny Cash all "just happened through," as Hank said. You get why. It's almost a lost world that's been preserved in time, and the food is incredible: these giant steaks (which, by the way, were perfectly cooked), mind-blowing French fries, Aunt Flo's salad that's called "wet salad" and the magic trick is that the lettuce somehow stays crispy.

Part of the secret is what everything is cooked in. The flavor of the fries comes from the ancient iron skillets they're fried up in. The salad is so great partly because of the bowl everything is tossed in; the bowl

stays seasoned. There was that pot on the stove with the cheese, all burnt and caramelized and dripping down the sides. It was layered like a work of art, that pot. That's the thing, one of the miracles of this place.

But my favorite miracle is Flo herself, who within five minutes of meeting with me proposed shacking up.

A Patch of the Cheap Stuff (For Julia)

Makes 1 cocktail

A patch is a resupply of your original drink, a Southern colloquialism. Julia liked to drink out of styrofoam cups at Doe's, as do I. I personally poured her hundreds of Dewar's and water there. And yet she always had a very ample supply of fine wines in her bag whenever she was there—or anywhere else, for that matter.

Once your three fingers of Scotch are poured over the ice, and it kinda settles in, put in an ample dose of water. With Julia, you were always in for the long haul. No need in knocking out too early, there's way too much fun to be had. Never was our first rodeo. **—Hank Burdine**

3 to 4 cubes of ice, straight out of the ice tray

3 fingers Dewar's White Label Scotch

Tap water

Put the ice in a plastic or Styrofoam cup (8 ounces/ 240ml) or whatever you have around. Add your Scotch, then top off the whiskey with a little water, to taste.

Tip "Three fingers" of alcohol is measured by wrapping your hand around the cup, starting with your pinky at the base of the cup, and filling roughly to the top of your middle finger. Here, the volume is much smaller than the typical "three finger" pour due to the ice.

Look at these people in the South.

I loved being here. These people don't know me, they don't have to like me automatically, but they couldn't have been more welcoming. It's not just me. They seem to truly love each other as much as they love and welcome strangers.

Isn't that how the world should be?

With a lot of love, in memory of Julia Reed

22

Hawaii

I've been to so many beautiful places, but nothing feels like Hawaii: the stunning landscape, the incredible food, and mostly, the spirit of Aloha.

Hawaii was the perfect last episode for our first four seasons in the series. It's an ultimate ideal. It's paradise. If, like me, you watched *The Price Is Right* or *Let's Make a Deal* growing up every day after school, you knew what the grand prize was going to be at the end: "You're going to Waikiki, beautiful Honolulu, Hawaii!" So it always seemed like the dream place to go on vacation. And it really does feel like that when you get there. So many parts of it are completely unspoiled.

Honolulu is an international city, with such a diverse population, and food-wise all of the greatest hits of the Pacific Rim are here. But there is also so much incredible indigenous food. And, the islands are diverse in terms of not just the people, food, and topography, but the climate. There are these different microclimates on each of the eight islands. You can go to Honolulu, a bustling city, then drive down to a beach and be in the most rural surfer's paradise or head out to a ranch that feels like you're in an idyllic fantasyland of the American West.

For me, it was also the perfect place to end the season because Hawaii seems like a good place to retire. It's both easygoing and gorgeous, and the locals don't moan at my bad jokes. But honestly, you know what my favorite thing to do in Hawaii is? Just sit outside at night. That's it. You literally understand what the phrase "balmy breezes" means. The air smells good, it feels good, it's like a big, warm hug.

· · · ·

I always say you've got to try something at the source, but I have to admit, I wasn't very excited about poke before I had Josh Schade and Erika Luna's version at their tiny shop, Ahi Assassins. The poke I'd had on the Mainland was kind of mish-mosh with all kinds of stuff in it. I always thought if this fish was really good, it would be sushi. At Ahi Assassins, their poke is sushi-grade. I now love poke.

Fisherman Ahi Poke

Serves 4

I grew up in a family of fishermen. We're the guys who catch, skin and blood, and cut up the tuna; the fishermen, fish cutters, fishmongers, and poke mixologists. My wife, Erika, deserves the credit on that last one. She's the reason I'm still in this business.

If you've never had fresh wild hook-and-line-caught ahi tuna, you've never had "reel" poke. (Poke is the Hawaiian word for a dice, a cut.)

Find a fisherman or a good fishmonger. You want sashimi- or poke-grade ahi steak trimmed of blood and skin and cut from the center of the top or bottom quarter loin (the most desired cuts). Get some fresh local seaweed (or go with dried) and Hawaiian kukui nuts (or use macadamias), and grab an onion (dealer's choice: red, white, yellow, sliced or diced). Invite a friend over, kick back, put on some Bruddah Iz, crack your beverage of choice, and share the experience of real Hawai'i poke making and partaking served with an extra scoop of the Aloha Spirit. Feeding friends, family, and communities fills our bowls and souls . . . and keeps our boats fueled and afloat.
—Josh Schade

1¼ pounds (560g) sashimi- or poke-grade ahi tuna steak	2 to 3 tablespoons Chile Pepper Water, recipe follows
½ medium red, white, or yellow onion, shaved or very thinly sliced	2 teaspoons toasted sesame oil
¾ cup (60g) fresh seaweed or 1 ounce (28g) dried seaweed	½ teaspoon coarse sea salt
1 to 2 Hawaiian or Thai bird's eye chile peppers, roughly chopped	⅓ cup (40g) toasted kukui or macadamia nuts, finely chopped, preferably unsalted, divided
	1 green onion, finely chopped

Trim the tuna of any residual skin and blood, rinse the flesh under cold water, and pat dry with paper towels. Slice the tuna against the grain into strips about 1 inch (2.5cm) thick and cut each strip into roughly ½-inch (12mm) cubes. Refrigerate the tuna while you make the poke.

Put the onions in a small bowl, cover with ice water, let soak for 5 minutes, and strain.

Rinse the fresh seaweed under cold running water and roughly chop the seaweed into bite-size. pieces. If using dried seaweed, crumble or break apart the pieces with your hands (do not rinse).

In a medium bowl, mix together the chile peppers, Chile Pepper Water, sesame oil, and salt. Add the tuna and use your hands to gently mix the tuna with the seasonings. Add the onions and all but about 2 tablespoons of the seaweed and kukui or macadamia nuts, and gently mix again. Season the poke with salt, if needed, and transfer to serving bowls. Scatter the remaining seaweed over the poke, sprinkle the green onions and remaining kukui or macadamia nuts on top, and serve.

Chile Pepper Water

Makes about 1⅓ cups (320ml)

3 to 4 fresh Hawaiian, Thai bird's eye, or habañero chile peppers

1 garlic clove, smashed

2 tablespoons distilled white vinegar

Remove the stems from the chile peppers and slice the peppers into rings. Put the chiles, garlic, and vinegar in a 12-ounce (360ml) or larger jar.

Bring 1¼ cups (300ml) of water to a boil in a small saucepan. Carefully pour the hot water into the jar, cool completely, cover, and let cure at room temperature for 24 hours. Store the chile pepper water in the refrigerator for up to 1 month.

Tips

- The saltiness of seaweed varies widely depending on whether it is fresh or dried (and the drying process), so adjust the amount of added salt to taste. Look for dried whole-leaf kelp at Asian markets and online (don't substitute pressed seaweed sheets, which are typically seasoned and roasted).
- Kukui nuts (also called candlenuts) can be difficult to find outside of Hawaii; unsalted macadamia nuts are a good substitute. If only roasted, salted macadamias are available, reduce the salt in the poke.

You either get more adventurous as life goes on, or the opposite happens to you.

By the time we shot the Hawaii episode, I was as adventurous as I'd ever been. Ask Monica. It's terrifying at first, to try something outside your comfort zone. Then it gets a little easier, each time you try something new. And every time Richard presents me with something new to do, I say no, and then he convinces me to do it, and then he's right. Stupid Richard.

In Hawaii, Richard wanted me to go out with a bang, so he set me up for not one, but two outdoor adventures: that paddle canoe trip with my new friends from the Ka Māmalahoe Canoe Club, and later in the episode, that very high zip line tour across the jungle. Actually, three adventures, if you count the Jeep ride.

Once in a while you meet someone who is just light, and love, and warmth, and beauty, and everything that's sweet about living, all wrapped up into one cute little package.

The entire show really is about the characters we meet, and Uncle Clay sums up my ideal philosophy of the world if the world was an idealized Garden of Eden. I think I'm pretty positive, but Uncle Clay makes me look like Ebenezer Scrooge. His sheer unbridled joy is incredible. I've never been hugged more in my life than I was in that shave ice shop, Uncle Clay's House of Pure Aloha. I even took a picture of his motto on the wall so I could keep it with me.

. . . .

You can't make real shave ice unless you have one of those shave ice machines, so Uncle Clay came up with the fruity iced tea slushy on the next page for you to try until you can get to Hawaii.

The Hānai Son.

Pineapple-Strawberry Plantation Iced Tea

Serves 8

Aloha! If I could, I'd build a house big enough for every member of our One World 'Ohana to live together in—yes that includes you! And, of course, so I could serve every person a delicious shave ice. Since that's a bit difficult, hopefully this recipe will give you a taste. Plantation, or pineapple, iced tea is popular all over Hawaii. Our version with fresh pineapple and strawberries gets you close to House of Pure Aloha's shave ice using everyday home ingredients and equipment (we'll just have to all use our imagination to fill the gap). Make the pineapple tea and strawberry syrup ahead so they have time to chill, and you're ready to share the Pure Aloha (our way of expressing unconditional love). Sending my purest Aloha from my heart and my house to yours! —**Uncle Clay**

4 black tea bags, preferably orange pekoe

½ cup (100g) granulated sugar, or to taste

1 large pineapple, peeled

2 cups (8 ounces/225g) strawberries, stems removed

10 to 12 mint leaves (optional)

4 to 5 cups (950ml to 1.2L) crushed ice or ice cubes

In a medium pot, bring 1 quart (950ml) of water to a boil. Turn off the heat and add the tea bags. Steep the tea for 4 to 5 minutes (longer for a stronger flavor, if desired). Remove the tea bags and let cool completely. Transfer the tea to a large (3-quart/about 3L) pitcher, add 1 quart (950ml) of cold water, and set aside, or cover and refrigerate overnight.

In a small saucepan, bring ½ cup (120ml) of water to a boil. Add the sugar, stir until dissolved, and set aside to cool.

Slice the pineapple in half lengthwise through the middle, then cut each half lengthwise so you have four quarters. Cut one of the quarters into eight triangle-shaped slices, then cut a small notch in the core (the bottom of each triangle) so the pineapple slices will slip over the rim of a glass.

Remove the core from the remaining pineapple sections and juice the flesh in a juicer. Or, roughly chop the pineapple, put the flesh in a blender with 2 to 3 tablespoons of sugar, and ½ cup (120ml) of water, and purée until smooth (do this in batches if needed). Add 2 cups (480ml) of pineapple juice to the tea (reserve any remaining juice for another use). Cover and refrigerate the tea and pineapple slices for at least 2 hours or overnight.

Meanwhile, put the strawberries and mint leaves, if using, in the blender, blend until smooth, then add the sugar syrup, and blend again until well combined. Cover and refrigerate the strawberry base for at least 2 hours or overnight.

When ready to serve, slide a pineapple onto the edge of eight large (16 ounces/480ml or larger) cups. Put the strawberry base in a blender, add 4 cups (950ml) of ice, and pulse until the ice is finely ground; there should still be flecks of ice visible. If the mixture does not have the consistency of a thick slushy, add about 1 cup (240ml) of ice.

Immediately divide the strawberry shave ice among the glasses, stir the pineapple tea until well combined, and top off each glass with about 1¼ cups (300ml) of tea. Now sprinkle on as much Pure Aloha from your heart as you like, and serve.

Tips
- "Orange pekoe" refers to the quality of the leaves used in a black tea, not the flavor. Most mass-produced black teas, including Lipton (a blend of orange pekoe and pekoe), either regular or decaffeinated, can be used.
- If you don't have a juicer, adding a little sugar to the pineapple flesh when blending it with water keeps the sweetness on par with a fresh juice, but if you prefer a slightly less sweet tea, omit the extra sugar.

There are some things even Richard can't get me to do.

Surfing a giant wave is one of them.

So when we went up to Oahu's North Shore to see the Pipeline, the most famous wave in the world and where the surfing world championships are held every year, I conveniently arrived just in time for breakfast. Jenn Marr, who's lived here since she was a teenager and now acts as the surf mom for all the young athletes at the Volcom House, and her adorable granddaughter, Lei Aloha, met me on the beach. Watching those kids riding these massive waves like it was a walk in the park, and sitting down with them to share that incredible breakfast together afterward, was one of my favorite moments on the series. That experience was so outside my lifestyle, and I hadn't even traveled halfway across the world. Hawaii is right across the ocean from California, the flight takes about as long as from New York to LA. The moment I got to the beach, it was like all worldly matters fell away. It was just me, the waves, and this wonderful family I had sat down to share a meal with, bonding over food and laughs. This can happen to you!

It's like a big family, the whole Aloha spirit. Everywhere you go, you're a little bit home. —**Jenn Marr**

If you watch the series, you probably look at me and go, "Wow, that is an adventurer. A stud."

The truth is my most adventurous moments on the series mostly occurred close to sea level: riding a motorbike, rowing a gondola, jumping into an ice-cold ocean, paddling a canoe. Zip-lining through the trees a couple of stories above the forest floor is not in my wheelhouse.

The hardest part wasn't the actual zip-lining. The instructors ease you into zooming down the ropes by going slower on the first few runs. It was that in between each ride, your instructor says, "Now you're going to go across that bridge over there." Okay, I can do that. What no one tells you is there are big, gaping holes between each plank *and* you can see right through them to the jungle floor far below. Then suddenly, you get across, get ready to zip down the line, and you're in the top of the trees … and it's absolutely beautiful and, yes, somewhat terrifying. But only at first. By the last ride, I was calmly talking about where lunch would be.

. . .

There's no better recommendation for a restaurant than the regular customers. In that scene at The Feeding Leaf, those ladies at the table next to me said they went there *every day* for the Japanese hand food that Tracey Apoliona and her executive chef, Brightwell Youngstrom, turn into a multicultural mash up on your plate. Get the chicken and waffles, and you'll understand why it's the restaurant's most popular dish. Amazing fried chicken, a sweet sauce, savory waffles … you can't go wrong with this recipe from "Tracey!"

Ben Rosenthal, one of my all-time favorite eating companions in the world.

Like many of us in Hawaii, Brightwell and I were always taught to share food with as many people as we could when we were growing up. More important, we were told to feed people during both the good and hard times. We pride ourselves in being able to tell stories through our food. I hope that as you enjoy this recipe you feel a little bit of the "Aloha Spirit" with you, wherever you may be.

When you cut up the chicken, some of the skin will separate from the meat. Don't throw it away! Fry them up with the chicken to get the yumminess from the crispy skin. He lau maʻona! (The leaves that feed!)
—**"Just Tracey" Apoliona**

Tracey's! Fried Chicken and Waffles

Serves 4

Aloha from Kailua Kona, Hawaiʻi! I am so happy to be able to share my love of island cooking with you. This recipe is a collaborative dish that came about from working with our executive chef, Brightwell Youngstrom. It combines our own family histories and traditions (Grandma's waffles) with our twists. Japanese furikake (a mix of dried seaweed, sesame seeds, and seasonings) gives the waffles that savory umami flavor, which pairs well with the spicy-sweet Korean-style fried chicken and hot pepper syrup.

2 to 2¼ pounds (about 1kg) boneless chicken thighs, preferably with the skin

2¼ cups (270g) all-purpose flour, divided

½ cup (120ml) Hawaiian-style soy sauce, such as Aloha Shoyu

1 cup (200g) plus 2 tablespoons granulated sugar, divided

1 tablespoon mirin (sweet rice wine)

1 tablespoon sriracha

1½ teaspoons toasted sesame oil

4 green onions, finely chopped, divided

2 tablespoons furikake seasoning, plus more for serving

1 teaspoon baking powder

¼ teaspoon fine sea salt

1¼ cups (300ml) whole milk

2 large eggs, lightly beaten

2 ounces (½ stick/55g) unsalted butter, melted and cooled

Vegetable oil, for the waffle iron (if needed) and frying

2 to 3 tablespoons Chile Pepper Syrup, recipe follows

Cut the chicken into bite-size (about 1-inch/2.5cm) pieces. Put the chicken, any pieces of skin that have separated from the meat, and 1 cup (120g) of the flour in a large bowl, and toss the chicken in the flour until well coated.

In a medium saucepan, combine the soy sauce and 1 cup (200g) of the sugar and cook over medium heat, stirring once or twice, until the sugar has dissolved, 2 to 3 minutes. Transfer the soy sauce to a medium bowl and let cool. Stir in the mirin, sriracha, sesame oil, and half of the green onions, and set the sauce aside.

In another medium bow, mix together the remaining 1¼ cups (150g) of flour, 2 tablespoons of sugar, furikake seasoning, baking powder, and salt. Use a fork or whisk to mix in the milk, eggs, and melted butter (make sure the butter is cool or the eggs will curdle) until the batter is just combined; it should be lumpy.

Preheat the oven to 250°F (120°C). Preheat a waffle iron, preferably nonstick, over medium heat according to the manufacturer's instructions. (If the waffle iron is not nonstick, use a pastry brush or balled-up paper towel to lightly brush both sides lightly with vegetable oil.) Pour ¼ of the batter (about a generous ½ cup/135ml) onto the iron, close the lid, and cook until the waffle is golden brown, 3 to 5 minutes; the time will vary according to the waffle iron. Transfer the waffle to a baking sheet and repeat the process to make three more waffles.

Lay a baking rack on top of a sheet pan. In a large cast iron skillet or Dutch oven, heat about 1 inch (2.5cm) of vegetable oil over medium-high heat. When the oil is very hot (about 325°F/165°C), add about ⅓ of the chicken (do not crowd the pan) and fry until one side is golden brown, 2 to 3 minutes. Use tongs to flip the chicken and fry the other side until golden brown and the internal temperature reads 160°F (70°C) on a digital thermometer, about 2 minutes.

Transfer the chicken to the baking rack–lined sheet pan to keep warm in the oven while you fry the remaining chicken in batches. Put the waffles in the oven to rewarm while you fry the final batch of chicken.

Transfer the fried chicken to the bowl with the sauce and toss the chicken in the sauce until well coated. Put a waffle on each of four serving plates and divide the fried chicken among each waffle. Sprinkle a generous pinch of furikake seasoning and the remaining diced green onions over the chicken and waffles, drizzle a little Chile Pepper Syrup on top, and serve.

Chile Pepper Syrup

Makes about ¾ cup (180ml)

1 cup (200g) granulated sugar

1 fresh Hawaiian, Thai bird's eye, habañero, or similar small hot chile pepper

In a small saucepan, combine the sugar, chile pepper, and ½ cup (120ml) of water. Bring to a low boil and cook until the sugar has dissolved and the mixture has slightly thickened, about 5 minutes; it will thicken more as it cools. (Do not let the syrup brown on the edges; it will solidify if caramelized.) Let the syrup cool completely, transfer to a jar or storage container, cover, and refrigerate for at least 2 hours or up to 2 weeks.

Tips
- Use the leftover Chile Pepper Syrup in cocktails or sparkling drinks.
- If skin-on boneless chicken thighs aren't available, use skinless thighs or debone about 3 pounds (1.4kg) of whole thighs (save the bones for soup stock).
- Hawaiian-style soy sauce is milder and less bitter than many widely available Japanese-style versions.

Phil: Oh, hello there! We're in Hawaii.

Max: Are there hula dancers?

(*Phil hums a tune and does a hula dance with his hands.*)

Monica (*singing*): "Oh, we're going to the Hukilau . . ." C'mon Max.

(*Monica and Max do a hula dance with their hands.*)

Max (*waving hand in his face*): Eh.

Phil: That's it. He just did the "Jewish hula." Every Jewish hula ends like this. (*waving hand in front of his face like Max*)

Monica: We're noting all the activities . . .

Phil: Are you proud of me?

Max: When you were running down the wire zip-lining, is that like skiing? Or what is this for?

Phil: There's no skiing there, I'm in the treetops. That's how you get around. At first, I was nervous.

Monica: Were you scared?

Phil: Yeah, at the first one, they give you like a baby one, but it's terrifying. You go a thousand feet in forty-five seconds. And by the end, it was great. I'd do it again. You want to do it, Monica? I'm gonna do it with you.

Monica: I did it once before. It's really exhilarating.

Phil: What do you mean? You did it before? With who?

Monica: You didn't come, you stayed in the hotel. That's what I'm saying. Now he does everything. He rides the horse. "Oh, no, I'm not riding the horse." He does the zip line. "No, I'm not going to zip-line." Does the ropes course. "No, I'm not going." Now he does it.

Max: 'Cause you're not there.

Phil: Because I'm on television. I'm now fully an outdoorsman with everything.

Max: What else?

Phil: You have a joke for the people?

Max: I can tell you an old joke. There were two couples, and the men sit in their living room. The women sit in the kitchen, and they're talking. And Harry said to John, "John, we went to this restaurant today and the food was delicious." So he goes, "Yeah? What was the name of the restaurant?" "The name of the restaurant. Uh, uh . . . I forgot already." "You were just there this afternoon. How could you forget the name of the restaurant?" "Wait, wait, what's that flower called? It's red . . . it smells good . . . it's got thorns on it." He said, "You mean a rose?" "Yeah, yeah, that's it! Hey, Rose, what was the name of the restaurant?"

Phil: He's still got it! Give me the Jewish hula!

Our last dinner was at Kahua Ranch.

The ranch is on the northern tip of the Big Island, and when you get there, you're transported to a whole different world. You're literally sitting in the clouds in a place that feels a little like what we call the American West on the Mainland, only this is the fantasy version you'd see in a movie. The great chef Peter Merriman gets his sheep and cattle here, so he joined me, and he brought along his longtime executive chef, Neil Murphy; both have called Hawaii home for more than thirty years.

That scene sums up everything I love most about doing this show, about meeting people from all over the world, connecting with them over food. Like so many other magical places I've fallen in love with by stepping outside my everyday world, some people fall so in love with stepping into somewhere else, they actually move.

It's hard to define the "Aloha Spirit" that you feel everywhere you go in Hawaii.

Come to one of America's great states and get to know the local people. You may never want to leave.

Don't say I didn't warn you.

One more recipe:

Uncle Clay's Pure Aloha Oath

I solemnly promise
To live every heartbeat of my life
From this day forward
With Pure Aloha.

Every single word that comes out of my mouth
And every single action, be it large or small
Must first come from my compassionate heart
And be supported by my thoughtful mind.

With an open heart and an open mind
I will unconditionally love
Every person who crosses my path in life
As a fellow member of our one world 'ohana.

If I truly try my best to do all these things
I will become the person I was born to be
Filled with inner peace and complete happiness.

Living every heartbeat with Pure Aloha
I can
Bring love into the hearts of others
And make our world a better place.

Nonprofits and Community Organizations Featured in Seasons 1 through 4

Elephant Nature Park, Kuet Chang, Thailand
elephantnaturepark.org

The Roots of Music, New Orleans, Louisiana
therootsofmusic.org

The Yolcan Project in Xochimilco, Mexico City, Mexico
bach.yo-yoma.com/partners/yolcan/

Row Venice, Venice, Italy
rowvenice.org

Food For Soul, Modena, Italy
foodforsoul.it

Harvest Youth Project, Hout Bay, South Africa
harvestyouthproject.com

Central Park Conservancy, New York, New York
centralparknyc.org

Project Soar, Marrakesh, Morocco (various locations)
projectsoar.org

Urban Growers Collective, Chicago, Illinois
urbangrowerscollective.org

Liberty in North Korea, Seoul, South Korea
libertyinnorthkorea.org

Diamantes na Cozinha (Diamonds in the Kitchen), Rio de Janeiro, Brazil
diamantesnacozinha.org

Family House, San Francisco, California
familyhouseinc.org

Delta Arts Alliance. Cleveland, Mississippi
deltaartsalliance.org

Acknowledgments

Special thanks to:

Everyone at Zero Point Zero and everyone at Netflix who works on *Somebody Feed Phil*.

Our fantastic crew; all our local fixers, drivers, and assistants; and all the wonderful people who work on every episode.

All the great people who worked on this book at Simon & Schuster, especially executive editor Justin Schwartz and editorial assistant Emma Taussig, art director and cover designer Patrick Sullivan, and Jessica Preeg and Molly Pieper on the publicity and marketing teams.

Brandi Bowles at UTA, who made this book happen for all of us, and thank you to Angela Rinaldi as well.

Our incredible creative team: book designer Debbie Berne, recipe photographer Ed Anderson, food stylist Valerie Aikman-Smith, cover photographer Jake Chessum, and the world's best brother (don't tell him I said that), Richard, for all his great behind-the-scenes photography.

Everyone else who made what you see on these pages possible—not only the chefs who shared their fantastic recipes but also their staff, family members, publicists, and so many others who answered every email and phone call. Back in LA, Erin Champion, who always tracked down anything that was needed with a smile—and, most of all, our families, for listening to us talk on and on about this book for more than a year.

And to everyone who has helped us everywhere we've been, and to all the friends we've made:

Thank you

Khàawp khun

Cảm ơn

Toda

Obrigado

Gracias

Grazie

Tak

Dankie

Choukran

Gamsahabnida

Merci

Terima kasih

Mahalo

—Phil and Jenn

Index